POWERHOUSE
PRINCIPLES

SOUTH OF FIFTH STREET,
Miami Beach, Florida (Icon
South Beach, Murano Grande,
Portofino Tower, Yacht Club at
Portofino, Murano at Portofino)
© billwisserphoto.com

POWERHOUSE PRINCIPLES

The Billionaire Blueprint for Real Estate Success

JORGE PÉREZ

WITH A FOREWORD BY
DONALD J. TRUMP

A CELEBRA BOOK

CELEBRA

Published by New American Library, a division of Penguin Group (USA) Inc., 375 Hudson Street,
    New York, New York 10014, USA
Penguin Group (Canada), 90 Eglinton Avenue East, Suite 700, Toronto, Ontario M4P 2Y3, Canada
    (a division of Pearson Penguin Canada Inc.)
Penguin Books Ltd., 80 Strand, London WC2R 0RL, England
Penguin Ireland, 25 St. Stephen's Green, Dublin 2, Ireland (a division of Penguin Books Ltd.)
Penguin Group (Australia), 250 Camberwell Road, Camberwell, Victoria 3124, Australia (a
    division of Pearson Australia Group Pty. Ltd.)
Penguin Books India Pvt. Ltd., 11 Community Centre, Panchsheel Park, New Delhi - 110 017,
    India
Penguin Group (NZ), 67 Apollo Drive, Rosedale, North Shore 0632, New Zealand (a division of
    Pearson New Zealand Ltd.)
Penguin Books (South Africa) (Pty.) Ltd., 24 Sturdee Avenue, Rosebank, Johannesburg 2196,
    South Africa

Penguin Books Ltd., Registered Offices:
80 Strand, London WC2R 0RL, England

First published by Celebra,
a division of Penguin Group (USA) Inc.

First Printing, May 2008
10 9 8 7 6 5 4 3 2 1

CELEBRA and logo are trademarks of Penguin Group (USA) Inc.

LIBRARY OF CONGRESS CATALOGING-IN-PUBLICATION DATA

Pérez, Jorge, 1950–
    Powerhouse principles: the billionaire blueprint for real estate success/Jorge Pérez; with a
    foreword by Donald Trump.
        p. cm.
    ISBN 978-0-451-22372-2
    1. Real estate development   2. Real estate business.   3. Real estate investment.   I. Title.
    HD1390.P47 2008
    333.3068'4—dc22   2007041641

Set in Minion
Designed by Jessica Shatan Heslin/Studio Shatan, Inc.

Printed in the United States of America

*To those whose continued support make it all possible:
my wife, Darlene; my children, Christina, Jon Paul,
Nicky and Felipe;
and my partner and best friend, Steve Ross*

ACKNOWLEDGMENTS

While there are many people who are instrumental in my everyday business and life, there are only a handful who helped me develop and craft this book: my wonderful wife, Darlene, whose opinion was always brutally honest and infinitely constructive; my assistant and friend of many years, Alicia Rufin, who helped me immensely with everything from proofreading to obtaining photo permissions; my editorial maven, Andréa Montejo, for helping to clean up and mold the manuscript; my confidant, Isaac Lee, whose comments and expertise were very helpful; my esteemed colleague and dear friend, Donald Trump, for his kind words, advice and encouragement to write this book; and my publisher, Raymond Garcia, for his guidance, vision and insistence, which ultimately convinced me to undertake this project and not pass as I had done several times before.

Finally, I'd like to thank the entire team at Penguin Group (USA) and anyone else whose dedication helped see this book through to its fruition.

CONTENTS

FOREWORD

The one person who could teach me something about real estate is Jorge Pérez.

In this book, he does.

Jorge and I have worked on projects together several times over the years. Every time, he has impressed me with his passion and his vision. He dares to dream, and to make those dreams real. The result has changed lives, and cities.

His efforts have earned him the acclaim of his peers, won him awards, and made him one of the richest men in America.

His buildings stand as examples of beautiful design woven with the best amenities and the highest quality. He gives his customers places to live that are truly—as he has named so many of his projects—Icons. They are each as much pieces of art as the museum-quality artwork he is famous for filling them with.

In these pages, he reveals his secrets of successful developing—the nuts-and-bolts principles that are fundamental to becoming a billion-aire, the tactics for negotiating, the strategies for maximizing sales, the construction techniques for building the best, and the management methods for a fruitful—and long-lasting—future.

In short, he teaches you everything you need to be a true apprentice developer—and *not* get fired! Jorge has taken all the lessons from the school of hard knocks and given you a leg up on the competition, and a tremendous head start in becoming as successful as him. Or me!

—DONALD J. TRUMP

POWERHOUSE
PRINCIPLES

INTRODUCTION • THE SIMPLE SECRET TO MAKING YOUR FIRST $1 BILLION

*"You never go broke
from making a profit."*

I didn't set out to become a billionaire. I didn't intend to make the top 200 on the Forbes 400 list of richest Americans.

But I did. And if I can do it, you can, too.

I started with nothing. Or next to nothing. I was an immigrant kid who came to Miami with $2 in my pocket. Today, I am a billionaire.

Believe me, you can do it, too.

I did it with real estate. I made $1 million the first year, with no money down. I was twenty-seven years old. Since then, I've never had a year that my company didn't make money.

It taught me a simple fact of life: You never go broke from making a profit. In other words, you make money by making more than you spend, not by posting losses.

It also taught me that if you want to be rich, real estate is one of the best ways to do it.

I truly believe that if I started again and you gave me nothing, I would make you $1 million that first year, just like I made $1 million that first year, in 1979. And I'll tell you what, $1 million in 1979 was worth a load more than $1 million now. It wasn't easy taking the plunge. I was afraid of leaving my secure job and going out on my own with a family to provide for. I was afraid of failing. You know, the fears anyone with any sense should have.

But I believed in the power of real estate and I believed in myself. I had seen how others made money in real estate, and I believed I could do it, too. And without putting up a single cent of my own, I made $1 million.

I believe you can, too.

This book will show you how. It's a step-by-step guide, complete with examples and detailed case studies, to show you exactly how to do what I did.

If you've got some money to invest, that's great. If you're like I was, and you're starting with zero, you can still make $1 million or more in your first year. I'm proof.

I'm also proof that it takes a tremendous amount of discipline, dedication, and determination. You have to want to succeed, at whatever it is you're passionate about, more than anything. *Anything*. I mean it.

Forbes magazine once asked me to offer my advice for young entrepreneurs. I said, "Have great focus, set high but achievable goals, and work *extremely* hard at achieving them."

Everybody's looking for a secret formula nowadays. Everybody wants to know how to get rich quick, with no money down. It can be done. I know it can because that's how I did it. But don't kid yourself: There's no magic pill. Nobody will do it for you. I can show you how, and will in the pages to come, but the bottom line is that it's up to you.

I believe that getting rich at anything takes about 25 percent luck, 25 percent brains, and 50 percent hard work.

Whatever you do that is going to bring you money—unless you do something that is illegal or get incredibly lucky, like win the Powerball—is going to require a tremendous amount of work. A tremendous amount of discipline. And a tremendous amount of knowledge.

That lesson needs to be clear. That was the first thing I said when I was asked to write this book. Whoever thinks they are going to read something and tomorrow say, "I'm just going to buy a building and quit my job and go look at this once a month and become a million-aire," is absolutely, *absolutely* on the wrong path.

You have to become an expert in the area that you are going to be functioning in. If you decide to do affordable housing, like I did when I started, you better know all the city programs, all the city financing, all the federal and state programs, all the federal and state financing that is available to you in order to make that project happen.

That requires an immense amount of research. It requires sitting down, having the vision, and drawing up a plan. Asking consultants to step in and help you in all the areas that you're not an expert in—which are going to be many. Pick their brains. Pick their brains. Pick their brains.

Then you modify your plan based on what you hear from the consultants. You go and test it out in the market and do your market research. And you find all the resources out there that could possibly make your project a success.

Hard work? Absolutely.

Impossible? No.

Will it make you rich? Without a doubt.

Since I started in 1979, I have built more than sixty thousand apartments and condominiums. I have developed or am developing projects in Miami, Orlando, Tampa, Atlanta, Los Angeles, and Mexico, to name just a few places. My projects include everything from small, federally subsidized housing units to market-rate apartments, multimillion-dollar luxury condominiums, and mixed-use minicities combining commercial, retail, and residential space. When *Time* magazine put me on the cover, they called me the "Trump of the tropics."

If you read this book, can you do it, too? Absolutely—if you're willing to plan and stick to that plan and not take no for an answer, and if you're willing to work as hard and stay as focused as I say you need to be, you will be successful and the answer is yes.

Thomas Edison, the great inventor, said, "Genius is one percent inspiration and ninety-nine percent perspiration."

I really believe that.

But the perspiration and hard work need to be accompanied by credible ideas.

Because, remember, you can work in a factory or a mine and say, "Hey, I want to do better than the next miner. Instead of eight hours, I'm going to work fourteen hours."

That's going to bring on the perspiration, all right. But all you're going to do is work a little bit more. And that's okay, too. But if you want to make a lot of money you need to power up a larger plan and make that perspiration truly profitable.

So the first thing you need is an idea. What do I want to do? Where are the opportunities?

Look around; this is an open, open market. Opportunities are immense. Real estate is one market that is very open. There is a lot of money that wants to go to real estate. There are a lot of lenders and a lot of investors who want to put their money in it. People like to be in real estate, as opposed to investing in something nebulous, like when somebody comes up with some idea for a "great invention."

If somebody comes to you and says, "Hey, do you want to be my partner in this warehouse?" you can feel it. You can touch it. You can go to the site and look at it. It's not an idea. It's not a dream. It's a very tangible reality. In real estate, you always have the warehouse there. You have the palpable, perceivable, touchable assets. You can go to people and say, "Hey, I own that warehouse or part of that warehouse."

And that's why people are very, very attracted to real estate. It's one of the most secure investments. It withstands time. Unless you pick the wrong location, very, very, very few real estate investments that I know of go down over time. They tend to go up.

So it will continue to be a business that attracts a lot of money from both the lending side and the investment side. That makes it simpler for people with a good idea and the capacity to work and execute to make their dreams a reality.

Having a dream isn't enough. You've got to plan it out in a realistic way, and create a road map that will take you to the end.

There is a multitude of real estate opportunities out there that allow you to start small. You can start small with an office building. You can start small by building a warehouse.

In this book, I'll show you how to decide what's best for you, and how to develop your plan once you figure out what you want to do. Then I'll show you that whatever the plan is, you have to stick with it.

For example, I just mentioned warehouses. Well, if you do your research you might find that it costs you $100,000 to build a warehouse. You talk to a broker and find out that 95 percent of the warehouses in the county are leased. Therefore, chances are that if you get the right location and the right leasing person, you're going to lease it, as long as you're not a total moron. The broker can also show you what other warehouses are renting for, and you might learn that if you lease yours at the going rate, it will bring in a hefty income. In almost every sizable area there are hundreds of investors who want to invest in things that give them a steady income. So, based on the income you know warehouses bring in in your area, you might be able to sell yours for $150,000 instead of the $100,000 it cost to build.

That, then, forms your plan: (1) Build a warehouse for $100,000 or less; (2) lease it at a rate that brings in a good income; (3) sell it to an investor for $150,000.

Do your research and develop a detailed plan like that and I assure you that most of the time it will work. Now, it's up to you to prepare the right game plan and get the right advisers, who will lease and manage it for you. And you'll need the right construction person, so you don't get screwed during the construction. Then you find the investors and lenders and you pump them up. You've got to transfer that dream of yours to all their minds so they all believe in you.

Then, after you've done your research and tested what you're going to do in your market, you find your piece of property. That's right; as I'll show you in these pages, the property comes *after* the plan, not before. It's up to you, with your advisers, to find the best location that fits your plan, so that warehouse is not in a secondary location that nobody wants to go to.

And then you have to take the plunge. Sooner or later, you have to take the plunge. And when you do, you better be ready to take the hits, to have a thick skin and to work really, really, really hard at achieving that goal.

Once you pick whatever the investment is, stick to it. It can be affordable housing. It might be buying a building and rehabbing it. It might be through strong management—reducing operating costs and increasing income to increase the net revenues, and then selling it for more—stick to it.

It doesn't matter. Whatever the plan is, stick to it. Maybe your goal is to start with one house on a Federal Housing Authority program that you can buy from the government for $2,000 and are going to put $5,000 in—you've already studied the market and can get $15,000 after you finish, or you can rent it for $400 a month.

Great! Stick with it.

Don't switch in the middle of it all. Don't look over at something else and say, "Oooh, that looks good. Let me try that." Stick to your plan. Make it a reality. If you do that, you will be successful.

If you get distracted, if you don't listen to the people you should be listening to, if you don't get help from the people you should get help from, or if you're not willing to work twenty-four hours a day to try to achieve it, then I don't care what you say, it isn't going to happen.

It isn't going to happen by attending seminars that tell you, "Rah-rah! You can do it!"

It's going to happen by sticking to a plan and achieving your first goals first. There are very, very few times in which people start running before they start walking. Bicycles have training wheels on them for a reason; you need to learn how to pedal and steer before you take them off and go on a two-wheeler.

In the pages ahead, I'll show you how.

If you're relying on luck, then you don't need me or anybody. Just play the lottery. You know, you might hit it and you might become very rich.

The great majority of the time that's not what happens. The people who make it, the successful people you hear about and see with all the things you want in life—a nice house, a nice car, money for your children—are the people who have a little luck and a big idea, and who try and try again.

Look at the great politicians—sooner or later in their careers they've had a defeat. They've experienced what it means to be beaten. And they become better because they have. They understand what the pitfalls are, and the strong ones say, "Now I'm going to be much better."

So as you start this, you can't give up when the owner of a piece of property you want to buy says he won't sell it to you.

You have to pick yourself up and go out and find another one. That's all. You thought you were done, but you're just going to have to keep looking.

You can't give up when a lender says, "I'm not going to give you this loan," and you think nobody in the world is going to give you a loan.

You can't think that way. It's going to happen. There will be plenty of nos, especially in the beginning. You can't give up. If you really believe it, you will succeed. You've got to find and surround yourself with people who believe it, too. As I'll show you, when the going gets tough, that's when your passion and persistence and hard work are going to be what gets you through.

One of my favorite quotes about what it takes to succeed comes from President Calvin Coolidge, who said:

"Nothing in the world can take the place of Persistence. Talent will not; nothing is more common than unsuccessful men with talent. Genius will not; unrewarded genius is almost a proverb. Education will not; the world is full of educated derelicts. Persistence and determination alone are omnipotent."

I'm proof that he's right.

As I said, I was an immigrant kid who came here with nothing. My parents lost it all in Cuba. I watched them start over from scratch and it scared the hell out of me. But it also made me damned determined. I had one clear goal: I wanted to be sure that what happened to them would never happen to me. Never.

I call it "the Cuba Fear." It drove me to succeed, to work harder than anyone else, to put money away, to have security for myself and my family. Always.

I remember watching a soldier at the airport in Havana, as we were leaving, stripping the jewelry off my mother's hands. He knew we were leaving and we weren't allowed to take any valuable belongings with us. My aunt and my grandmother were there and they were sobbing out loud. I was ten when Fidel Castro seized power and my father was forced to give up his pharmaceutical company and all our family holdings and take us into exile in Colombia.

Ironically, we hadn't been back in Cuba that long. When I was born, my father was a successful multinational pharmaceutical company executive in Argentina. But we went back to Cuba when my grandfather died, and my father put everything into founding his own business. It did well and we lived comfortably, with maids and a chauffeur. My mother never worked. She was a dilettante—she spent her time studying, studying, studying; reading, reading, reading; just for the sake of knowledge.

I always say, people can tell you things a million times and you can understand them conceptually. People can tell you an education is so important because it's something no one can take away from you. You hear that all through your life and just shrug it off. But sometimes you have shocking experiences that make you understand how real it all is. In my case, it was Cuba that made all of those lessons real.

When the guards pulled the rings off my mother's fingers and my father had to go back to being a simple salesman lugging his bag of samples from doctor's office to doctor's office, I learned how true it is that education really is something no one can take away from you. Very soon after we left Cuba, my mother, a woman who had never worked before in her life, was able to get a job as a teacher, all because of her educational background.

So education became very, very, very important to me. And that's why I pursued it and why I was a straight-A student in college. Because the fact is that you can face difficulties, either your own or those due to external circumstances, such as Castro, but if you're prepared with a great education, no one can take it away from you. They can take your job. They can take your possessions. You can go broke. But if you have a solid education you can pick yourself right back up and do it all over again. I can go into one of these jobs, with hundreds of millions of dollars at stake, and I can go totally broke. But you know what? I will be ready to start again immediately, all because I have that solid educational background.

Education is what brought me to the United States. I wish I could say I already had my plan in mind—that I was going to get my degree and build an empire, or cure cancer, or whatever. But I didn't. I was chasing a girl.

My high school girlfriend was coming to Miami to study and I followed her. Since I couldn't afford tuition I figured out how to win a scholarship to what was then called Miami-Dade Community College. When we finished junior college, she went to Fairleigh Dickinson College in New Jersey. I got into C.W. Post to be near her.

Back then, I still wasn't thinking about becoming a developer, at all. I studied philosophy, and was greatly influenced by the writings of the existentialists, particularly Jean-Paul Sartre. I found great appeal in his idea that life begins with a clean slate and it's up to each of us to write our own history, and to be an example for others.

But by the time I was in graduate school at UC Berkeley, I found my entrepreneurial bent. Actually, I was forced to find it. I had saved all this money to get me through the first year, until one day three of my friends and I decided we were going to buy a car. We bought an old Volkswagen minibus and drove across the country, sleeping at friends' places and crashing with different people, until we got to Las Vegas. And there, I blew everything I had saved, like $8,000 or $9,000, in a casino. They had to drag me out. I was down to my last $300, and my friends were saying, "Stop! You can't spend that."

Because of that, instead of having my leisurely semester, I had to work in the Big Bear Car Wash washing cars. I learned what it meant to be stupid with my money, and I became extremely fiscally conservative. From early on, if I made $10, I would put $2 or $3 in the bank. I remember even having arguments with my ex-wife over it. I was so disciplined about that: "No, we don't go to the movies this weekend. No, we don't go out." I would always put some money away. And to this day I do that in the company.

But I also learned that I could make it on my own. I could support myself and go to school. I came up with all these crazy ideas to make money while I was in college. One time, for example, a few of us got together and bought this company that made stuffed animals and was going broke. We got all these stuffed animals for like 10¢ each. We paid students to store them for us in their dorm rooms until we found a cheap little warehouse. And then, around Valentine's Day, I went from college to college all over the area selling these stuffed animals. I made a lot of money and I proved to myself that I could do it. It had nothing to do with real estate, but I showed myself that I had the ability to produce.

Eventually, I realized I needed a degree in something practical. I had always had an affinity for cities and how they were designed, so I went to the University of Michigan to study urban planning, which eventually led to my first job in Miami, in the city's planning department.

I was just a kid, barely in my mid-twenties, when I started there. In fact, I knew I looked like a baby and that that hurt my credibility, so I grew a beard. But even then, I was thinking of bigger things. I was determined to work harder than anyone else, and was always thinking about the possibility of creating something of my own and making it a success—whether that meant monetarily or in the way it impacted a community. So I think the constant exercise of doing that sort of prepared me for when I actually took the plunge of doing it on my own. I had worked it out in my mind many, many times. It was just a matter of making it a reality.

I was always learning. Every day I was laying the groundwork for the next step, even if I didn't know yet what that next step was going to be. I learned from reading and seeing what others were doing. I would go and see what the developers were doing and checked how they built their projects. Even though I was a do-gooder planner helping to make the city a better place to live, I was always visualizing opportunities. No matter what you're doing, always keep your mind open to opportunities.

One day, after I had been there for a couple of years, a consulting company offered me a job. They wanted me to head their market analysis division. Now, I had no idea how to do market studies, even less how to run an important division in one of the premier real estate consulting firms, but I wasn't going to tell them that. So I told them I needed to give my bosses a month's notice instead of just two weeks, and I said, "You know, everybody does their analyses slightly differently. Let me have some of yours so I can see exactly how you like yours done." So I grabbed what they gave me and I studied them twenty-four hours a day for a month. I didn't sleep. By the time I went to work for them, I could do market studies better than anybody else.

I learned and grew a lot there, yet soon enough I realized that what I was doing for them was making somebody a lot of money—and that I could do it for myself if I wanted.

My first solo project was the renovation of a twenty-one-unit federally subsidized project. It was a wonderful, terrifying experience: Every day I ran into new problems and every night I went to bed afraid I was going to fail. But I didn't. I learned a lot, made a tremendous profit, and dove right into the next one. After a couple of those, I moved into market-rate apartment buildings. Then luxury units, then condos, and the rest, as they say. . . . With every project I learned that I could play on that level, and I gained the experience to go to the next. It's a matter of taking larger steps as you become more experienced.

So I was always, even when I was a planner, learning how to get from point A to point B. I was driven. I always had an idea that I was meant to do something that was important. With all of my fears and everything, I just felt I wanted to make a difference. And as a young man I didn't really know what that would be. But it was something that had to have some value.

Then I started experiencing success. And success wasn't just in business. That's why I always say you should sell your first project as soon as possible, so you experience success. Not only to build a track record, which is very important, but also so you build yourself up. So you start feeling good about yourself. So your self-esteem grows. So you start believing, "I can do it!" Not just thinking it, but believing it.

You can. I didn't know any of this when I started. I learned by making up my mind that this was what I wanted to learn, that this was the area where I was going to make money fast. I had to. I had a family to feed.

You've got an advantage over me, even if you don't have any more money than I did when I started. I didn't have anyone to show me how. You do. In this book I will provide you with all the tools you need to make it big.

ONE CITYPLACE,
Atlanta, Georgia
Methanoia Studio
www.methanoia.com

1 ▪ MY FIVE GUIDING PRINCIPLES

"If you don't really love real estate,

you shouldn't be in this business."

I can show you how to succeed in real estate; but only you can make yourself a success. It's like a professional sport—knowing the rules doesn't mean you can play the game. What it takes comes from inside.

In my life, I've found five guiding principles that propel me to success. And I believe that if you make these principles your own, they will give you what it takes to succeed as well. They provide the foundation. The rest of what I'll show you in this book will show you how to play the game. These principles will teach you how to win.

Someone once said, "If you love what you do, it's never work." I don't know about that. What I do is tremendously hard work. But I am totally, unwaveringly, and absolutely dedicated to it.

If you don't feel that kind of passion for what you do, you should do something else.

You have to want to be the best, and that takes discipline, hard work, and an unfaltering attention to details. It takes complete and utter devotion. As I already told you, I wasn't thinking about becoming a billionaire when I started, but I believe that if you truly want to succeed as I have, you need integrity and loyalty as well.

But, first and foremost, you need passion.

Principle #1: Passion

Have a love for what you do. The passion for what you do inspires you, drives you, makes you tenacious.

That's true not just in real estate but in all your endeavors in life. My friends tell me they love to hang out with me because of my passion and joie de vivre. To me, every restaurant is the best, every party is incredible, every exhibit is *awesome*! Those aren't just words. I truly feel it. I have a passion for life, and a passion for what I do.

When you feel that kind of enthusiasm, that fervor, it's like a fire burning inside that fuels you and propels you. Your intensity increases and you want to enjoy and achieve to the greatest extent possible. This is what drives you to be the best—not just in the eyes of others, but to yourself. Passion builds desire and also self-esteem.

Think about it: You can find a job you "like," get up and go to work every day and be "happy," but it's probably not something you'll want to dedicate your life to. If you're passionate, however, you'll work around the clock if that's what it takes, and you won't complain—you won't even mind. Passion is when working hard inspires you to work harder. While others want to do their jobs and go home, you won't be happy unless you're the very best. And every day, you'll want to be better.

So, before we even get started, I have to tell you: If you don't really love real estate, you shouldn't be in this business. I tell my children that all the time. If you don't love it, pick something else; pick something that you do love.

> Passion is when working hard inspires you to work harder.

I love the excitement of creating a project that changes the way people live—something that is unique, beautiful, and visionary. I love bringing together the best designers and architects I possibly can and working with them to produce a place that is so imaginative and far-sighted that it transforms landscapes and lifestyles. I love looking at a piece of land or a building and seeing something no one else does—and then making my vision a reality.

That's what gets me going. It doesn't matter if we're talking about the most magnificent luxury resort in the world, or a small, federally subsidized apartment building. To see the possibilities that no one else saw, and to create something that will make life better for the people who live there, ignites my passion.

How do you know if you're the same? It's easy. Do you get excited thinking about building your first four-unit condo building and giving people who couldn't otherwise afford it a place to live? Do you find yourself looking at a run-down apartment building next to a highway and see yourself transforming it into an inviting medical office complex with easy access to nearby hospitals? And does the thought of it get your blood pumping? That's passion.

Passion is what allows me to see, visualize, and get totally focused on a project. It gives me extra energy. It gives me the feeling that what I am doing is the most important project in the world. I listen to other people carefully, but when I know they're wrong, I don't doubt myself. And that's a very important thing, because that's what drives you to success. Because if you question yourself, or let others make you doubt, then you will tend to let go. And what you can't do is let go.

So the passion carries you, and carries others—employees, lenders, partners, investors—into achieving the results. It helps me make something that's good, great. Because of my passion, I'll take that idea and I'll play with it to the largest degree possible. I'll take a piece of land, for example, and I'll say, "My God! This is incredible!" I envision all the magnificent possibilities, instead of limiting myself to what is likely. I look at it in terms of, "What could this be if there were almost no restraints attached to it?" And I get everybody around me to think the same way.

But beware of letting your initial excitement blind you. There's a duality to that passion. Because no matter how fantastic I think an idea, or a piece of property, or anything is, there's a part of me that holds back. There's always a part of me that says, "You can't totally fall in love. If you fall in love, you're going to make mistakes. When you fall in love, you forget about things that are important."

So what you need is a measured passion—passion tempered with practicality. You can never, never forget in the passion of the moment about the reality and the pitfalls.

A problem that sometimes arises with the people in my company, or my partners, is that as I display my passion for a project they get so turned on by it and it's so contagious that they fail to see the other side. They will fall in love with the concept and be blind to the drawbacks. They will make the mistakes of passion. So when I come to them later and say, "Well, that's a *stupid* thing!" they'll be totally shocked. They'll sputter, "But, but, but, you . . . you said that."

Because what they don't see is what's happening inside me. As soon as I fall in love, the logic steps in. I start analyzing, questioning, weighing everything that made me feel that way against the cold, hard facts. And, through that process of looking at the reality, I start chopping it down to a level that mixes the passionate with the practical until I arrive at what is possible.

When I'm doing a project, I don't tell my marketing people, "Hey, look, I've got a five-dollar budget, so don't think too much. We can't do too much. Let's keep it simple." No. I want to create the greatest campaign, regardless of the budget. I want them to free-flow and think and think and think. I want to instill that passion in them that I have, so they can create grand ideas. I don't want to take their passion and their creative juices and in any way curtail them during that creative process.

After they come up with their pie-in-the-sky visions, then we start scaling back until we find the place where their dream and the budget coincide. After they finish everything, I explain the limitations of the job and together we take all the great concepts we came up with and adapt them to a workable, financially viable solution.

When you're starting out, you should forget that you only have a limited amount of money. You should ignore the people who are saying, "What are you doing? Are you crazy?" If you don't, you'll stop yourself. If you're going to jump, you have to believe you can fly. You can't listen to the people who are afraid of falling.

Without the vision and the passion you won't be able to sell your ideas. Even if you have a limited vision that will curtail some of the things you can actually do, you have to treat it like the greatest project in the world. Even while I'm thinking about the pitfalls, I can't go to the bank and to my investors and say, "Hey, this has got all these pitfalls." Because then they're not going to buy in. You don't go to a lender and say, "I've got the greatest job in the world for you to finance. Nevertheless, the market is not really that good, and the project has all these potential problems."

You've got to think of all of those things and be prepared to deal with them and to answer their questions, but you can't let challenges stop you.

> Don't let challenges stop you.

I remember one time, we were looking to buy about six thousand acres outside Cartagena, Colombia. The first time I went to visit the place, I took a bunch of people, including architects and friends and so forth.

At the site, I started seeing everything we could do with this beachfront land. I started visualizing how great it could be. And what I could do. I could bring in an equestrian center here and tie it in between the farm and the beach. I was so passionate that everybody got completely hooked on the project. The Colombian partner we were thinking about working with was ready to put up a $300,000 down payment, and he was so excited about the plans that he almost did it without asking for it to be returned if the deal didn't go through.

We stayed in Cartagena for two or three days and I kept on going back to the site and looking at the beach. They were totally shocked when on the third day I said, "I don't think I want to do this job."

What happened was that, by then, my practical side had kicked in and led me to reality.

But there I was with all these people shaking their heads and saying, "But I thought you told me the beach was incredible."

And I said, "Yes, but when I said that I hadn't actually put on my bathing suit and gone out there and found out that it's more mud than sand. And I hadn't done my analysis and found out that every lender and everybody I spoke to in the United States told me they would be petrified to come to Colombia because of the current political situation."

So, after all the initial excitement, the reality overtook the passion that had gotten me excited about the job.

First, always, you need passion. Then, as you investigate your ideas and attempt to make them coincide with reality, you might change your plan or end up discarding it altogether. Or you might find out that your passion totally checks out and you can say confidently: "I'm in the right location and I'm in the right place and I'm in the right program."

But without the initial passion you're never going to get to that level. Because if you want to get everybody to be on board with you, you have to believe it deeply yourself. If you doubt, so will everyone else.

I don't know who said it first, but it's true: "Failure is not in falling down, it's in not getting up again." You're going to get knocked down. You're going to feel defeated. You're going to hear a lot of nos. A lot. I still do. But when I'm down I know I just have to get up and regroup. I have to rethink it differently and give more to the next battle so I do better.

When I would go to a lender, particularly in the beginning, and they said, "No," I wouldn't just quit. You don't just give up, you learn from that no. When you go to them and say, "Okay, I've got this great job and I'm going to do the construction like this and it's going to produce such and such revenue," and the lender says, "No," ask why. Don't just take that no. Say, "Can you at least tell me why?" He may have any number of reasons: He might feel you don't have enough equity. Or that your contractor is weak. Or he might not believe your income projections.

Listen to that lender's reasons and use them to prepare better for the next lender you go see. If there was a contractor problem, an equity problem, or whatever, you can look for ways around it. You can build your case into a more solid presentation so that you can answer better for the next lender. You have to keep on fighting, and keep on fighting, until you find the one that believes in your idea enough to give you the loan.

When I was starting out in the affordable housing business, if I had taken no for an answer I would never have gotten that first job built. There were two *huge* obstacles: we were doing rentals, and we were doing affordable minority housing. Nobody wanted this in their neighborhood. Even the poor people who would benefit from it many times didn't want it in their neighborhoods. The lenders were petrified of lending in those areas. So they wouldn't. It's what was called redlining in those days. The cities were very difficult to deal with because they listened to all the naysayers who would come in and say, "Not in my neighborhood. We're not going to vote for you if you do it."

So I had to build a fortress around me and keep on going until I hit my goal. How? Never say, "No." Never believe it can't be done. Say, "How do I get the best consultants? How do I make the project look the greatest? How do I convince the neighborhood residents that this is going to increase their property values? How do I convince the politicians that this is going to be a plus in the vote column and not a minus? How do I convince them that this is going to make this a better city in the long run?"

You will hear many more nos than yeses. If it were any different, believe me, everyone would become a real estate developer.

It's important, as you grow, to understand exactly what you need to succeed. How much money. How much preparation. How to set up your presentations. But then, remember, it's a long road. So just keep your eye on the light at the end of the tunnel and keep building a better and better road to get you there. And then just don't give up. You can't give up.

Just because you hit a roadblock doesn't mean you're not going to win. It just means it's a little harder and longer and you just have to gather all the troops and go at it. But, if you keep at it, if you let your passion carry you forward, you're going to win a lot, too.

So, when you hit a stumbling block, you can't waste your time being negative about it. You can't beat yourself up over it. You learn from it and make yourself better for the next time.

I worry all the time. If I'm getting ready to make a presentation to ask a lender for money to build a project, I worry. If I've got the construction under way on a new building, I worry. But it's not like I just worry for no reason. The worry does two things: it makes me extremely competitive, in that I want to make sure that my job will be the best, and it keeps me out of trouble, because I tend to think about all the negatives that can happen. I worry about things that are real. I worry so I can prevent problems before they happen.

> Worry about real problems that you can prevent before they happen.

That keeps me on my toes and very, very sharp and very receptive to ideas. And I push the people around me to think along those lines: "Don't give me the good news. I can see that. Where are our pitfalls?"

You have to concentrate on that. Ask yourself: "Where did we go wrong? What part of the due diligence didn't we do? I know this site is great, but did we cover everything? Is the title right? Did we really do the market study correctly to know that we can get these prices? Did we really see what the contractor did so that we priced it out correctly?" Don't leave it for tomorrow. Do it now. That's part of worrying.

I also know there are certain things I can do something about and certain things I can't. There are two great philosophers, Epictetus and Marcus Aurelius, who explained that a lot better than I do. One was an emperor and the other was a slave. And they basically said, "You take what is given to you. Some things you can change and some things you can't change. You need to concentrate on those things that you can change." I hope I'm intelligent enough to worry only about the things that are within my power to change and not about the things that are givens.

So I'll worry long before I make that presentation so that I can make sure I've covered all the issues and made it the best I possibly can: Are the numbers right? Do I show the contractor's credentials effectively? Is the architect's rendering powerful? Are the plans complete? Can I answer every question the lender is going to have so I can convince him to give me the loan?

If not, I'd better learn the answers, fix the plans, or whatever *before* I get in that lender's office. Because if I worry about something, I need to act on that worry. Then, once it's taken care of, I can let it go. The worrying reminds me that you don't put all your eggs in one basket, hoping that your plan is going to work out exactly. You build contingencies. And you can't be overoptimistic. You have to expect things to go wrong.

That's very different, though, from spending your time being negative. What good does that do you? That's just a complete waste of time. Or, worse, it's a way of undermining your confidence and fueling your doubts until you quit. No! Don't do that. Learn from your experience. Do it better next time.

You can't get discouraged. I know that's easier said than done. It takes a tremendous amount of heart and knowledge to get through the hard times. But that's where your passion comes in again.

People get defeated by failures, by losing battles, by buying properties that don't go well. In order for me to get up every day and create and lead the company, I can't be in a negative frame of mind, particularly in areas where there is very little I can do to change the situation. Problem jobs, even though they may be a very small proportion of your overall financial situation, can end up taking a much larger chunk of everybody's time. So I'm much more inclined to take the first loss than to keep the cancer growing and try to fix it.

The Las Ramblas project we were involved with in Las Vegas is the perfect example. Before that, we had never been unsuccessful in a job. But after we bought the land and formed our partnerships to go forward, two things happened: One, the construction costs we planned for shot up to almost three times what we thought because of labor unions and other problems. And, two, the market slowed and the demand for condominiums became much lower than we had predicted, while the supply became much greater. So there was a huge imbalance.

And I thought, and I thought. I had a lot of sleepless nights, because we had never given deposits back and we had never sold a piece of land in a job we had worked so hard on. It was consuming me, distracting me from other projects I had going on at the time.

I consulted a lot of friends to see what my options were. Finally, I told myself, enough is enough. I didn't want to deal with the negative thoughts, and probably fail because of market conditions I had little control over. I decided I wanted out.

It was a very, very tough decision to let go of the project, to have a failure in a project, but I had to cut the losses and cut the negative thoughts.

You can't dwell on areas that are very, very negative and very, very problematic, because they are going to totally consume you. I always say, "Your first loss is your best loss." Take it. Learn from it. Move on. Be better next time.

> Your first loss is your best loss. Learn from it.

Passion made me see the possibilities of Las Ramblas in the first place. Reality pushed me to pull the plan together—to bring in the architects and the designers, to line up the partners, and to go after the necessary permits. But when the market realities changed, I knew we had to pull the plug.

That didn't reduce my passion for the project. And if the market realities (which we'll go into later) hadn't changed, I would have gone forward and it would have been a wonderful project that would have redefined the Las Vegas lifestyle. But Las Ramblas proves how your passion and reality must constantly be balanced.

Think of it this way: a sculptor may want to create a magnificent piece that stands fifty feet high. But if all he's got to work with is one twenty-foot block of marble, it's pretty much impossible. His passion won't make the marble longer. He's got to modify his vision, or wait until he finds a fifty-foot piece.

It's the same with real estate. Use your passion to imagine the greatest project you can; use reality to guide you to create the best that is possible. Never lose either. Passion will keep you going as you run into the obstacles that always crop up. It will give you the strength to believe in yourself and to withstand the critics and naysayers. But paying close attention to reality—and the changes in conditions that affect your project—will keep you from driving off a cliff.

PRINCIPLE #2: DISCIPLINE

If you're going to play the game, you've got to think you're playing at the highest level and you're the best. If I don't think that then it's not fun for me.

Being the best takes discipline and absolute dedication. If you're passionate about what you do, that isn't hard. If you're not, every day will be a chore. Eventually, you'll quit.

You have to be like an Olympic athlete. They love what they do so much that they'll get up every day, train for hours, run, sweat, fall down and get back up to try again. They do it only with the thought of that gold medal, of being the best in the world.

When he runs faster than he ever has before, an Olympic sprinter will smile, think through all the things that contributed to that success—how his muscles felt, what was perfect about his stride, how his breathing came in perfect synch—so he can engrave it in his muscles and his mind. Then he'll turn around the very next time and try to beat that time.

Every day, the Olympian practices to beat all the other competitors he'll be facing. But even more than that, he runs against himself. He wants to be the best. And, when he is the best, he wants to be better. So he doesn't skip practice. And he doesn't hold back.

Talk about discipline and devotion.

You shouldn't do any less, no matter what you do. If you want to be a developer, you have to be just as disciplined. You have to learn all you can about the area you're going into, study the competition, and make every project the very best it can be. You have to make the best presentations, do the most research, and remain totally, totally focused on your goal.

Most people get distracted, and even if the distraction is only for a few minutes, they lose their focus. It's very hard to come back to the idea. So while you're hitting it don't move away from it. If you do, you will have lost the intensity of the moment and that level of hard work that it requires.

I think that maybe the one characteristic that separates me from most, and makes me a successful person, is my total dedication to the task at hand.

I'll give you an example. We were in Atlanta going over a big new project we were doing called CityPlace. We had architects and engineers and everyone there. I brought several of my people up from

Miami to walk through with me, along with the president of the bank that lent us the money for the project.

I was walking through the project with the engineers, going over the plans, comparing the ideas we had on paper with the reality of the site. I'd say, "Look at where the cars are coming from. Our building won't be seen this way. Move the entranceway over here." That level of detail. It's very important to me. I believe that being the gadfly, the guy who goes around searching for the truth, is an important role of the leader of the company who wants to stay on top. You've got to shake that tree and you've got to make people think.

While I was doing this, I noticed that two or three of my guys weren't paying attention. They were standing there with the lender, talking about the basketball game or something like that. And I exploded!

I said, "Hey! You know what? I'm not wasting my time here, and if you guys want to"—I'm yelling at the lender, too—"then do me a favor and get the hell out of here. Because the reason I'm doing this at my age is not only to make the project better, it's so you guys understand what it is that is going to make the project better."

From then on everybody was taking notes and watching carefully as we continued through the rest of the project. And the thing was, I was so totally focused that I didn't even think about what I had done—until later, after we were done. Then the local bank officer who had arranged for the bank president to come along came over to me and said, "Jesus, Jorge, that guy is the president of the bank! And the way you were yelling, even I got scared and started paying attention."

I hadn't even thought of it. Because I was working, and when I get focused I don't care if it's the president of the United States. We are there for a purpose and we were all supposed to be working. Still, though, the president of the bank!

I said, "Oh, no. Did I insult him?"

"No," he said, "are you kidding me? He loved it. He learned from it."

Good. I'm glad. Because I truly believe you need that kind of single-mindedness to succeed. Success requires discipline. It requires total focus and attention to details. I do everything with that same kind of intensity, that passion, that discipline.

When I go to the tennis court, for example, I know I'm not Roger Federer, but when I'm there I am going to be the very best that I can be. I will practice and try with every ounce of strength. If not, I'm not even going to the tennis court.

When I get on the treadmill in the morning, I'm going to see how well I can do in thirty-two minutes, even though at the end of five minutes I want to quit. You can never say no. You can never give up. I know in the back of my mind that my record is whatever, so I'm going to strive to push myself harder than that. I'm going to strive to achieve. If I don't, I will promise you that every time I go there, after five minutes I will say, "I'm done."

I can go there and say, "You know, you're fifty-seven years old. You look pretty good, you know. Look at everybody around you." But I go, "Nah! I don't want to hear that." I don't want to hear that I'm fifty-seven years old and because of that I don't need to play this way. I'm going to be the best fifty-seven-year-old man there is. I know I'm not twenty-three. But within the playing field I'm in, I would be very, very competitive. I have to be, or my desire greatly diminishes and I won't do the job. That striving for being the best has to be there at all times.

I apply the same drive in my work. If you want to get rich in real estate, you have to want it more than anything else. But wanting it isn't enough. You have to be dedicated to your dream. That means poring over the details. That means being willing to push yourself—always—to be better than the competition. That means not resting on your laurels and just repeating the same old building designs in new locations. You have to stay sharp to continue to succeed. A boxer who doesn't train as hard as he can before every bout won't be champion for long. A developer who isn't disciplined won't be either.

PRINCIPLE #3: HARD WORK

Success takes discipline. And it takes hard work. Those two are inseparable.

Discipline involves total devotion. It makes you strive for perfection. Without it, you go from a capacity of being great to staying average. But it's not enough to show up at the gym religiously every day, you have to put in the hard work it takes to be better today than you were yesterday.

When I was in college I had to be an A student. When I went to the city of Miami, right away I was determined to work harder than anyone there. I consciously tried to do better than anyone. I was in a race against myself. Can I achieve that? Can I go to a neighborhood meeting and—even though I'm petrified—get people to understand why it is that they need to spend money on a sewer instead of on landscaping on the street?

And I worked harder at achieving that than anyone else.

As I think back, I was really always preparing myself for what was to come. I was always laying the groundwork that would lead me to where I wanted to go. Even when I went to the city of Miami, I was immediately not just thinking about doing my job, I was thinking about how my job would allow me to progress.

Someone else might have been happy to go there as a planner and say, "I'm a planner. I'm going to do planning." And that's all they would ever do.

To me it was: "I'm a planner, but I'm a planner in the context of a much larger organization." I had to understand how the government organization functioned. I had to understand how the neighborhoods functioned. I wanted to understand it all in order to become the leader I wanted to be.

You need to get into the mind-set that says: "I can reach that next step. I can work harder than anybody else. I am smart enough to go to that next level. And, if I don't, I am no worse off for trying. I am back to where I was, just a little smarter."

The only real defeat is not trying. Even the greatest superstar needs to take several shots before that three-pointer goes in.

> ## The only real defeat is not trying.

Of everything you need to succeed, I think hard work and dedication are the qualities that carry you to the end. You can't do it without luck, and you can't do it without brains. But there are a lot of smart, lucky people who just don't get anywhere—a lot smarter and a lot luckier than me.

When I think of success, I think of a person who has the drive and the determination to pursue his dream. I think of the person who wakes up and says, "You know what? I don't want to drive a truck anymore. What if I bought three trucks and got other people to drive them for me?" And they don't let up. The successful person is the one willing to work as hard as it takes to put that dream into a plan, and to just go at it nonstop.

I think when people think about the keys to my success, that's what they think. They think of the passion, and the relentless pursuit, and the hard, hard work. In my case, when I'm pursuing a goal, I become so totally dedicated that almost anything I do in life relates back to it. I become a worker almost twenty-four hours a day. By that I mean not only do I get up and have my plan and work and work and have the phone calls I have to make, the studies I have to do, the interviews I have to carry out, the pro formas I have to pump out—all those things. But then every other thing I do becomes more work for me.

For example, I get up on Saturday and I read the paper. Almost everything I read in that paper somehow comes back into the ideas I have. If I read an article about how another person in another city did whatever, boom! I apply that. Whether I read a book, or I go to a seminar, or I attend a board meeting, if there's something I think will make what I'm working on better, I apply it. At board meetings, I'm constantly taking notes, writing down the great ideas that come from listening to the world around me. So I come back and I apply all that to my area of expertise.

When you become that dedicated, everything starts becoming your work. You're always studying your competition, always coming up with new ideas. What you want to do is really look and study your competition and then say, "How do I build a better mousetrap? What is it in my job that is going to make people (a) choose it, and (b) pay more for it?"

I always tell the young developers and the developers who are working for me, "When you think of the customer, put yourself in their shoes. You don't need to be a rocket scientist. What the hell would you want for yourself? You want the best."

So you've got to work hard and you've got to do whatever needs to be done. When I started out with my affordable housing buildings in Miami, there were a lot of times when I had to get my hands very dirty in those buildings—very dirty. I mean this is not like you start and you're going to be a white-collar worker and just do numbers.

I remember one of my very first lenders, Leonard Abess, who now owns City National Bank, he would love to come to building tours with me. And he would tell me afterward, "I have never seen the attention to detail, the attention to picking up papers. You go to an office and start putting all the furniture in place. You straighten the pictures if they're a little slanted."

I would go nuts because I had bought these blue-and-white uniforms for the workers at the buildings. This was affordable housing, but I wanted everybody to look nice and elegant. And if people were out of uniform, I would freak out. Just because it was affordable housing didn't mean I was going to give it any less. It takes the same amount of work and attention to detail as I give one of my multimillion-dollar projects today. If a plant in the lobby was dead and it hadn't been replaced I would get the manager and tell him to take care of it. Everything you can imagine on a property had to be perfect. And that takes a lot of hard work.

Leonard tells me he learned a lot about how to inspect things and how to do market analysis, and how to visit properties to see whether it was being done right or wrong, on those trips with me. He learned the value of that level of attention.

At the beginning he thought, "My God, the guy's a freak." But then we became friends, and he understood. He became my main lender, and he started giving me just unbelievable amounts of money, because he saw that passion and that attention to detail from the very beginning. I was proving to him that I was willing to work as hard as it takes to succeed. You have to do the same. It will make it easier to get loans from traditional lenders, or to convince investors. When they see that you'll do whatever it takes to make your projects a success, they'll be happy to give you the money you need.

Settling for less is something I just won't do. I beat myself up more than anybody else. Most of the time I'm not a happy guy. I'm not a settled guy. I'm a dissatisfied guy. Because I strive for perfection, and a guy who strives for perfection is never pleased with anything he's done.

So work became my life. And when you start, if it's going to be something you want to make a career out of, it's got to become your life. You've got to make it so much a part of it that it's seamless. You still go see a movie and you still go to dinner and you still enjoy your family, but you do it with those who are helping you build your company. You invite your lenders to barbecues, dinners, movies, parties, and birthday parties. You do the same with your partners, your investors, your architects, and your contractors. You should treat everyone who is part of your professional "family" like part of your immediate family. I was very conscious of that and very driven about it.

One of the reasons my first marriage was not successful was that I started having problems combining my family life with having to go every weekend to visit jobs and things like that, and then it started to become a strain. Even though I tried really very hard to make it family fun. Today, my wife, Darlene, takes a writing pad and my son Felipe, who's three, sits in the back and we go see jobs. We see the pretty girls who are in the showrooms selling the projects and Felipe comes in and flirts with them and they've got treats for him and everything is fun.

Get your loved ones involved in what you're doing or else you're going to have a real hard time. In the beginning I had two jobs—I was working as a consultant and I was starting my company. You've heard the saying: "The family that plays together stays together." It's true. But the family that builds their dreams together does too. If they feel like they're a part of what you're doing, it's much easier for them to support you and encourage you along the way.

Principle #4: Integrity

You have to have certain rules you live by that you don't bend. That's the morality. That's the integrity. Never do anything that is not right. Those things follow you and they form the parameters under which you act. If you can't do a deal within those parameters, then you walk away from the deal. If it meant that the only way I could do business in

Mexico, for example, was to stretch those parameters, then I would not do any business in Mexico.

When I was first starting out—and get ready, this can very easily happen to you—there were some inspectors who tried to get me to bribe them. In fact, on the very first deal I made in a city I won't name, I had an inspector who my people came to me about. They didn't know what to do because the guy was known for taking money and he was refusing to give us our certificate of occupancy.

I said, "Have him talk to me."

I went and met with him and I didn't wait for him to say anything because I didn't want to get in a position in which something illegal was even mentioned. I started right off with, "Listen, I don't know what is happening with our certificate of occupancy. It's costing me a fortune. My people are all worried and I know from you that you're a person who has the highest standards. Because if somebody would be delaying the permit because they would be expecting a bribe from us, or something like that, I would immediately go to the state attorney's office and denounce them. Because we will never do anything that's illegal."

The conversation changed right then and there. I got my certificate of occupancy the next day. The problem, if you ask me, is that he just hadn't had anybody call him on it before. And he knew that this was no bluff. The next day, I would've gone to the state attorney's office.

So, from the very beginning, everybody knew that we were the lily-white guys. We played the game by the rules. We were tough, but we were not going to bend the rules in any way that was wrong. We may get whatever tax opinions from our accountants and our attorneys so that we pay the minimum; it's not like I'm a fool and I'm going to pay the most tax. I'm going to have the best consultants in the world in telling me how I can legally and morally skin that cat. But I would never, and I would not allow anyone in my company to ever, do something immoral.

That's how you mix morality and integrity with business acumen. You're doing it really for self-preservation, but at the same time you're also doing it because it's the right thing. And doing the right thing ultimately helps you and the community.

That reputation is going to follow you forever. If you show people you'll break the rules even once, they'll never trust you. Why should they? You've already shown them you're willing to be dishonest when it's convenient. Don't do something wrong in the short term to get your goal. It will haunt you forever and hinder your company's growth.

If you show people you are honest, that you have high morals and integrity and you stick by those principles, they will want to do business with you. They will tell their friends and those friends will want to do business with you.

Most people, though, are shortsighted. You see it in teens. I see it in my kids growing up. I think particularly in this modern age, there is a great desire for constant gratification and short-term results. People will forgo the future to make a killing in the present.

When I do something, I'm very keen on not necessarily maximizing the profits in a deal. I'm more interested in maximizing the profits in a long-term relationship. I know that if I go to an investor I could push the deal to a greater extent for me. But I am cognizant of the fact that what I really want is to build the relationship with him so that in all of the future deals I have he'll say, "Let's do it with this guy."

That typically means leaving money on the table. That typically means treating that person well. That typically means maybe I won't make as much money in this deal—but I'll make a lot more money in all the future deals put together.

I do that with customers, too. I always give them the best, even if that means making less money for myself. Why? Because it creates a brand; people will talk about you as an honorable person. And, selfishly, it will give you future clients. People don't always stay in the first condominium they buy. If they have a good experience with you, they'll want to buy from you again. And they'll tell their friends. The word will spread, and when those friends or friends of friends are looking, they'll remember.

As a person starting out, it is going to be very hard to balance present profits and future profits, instant gratification and long-term gratification. It's a very difficult thing to do because many times the easiest way is to take the shortcut and make the money there. But as you prepare your plan, as you embark on your path, you've got to think about future relationships, about giving back. That's why it's important to send people gifts. That's why you'll want to spend some money to give somebody a bottle of wine and in doing something nice for them. You're not buying them off, you're remembering them on birthdays and holidays, and thanking them for being helpful. Treat them like family and they'll treat you like family. It's taking part of the proceeds you have and reinvesting them in the future.

So as you're starting out always think about building relationships. Don't just think about the money you're going to make now. Think about leaving part of the profits on the table so you can do the next deals in the future.

And, no matter what, always integrity. Treat people and your community right. You want to build a reputation for doing the right thing. It will reward you personally and professionally.

PRINCIPLE #5: LOYALTY

My first architect was a man by the name of Adolfo Albaisa. He did all my early jobs. He did them for nothing. He didn't get paid until I sealed the deal. Then he got paid. And we became best friends. Our families became best friends.

The same with my lender. I had a few lenders who also became my best friends. To this day, Leonard Abess, Adolfo Henriquez, and Carlos Migoya are my best friends. Some of them are still lenders and some of them are not. But they're my best friends. Or very, very good friends.

My contractor. On my very first job, one of the guys who helped me close the deal without charging me a cent was a contractor. As I grew, that guy did everything for us. Everything we did was through him. And he became a dear friend. So did his wife and children.

All these people became like employees in a way, but they weren't. They were like partners. And they were friends. And I proved to them over and over again that I was always there for them, just like they had always been there for me. They knew they could count on me because they knew that I place tremendous value on loyalty.

When I think back on what I know now, the one thing that comes out that the young in all their zeal tend to forget is: build long-lasting relationships with those who matter. It's like planting seeds in fertile soil and taking good care of watering them. It won't be overnight, but the results will come.

You build those by doing the right thing. By being there for people. By being loyal. I will not screw a friend in a deal. They all know that. They know I won't let them down.

Your friends and business partners should know the same about you. If you're loyal, they will trust you. Your lenders should know they are going to get their money back, and on time. That way, they'll be willing to lend you what you need, when you need it.

When I borrow money from a lender, they know they are going to get paid back. I have never defaulted on a loan. I have never even been late on a payment. As hard as that may have been to do—and, believe me, there were times when it was extremely difficult to get the money together to pay on time—I always did it.

I was building a credit history, sure, and I knew that was important. But I was doing much more than that. I was showing those lenders that I valued our relationship, and that I would always, always honor the terms of our agreement.

From early on, I understood the importance of relationships. And I knew that if I was going to build good relationships I had to prove I could be depended on. Remember the old saying, "A friend in need is a friend indeed." That's just another way of saying people appreciate loyalty. They want to know they can count on you. And if you do that, then you'll be able to count on them.

In graduate school I built great relationships with my professors. I wanted good grades so I knew that was important. But it wasn't hard; I liked them and they liked me. Then, when I was graduating, those relationships helped even more.

The head of the University of Michigan urban planning department was very good friends with a guy he had gone to school with. That was the head of the Miami Planning Department. And he called the guy and said, "I've got this bright young kid. You've got to see him." So my relationship with a professor got me the interview in Miami.

After I got the job, I became very close to my new boss. We had some things in common—we both went to the University of Michigan; my wife used to live near the Thornapple River, and so had my boss—so I used that to establish a relationship. A relationship that could lead me to grow. So when opportunities became available in the Planning Department, who do you think they were going to give them to? To those people who were close to them. I had my sights on bigger things, but I wasn't just using them. They wanted to control the department. So they wanted people who were loyal in key positions. I knew that. So I became part of their loyal team.

The same thing with the mayor. I knew the mayor wanted to have incredible programs that would benefit the community. So I met him and I said, "I believe in your programs and I think I can do this." And he said, "Unbelievable!"

So I developed these housing programs and he loved them. Those same programs I developed with the mayor were the ones I later used to start my first affordable housing project. I was the golden boy of the mayor and the city manager; and the city manager and the assistant city manager were still my Michigan guys. So I can say, yeah, I worked harder than anyone and I had the best applications, which I did, but my goodness, I had my relationships that I had worked really hard at, as well. And I was a loyal and trusted friend.

That's especially true of my relationship with my partner, Steve Ross. People are amazed that two people with such strong and different personalities have been such great partners for thirty years. We have been because of the complete trust and loyalty we have for each other. We are always there for each other, professionally and personally.

You need to think about the long-term effect of everything you do. You are building your future, every day. People who are seen as dishonest or disloyal, people who are lazy or undisciplined, won't succeed. At least not beyond one or two deals. The word—both good and bad—spreads fast. Make my five guiding principles your guiding principles, and you will have a tremendous advantage over your competition.

KEY PRINCIPLES

- Passion is when working hard inspires you to work harder.

- Don't let challenges stop you.

- Worry about real problems that you can prevent before they happen.

- Your first loss is your best loss. Learn from it.

- The only real defeat is not trying.

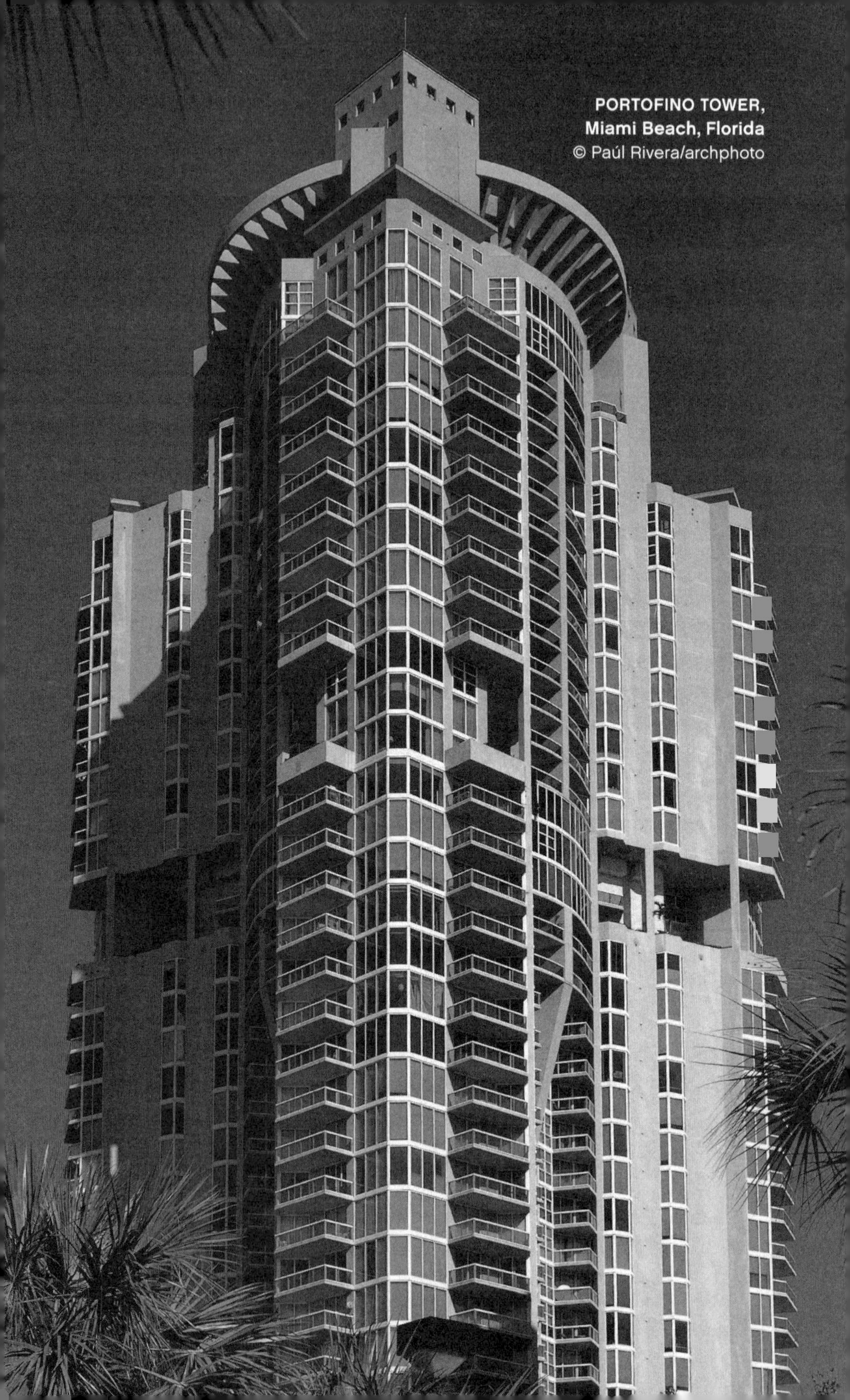

PORTOFINO TOWER,
Miami Beach, Florida

2 · STARTING OUT: THE FOUR KEYS TO SUCCESSFUL INVESTING

"The crowd is the untruth."

—Søren Kierkegaard

A lot of people think that the first thing you do after you decide you're going to go into real estate is find the property. They scan the classifieds, drive neighborhoods looking for FOR SALE signs, wander past brokers' offices scanning the flyers in the window.

They're wrong.

You start off in real estate by figuring out what you want to do. You have to decide what the best type of investment is for you. Before anything else. Before you find the property. Before you raise money.

First you decide what you're going to do. Then you learn everything about it. Then you go do it.

It makes sense, right? If you don't know where you're going, how can you get there? You'll be wandering in circles. You'll try one thing one day, change your mind, switch course, and head off after something else. The only place you'll end up is broke. Oh, you may get a lucky break along the way that will keep you afloat and make you think you're succeeding, but sooner or later your money is gone, your investors have lost faith, the banks won't lend you money, and your partners—if you had any—will be taking you to court.

If you'd rather be rich than broke and in court, you have to find the investment that's right for you. What that really means is, in many ways, you're finding yourself. You're finding your talent. You're finding that thing inside you that you were born with, that thing that was given to you and that you need to bring out.

Most people are afraid to uncover it. They're afraid of failure. They're afraid of ridicule. You can't be. You have to believe in yourself and take the plunge. You have to take risks.

In real estate, as in life, there are countless options. You need to know what it is you want to do.

For me, I knew it was affordable housing. But it very easily could've been market-rate housing or anything. I picked affordable housing for reasons that fit me. I knew I needed certain things.

I needed to feed my family, so I needed money fast. I didn't have any money to put up, so I needed an investment that didn't require any money from me. I didn't want to fail, so I needed something I could figure out how to do, and that had a reasonable chance of succeeding.

KEY #1: SEE WHERE YOU CAN SUCCEED

I didn't pick affordable housing right away. I looked around and learned about different things before I made my decision.

Only you can know what's right for you. Whatever it is, I recommend starting small. You want to walk before you run. You learn as you go. With every deal, with every project, you learn something new. It's like running a marathon, or lifting weights. You need to train. You need to work at it. If you try to bench-press seven hundred pounds your very first time, you're not going to be able to do it. And there's a really good chance you're going to get hurt.

It's the same with real estate development. Don't try to overachieve right away. Let's say you inherited $1 million; I wouldn't recommend taking it all and spending it on launching a three-hundred-unit luxury condominium project if you've never done anything like that before.

The worst thing you can do is risk that money without knowing what the hell you're doing. You might as well take it to Vegas and play it all on a single bet at the craps table. The odds are you're going to lose it.

That's why, even if your rich aunt died and left you a boatload of money, I would still give you the advice of starting small. So if you mess up you haven't lost your $1 million.

When I first started, it wasn't a three-hundred-unit job. It was a sub-sidized twenty-one-unit renovation in Little Havana, an area I already knew well because back when I was a planner in the city of Miami I had created a lot of its neighborhood programs. I knew a lot, but I still started with a twenty-one-unit job. It would have been crazy for me to start out with five hundred units.

So you have to ask yourself, "What can I really handle so I don't fail and go broke before I even start?" Don't think that you're going to be Jorge Pérez the first year. Jorge Pérez wasn't Jorge Pérez the first year. Not even close. He had to learn the hard way about everything before he could take the next step, too. It's all about stepping-stones. It's all about knowing, learning, saving a little bit, jumping up. Knowing, learning, saving a little bit, getting more relationships and jump-ing up.

That doesn't mean you have to stay small. As I told you in the intro-duction, I made over $1 million the first year I was in business.

That was out of necessity as much anything. I had to figure out how I was going to get money into the company very fast. I had to eat. I didn't have a salary. So it was very important for me to find the short-term income that was going to allow me to succeed very quickly.

So I picked two jobs that had finish lines that were very short term, as opposed to some of the other jobs that came later on, in which I had to start new construction from beginning to end and it would take me twelve to sixteen months to realize the fruits of the labor.

In some of the rehabilitation jobs we did first, within six months of the time we got in we redid everything and started seeing some dollars flow in. It was very important for me to manage that cash flow.

If I were starting all over, I would start in the same area again. Abso-lutely. I think there are still huge possibilities in affordable housing because federal programs allow you to make money without having to put a lot of your own money in. They give you a guaranteed income for units you rent to people with incomes below certain levels.

The key questions to federal programs are: How do I make the proper government applications for whatever I am going to do so that I get selected? And then, how do I draw up the plan so that it becomes economically feasible? Once you have that, then it becomes a question of finding the product—will you do single-family homes or FHA homes that have been abandoned? Or do you do multifamily rentals as I did?

The federal government has become a partner, in a way, in your endeavors. And once you achieve that success in getting funded, it will be quite easy to get investors and lenders to back you financially in order to achieve your goal.

The risk levels of affordable housing are much less than those for market-rate rentals and much less than in the condominium market, because there is a never-ending demand for this type of product. It's not like you're going to do a project in a lower-income part of town and rent it for $200 a month and there's not going to be people lining up to come in. There are always people who need apartments with cheap rents.

So when you're starting out picking your investment, it's very important to look at all the federal, state, and local programs that are available to help you make your plan work. You have to see where you can succeed most easily.

There are a lot of ways to do it. It might be flipping individual houses. It might be buying office buildings and improving them so you can raise rents or sell them for more, or both. It might be affordable housing.

It depends on you, and the market. At different times, market forces might make one area better than the others. If there's a glut of office space, you might not want to start there. On the other hand, there might be a glut of offices in general, but you might see that there's a real shortage of premium office space in a specific area and decide that that's what you want to offer. You have to see where you can succeed. That takes knowing what you think you'll be best at, and knowing what you like enough to stick with.

It might be federally subsidized housing, like it was for me. If it is, you'll have to have imagination and be willing to deal with all the bureaucracy that is inherently involved in government programs. But you can make money at it. Like I said, I made over $1 million the first year and I didn't put any of my own money into it. I started small, and I stayed totally focused on my goal.

> Start small. Pick an achievable goal, then be
> unwavering in your pursuit of it.

I recommend the same for you: Start small. Walk before you run. Pick an achievable goal, then be unwavering in your pursuit of it.

As I said at the beginning of this chapter, you have to know where you're going if you're going to get there. Once you do, you can't take your eyes off the target. You have to stay focused. And you can't deviate.

You're going to have to become an expert in whatever area it is you're going into. If it's market-rate apartments, you're going to have to learn everything there is to know about the market in your area, about what people like and want, about what kind of financing is available, about the costs, the competition, the trends, and everything else there is to know.

If it's office buildings, you're going to have to know how to increase the value of the property so you can increase rents, how to understand leasing and how to select tenants, and so on.

So choose what you think you'll be best at, and then keep at it. Don't lose sight of your goal.

But to be able to decide what you want to do, you have to know what's involved. And you have to know yourself.

KEY #2: KNOW YOURSELF

When I was starting, I did not only do subsidized housing; I tried a lot of different things. I would have different partners for different ventures and we'd go into certain areas of the city and decide to invest.

For example, we decided to buy property in South Beach, so we went looking for deals.

Back then, in 1979, South Beach wasn't the glitzy, glamorous spot you see on *CSI: Miami*. If you found a top model on Ocean Drive, she was probably lost. Miami Beach, including South Beach, was full of elderly retirees and decrepit old buildings.

But what a beautiful beach! I couldn't help but look at that and think it was the best-kept secret in real estate.

So I found a partner named Barry Goldmeyer and we started buying all these buildings on South Beach. He had more access to money. I had the desire, and the willingness to put in every afternoon and every Saturday I had looking for properties. At the time I had a full-time job and he didn't, which meant that I had to cut out my leisure life to concentrate on this.

After doing it for a little bit I realized that that's not what I wanted to do. I really could not take all my waking hours and go and find dumpy buildings on South Beach. Not because the idea wasn't good, but because I wasn't willing to devote that much time to that purpose.

There were two reasons: One, I couldn't have two full-time jobs at the same time; and two, I really lost interest in buying junky buildings to flip them. We used to do a paint job, for example, and flip them. And after a little while it just didn't do anything for me. I couldn't develop a passion for it.

Affordable housing, though, offered several things that were really important for me. As opposed to my South Beach venture with Barry, I could see the growth opportunities. I saw the possibilities of expanding to a national thing once I got my expertise locally—first in the city, then in the county, then in the tri-county, then in the state, then national. I couldn't see that in the South Beach buying. It was much more limited. And much less creative. There is only one South Beach, and there is only so much you can do with it.

I also felt incredibly satisfied by the public purpose of affordable housing. I was providing poor people with places to live at prices they could pay. And that was great.

To make it even better, the first units we rented went to the elderly. Going to visit those jobs and having those elderly people coming up and treating me like a son, thanking me and bringing a little Cuban coffee—it was like being in heaven. I sort of felt like the professional basketball player who says, "I can't believe they pay me to play a game I love." Well, I sort of couldn't believe I was doing what I did before as a planner working for the city and making two cents, and now I was making two dollars—and I was getting even greater emotional satisfaction out of it.

I learned a lot about myself. I learned that flipping buildings didn't give me the satisfaction I wanted. It wasn't right for me. I needed something that satisfied my social conscience, my need to be a do-gooder. Affordable housing fit that need. I was providing housing for the elderly, giving grandmothers and grandfathers places to live, at a cost that was within their means. And I could make money doing it. What could be better?

You decide. Only you know what's right for you.

> Only you know what's right for you.

As you look at yourself, you have to ask, "What is it that I really like that is going to make me thrive?" Because for you to spend all those hours working at it—days and nights and weekends—you better love what you're doing. Or else you're going to give up the first time someone turns you down.

So you've got to know yourself and you've got to know what you're going to like. Try to pick something that really turns you on, that sparks your imagination, that is not just about money.

KNOW YOUR GOALS

When you're selecting the best investment for you, you need to have a clear understanding of what it is you really want. That means knowing what you want to get out of what you're doing.

We already know you want to be financially successful; that's why you're reading this book. But do you want to do it by providing affordable housing for people? Do you want to do it by fixing up distressed properties and flipping them? Or is it more important for you to build up a portfolio of properties to pass on to your kids?

It might not be housing. It might be that you have a friend who owns an office building and that gives you an idea. Perhaps you've realized how office buildings that are in good locations and are fixed up trade for a higher multiple of income than worse buildings. You've noticed how tenants are willing to pay more in this building that's the same as this other one, just because it's rehabbed.

So, do you just want to buy one, fix it up, and sell it? Or do you want to fix it up, increase the rents, and hold on to it for a nice steady income?

No matter what area of real estate you go into, there are two basic types of investment, passive and active. While a passive investment requires very little investment on your part, an active investment needs your full attention. Knowing your goals will help you decide which is best for you.

Passive or Active Investments

A passive investment means you're going to find something that with very little involvement on your part will make you money. For example, you will find gaps in the market in which you can get a house, and by just doing a paint job, or just a few improvements here and there, you can remarket it and make money.

Other gaps in the market are ones in which you can hold on to a property because you know there's a market trend going toward your piece of land, because the development path is going there, and in a year you'll make money.

Another passive investment is when you buy an office and get someone to manage it well for you. You get an architect to maybe make a few fixes. But you're fairly passive and you can do it without it being your full-time job.

Then there's the active investment, in which you're going to do work. You're going to rehab it. You're going to learn of a program and you're going to make the application for government subsidies, and you yourself are going to be the reason for the creation of value.

The expectations of a passive investor are typically much lower than the expectations of an active investor.

I do a lot of things in which I'm an active investor. It's hard work, but I make a lot more money. However, that doesn't stop me from being a passive investor in many other deals.

For example, let's say I have a friend who is unbelievable at office buildings, but doesn't really have enough money to buy a building that I think is a good opportunity. But I know he's really good at it and he can be the active guy and change it around. So I will choose to move my money into this project I'm familiar with, and I will get greater returns than by just putting my money in a certificate of deposit in the bank.

It gives me a higher return because there is a greater level of risk. But I'm still pretty much of a passive investor in those scenarios.

I just bought a building in Houston in which one of the partners is the guy who's rehabbing the building. And I'm a passive investor. I'm passive, but I still go there and I look at it, I analyze, I tell them what I think the building has and what it needs. It takes some time, but not as much as my active projects do.

Similarly, I just bought a building in New York. Somebody else is going to be running it. We have a long-term plan for the building, but it's a passive investment. My returns on those buildings are going to be substantially less than my returns on my active projects. But it's a great long-term hold that will produce substantial economic and tax benefits without requiring my active involvement.

Here's how it works. On a condominium project, typically you put down 15 to 20 percent of the cost as equity. You borrow up to 85 percent of the cost. But when you sell, you typically make about 20 percent profit on the sales price, not on the cost. Now, the sales price is much higher than the cost. So that 15 percent investment can mean a 300 percent return on your money in a couple of years.

Let me give you an example that's really simple:

I am building a project for $100. I go to a lender and ask for a loan. He gives me $85 and I put $15 down. After that, I do all my work, and I end up selling for $130, because I typically look for between 20 and 30 percent on the cost of the project. So the difference between the cost ($100) and the sales price ($130) is $30. Because I had put down $15, and made $30, I made a 200 percent return on my investment, or ROI.

The fact is that by doing a lot of different things—by putting the land up as equity when I ask for the loan, and setting the value of it a lot higher than what I bought it for because that's what it's really worth—many times I can reduce my initial down payment to $10. If I still sell it for $30 more than it cost, then I triple my money. That's a 300 percent ROI.

That's how leverage works. The more I reduce that initial payment, the greater my return is going to be. The amount stays the same, but the percentage return is greater.

Now, if I make a passive investment and I buy a building at $100 because I think it's a great deal, the market is going that way, and so forth, I would never in a million years expect to put 20 percent down and make a 200 percent return. Forget about 300 percent. In a passive investment it's simply not going to happen.

Typically, when you're looking at investments that are passive you look at an internal rate of return (IRR) in the 15 to 20 percent range. IRRs are used to compare investments that yield returns over a period of time, after an initial cash outlay. If you don't know how to calculate the IRR, your accountant or chief financial officer can. You can then use the IRRs they come up with to compare investments and see which gives you the best return for your money versus the risk involved. As a passive investor you can pick good real estate people and friends of yours who know what they're doing and get IRRs that are much better than the IRRs you would get from a certificate of deposit, which are around 5 percent at the present time.

Returns are always a reflection of the level of risk and the amount of work you put in.

So I have some passive investments, which I do because I'm going to get those 20 percent IRRs, and a lot of active investments in which I do the project and get a 200, 300, or 400 percent return.

So what I'm saying is, when you pick what you want to do, you have to see if you should take the plunge into becoming an active participant and increase your returns, or if it's better for you to be a passive participant and invest in projects that don't require so much time but give a lower return.

Management or Development

You also have to decide if your goal is to hold a piece of property and manage it, or develop it and sell it. Which is better? It's up to you. My partner, Steve Ross, and I always have this discussion. He's much more of a keeper. I'm much more of a seller. He believes that in the long term by keeping, for example, apartment rentals, you maximize value. I think I maximize value by selling in hot periods.

Neither one is wrong. It's just the way you want to make your money. His way, you collect rents that more than pay the mortgage and bills and you're always making some money. For years and years.

The other way, you buy it, fix it up or build it from scratch, and sell it as soon as you can for as much as you can. Then you can take the profits and build an even bigger project, or more than one project. And so forth and so forth.

The truth is, Steve and I debate the merits of management and development, but I do both. I still own some of my first affordable housing buildings, and I make good money off of them. As you grow, you should consider diversifying your investments as well.

The big difference is, if you're going to hold on to a house or a building and rent it out, you're going to have to maintain it, collect rents, pay the bills, do the bookkeeping, and so on. In other words, you're going to have to manage it. You can do it all yourself or hire someone to do all or part of it for you, but the bottom line is it has to be managed. It won't just run itself. That requires work over the long run, while providing a steady income. Selling fast may not give you as much money as you might gain over the long haul, but it ends the investment of time in a project, and it gives you an immediate influx of cash you can use for other things.

It's up to you. Which do you like better—a generally steady income for the long term, or quick cash?

The other thing you have to keep in mind is that in every deal there are always some rules that you can't deviate from. If you do, you're going to get hurt. You need to know those basics.

In market-rate rentals, the overriding factor is marketing. There are lots of choices for rental apartments. So you've got to make that person who's coming to see you believe that yours is the best choice. That is done through two things: good product and marketing.

Without marketing, you're nowhere. You can have all the good product you want, but if you don't let people know it's there and it's great, they aren't going to come. It's not like they all say, "Hey, let's go take a look at Jorge Pérez's rentals." I wish they would, but it doesn't work that way.

You've got to let people know you're there, and that you're better. And, as we'll see in chapter 6, it doesn't stop with the ad. They're not tenants until they sign the lease, so an ad that gets them to come see you is important, but it's only part of what it takes. The way you present your product—the landscaping, the amenities, all the touches that work together—and the way you treat the customer work together to seal the deal.

In federally subsidized affordable housing, such as Section 8, marketing is not even an issue. Tenant selection is what is most important. We would put a little trailer up as an office before we opened the building up. Then we would go looking for the best tenants.

How? We worked with the churches. We used to go to all the churches in the area and ask them to recommend their best parishioners. The ones that had secure jobs. We used to go to the social service agencies and ask them to recommend their most reliable program participants.

We would put a lot of effort into getting the best tenants we could. Because the all-important thing when you're dealing with very-low-income housing is tenant selection. That is of overriding importance.

I learned that studying urban planning in graduate school and reading about what happened with all the public housing projects in New York and Chicago—projects that actually had to be blasted after so many years because they became so drug-infested.

So I knew that if you had a two-hundred-unit job, if you had five bad families or drug dealers who had garbage everywhere or didn't pay their rent and hung around telling everybody they didn't pay rent, the chances were that your project was going to go downhill. They would bring their friends. The good tenants would get scared and leave.

So it's a whole progression that happens, and you lose it. You can't get the right managers, because no manager in his right mind will want to deal with such a complicated situation, let alone be inspired to do a good job.

So the trick is to have very, very tough management. We were great at tenant selection, we were great at maintenance, and we had strict rules about apartment upkeep and inspections. So if by any chance we did get that bad apple, we would be able to get them to follow the rules or evict them quickly.

So if you choose subsidized housing, if that's what you decide you want to do, management is of extreme importance. Get the right people in and make sure they stay in.

That helps maintain the value of your property, which opens up options for you. You can continue to rent it as subsidized housing. Or, if you ever decide you want to sell it, you'll be able to get a higher price. It also allows you to convert it to a market-rate building if general market prices become attractive enough.

What Is Your Level of Risk Tolerance?

When I started out in affordable housing, I was terrified. I didn't show it, but inside, I was petrified. I mean, I had no idea if it was going to work or not. I had no idea if the costs were going to come in as projected or go way over; if I was really going to be able to sell the tax credits to syndicators; if the lenders were really going to be there; if I was going to be able to secure the buildings at the price that we said, with very little down payment and very small, returnable deposits.

You're probably going to feel the same way. It's natural. But you go through this and you succeed and the lesson is: Don't let your fears get the best of you. Let me tell you, I woke up every day and I said, "Oh, my God! Not only is this not going to go through, but everybody is going to hate me."

Every day, I would wake up worrying that I had made the worst mistake of my life.

Every day there were details and questions and problems that came up, and I was totally and absolutely frightened.

What I did was, I used that fear to become even better. I used that fear to work that much harder in making sure that all those gaps I saw were fixed. That fear drove me to perfection.

How do you handle fear? You can become paralyzed. Or you can allow it to energize you and push you to become better at what you do. You've got to learn the difference between the things you can do something about and the things you can't do anything about.

> Learn the difference between the things you can do something about and the things you can't do anything about.

When you've got a lot at stake, fear is part of it. The more you stand to gain, or the more you stand to lose, the more you're going to be afraid. And it's not just when you're starting out. The fear happens all the time.

While I was working on this part of the book, I had to run out to see one of the most expensive jobs we've done. It was under construction. And I went in there and there were huge, huge, huge problems. The imported kitchen cabinets were coming in damaged and all wrong. They weren't the ones the customers had ordered and they had nicks all over them. And having to wait for new ones to arrive was going to slow down the rest of the interior work in the condos. Some pretty tough decisions had to be made and none would totally solve the problem.

It was like I was back to my very first project and the same thing was happening all over again: You go and you see what's wrong and you think, "What in the world am I going to do?"

That's the way it is. But you have a choice. You can either be the person who freaks out or you can be the person who deals with it.

So instead of looking for who to blame, I came up with a game plan to solve my cabinet problem.

The next day I sent a guy to Italy to make sure the rest of the cabinets weren't coming the same way. I had the project manager on-site to keep the rest of the job moving forward. And I called the general contractor to tell him to get someone else in for the cabinet work.

So there you have it. You can either say, "I've got a problem and I blame you," or you can regroup and solve it.

That's what I've always tried to do. Get everybody involved. Stop everybody from thinking negatively. Stop everybody from thinking about blaming and get them to be thinking about how to solve the situation at hand.

Now, I'm not saying I won't fire someone who is to blame. But first, the most important thing is: Don't be paralyzed by the fear; fix the problem.

And, get ready, there are going to be problems. Because real estate always involves taking risks. But the level of risk varies, depending on the type of investment, the size of the investment, the resources you have available, and your experience. So going into it, you have to ask yourself, "How much risk can I handle?" That's a really important part of deciding what you want to do.

It's hard to go wrong building affordable housing, for example. There's always a demand for it. Don't get me wrong, there are still ways to mess it up, as I'll show you later on. But there's always a market for it, so that reduces the risk.

Same thing with buying a single run-down house and fixing it up to sell at a profit. If you buy it at a decent price in a fairly decent location, the chances are good that sooner or later you're going to at least get back what you put into it. You may have to hold on to it and rent it for a while. Or you may have to accept the fact that you're not going to make the profit you projected. You may even lose a little money. But it's only a little, so the risk is much lower than it would be if you were taking all your life savings and trying to build a whole subdivision from scratch.

It's a simple fact of life: The bigger the deals, the bigger the risks; but the bigger the rewards, as well. So I'm still scared every day, but I can't let that stop me. You can't either. The only way to succeed is to take smart chances. You have to take calculated risks. You have to do your research, get advice, and make your plan. Then it's up to you. Sooner or later, you just do it. And when that happens, you will be alone with only your passion and vision to carry you.

> **The only way to succeed is to take smart chances.**

But you can't just dive in blindly. You take measured risks. I will risk little bits of money before I risk a large amount to find out if I'm right or wrong. I do presales like crazy to find out if there's a strong demand for the product I'm offering before I take the heavy-money plunge. And I always try to give myself a backup plan. I always try to buy smart. I want to be sure the land I am buying is well priced enough so that if the job is not successful, I can still sell the land and cover my costs.

But always remember: Reducing risks is not the same as not taking risks. You take intelligent, measured risks. Fear is really good. Worrying is really good. As long as it makes you a better developer and doesn't lead you to inaction.

> **Reducing risks is not the same as not taking risks.**

The way I see things, there's only one way to fail: by quitting. If you mess up and you learn from your mistakes to do it better next time, that's not failing. That's learning from your mistakes. A scientist who's trying to find a cure for cancer doesn't look at all the things he tried that didn't work as failures. He just continues to try other things. That's not a failure, that's a discovery. And sometimes, while they're trying to cure one thing, they find a cure for something else. Columbus set sail to find a new route to India. He didn't. Did he fail? I don't think so. He discovered a New World. How can you call that a failure?

That's why you can't let your fear stop you. What I say is, use the fear to build yourself up and build your walls around you, to make you stronger. Be smart. It's not like a great warrior doesn't have fear. But he better get a good sword and a great suit of armor, right? You know what I'm saying. He is not stupid. The fear drives him to plan and to protect himself.

Then, when he goes into battle, he's taking a measured risk.

Ask yourself, "What is the risk?" Then go over it. Think it through.

In every project there's a number of levels of risk: There is financial risk. There is personal risk. There's image risk. There's relationship risk. Take each of these risks, one by one, and ask yourself how you can minimize them. And make the answers part of your plan. You include contingencies. This goes for everything.

When I'm looking at the financial risk, what I do is get all the best consultants I can around me and listen to them. I get all the market data around me and I look at it in great detail. After that, I take the lead. I don't just dive in to see what happens. I do extreme research and I surround myself with the best people. Then I take the risk. And I stay ready to make changes as I find things along the path that were not expected.

You constantly have to be reassessing your plan and your risk levels. And if all of a sudden you find your risk level has increased tremendously, you better be ready to either pull out or to lower that risk somehow. You have to maintain the flexibility to constantly change and reassess, reassess and change. Because there are very few paths that remain straight. There are very few plans that don't change. You try to plan for as many contingencies as you can, and you continue to always measure that risk until the project is sold.

I always tell my guys in the company, I want to have the most pessimistic guys in the world when we're doing the due diligence and analyzing the job. And once we do that and we take the plunge and we're totally at risk, then I need them to become the most optimistic guys in the world. Because you've already taken the plunge. Now you have to make the project an absolute success.

Now, when you're starting off, you have to look at yourself and decide what your risk tolerance is. Are you willing, and able, to take smart chances? You can read a thousand books, but if you don't get yourself ready to take some measured risks—and I always say *measured risks*—it will never happen. Nobody is going to come to you and say here's an opportunity. It won't happen. You've got to take it on your own and you've got to prepare the plan and do it.

In this country there is a great opportunity to make money if you go outside the security zone and the box. Entrepreneurship is highly rewarded. The guy who comes up and takes the risk and accomplishes what he was aiming for typically gets rewarded at a much higher level than the guy who just has a secure nine-to-five job. When you get out of the crowd and you step up, it carries some risks, but the people will notice and you will be rewarded for that risk. That's why I always say: risk/reward. They always go together in my mind.

Know that—you have to take risks if you want to get the rewards—and believe in yourself. You have to. Because no matter what you do, there are going to be plenty of people who are going to criticize and second-guess everything you do. When you make money, they're going to ask why you didn't make more. When you're going into a project, it doesn't matter if it's buying a single house to fix up and flip or putting together a deal on an office building you want to rehab and sell, there are going to be those who try to make you doubt yourself.

Don't let them. You have to listen to constructive criticism, but don't be discouraged by negativism or Monday-morning quarterbacking. There are two types of people in the world: those who do and those who sit back and analyze and criticize. Every time you throw yourself out there, you know very well that there is going to be a bunch of people who are going to point out whatever it is that goes wrong. And that's okay—just don't let it get you down.

The easiest thing to do is to not do anything. But to make it in business you must take the plunge into the abyss—just bring good flashlights!

Sooner or later, you have to take a "leap of faith," as the philosopher Søren Kierkegaard called it. You prepare and plan, learn and get advice; but you can never know for certain. You just have to do it.

> Prepare and plan, learn and get advice—but you'll never know for certain. You just have to do it.

Kierkegaard also said, "The crowd is the untruth." He was talking about "eternal truths," but I think the same holds true in the world of business. Conventional wisdom and moving with the masses is not going to lead you to greatness. In fact, going with the crowd is most likely going to lead you away from opportunities for real success. You might do well for a little while, but in the long run moving outside the mainstream will bring much larger rewards.

Think of the tech stock bubble. How many people lost money there? Let me tell you, the guys who took the losses were not the ones who got in in the very, very beginning. They were the ones who saw what was happening and said, "Oh, my God, look how great this is!" And by the time everybody thought the same, it was too late.

The first to get in on the Internet craze, the ones who got there before the crowd, did well. Especially if they got out when they saw the crowd growing. Because as the crowd grew, with more and more people blindly speculating, the prices went up and up. The bigger the crowd when you got in, the more it cost you to buy and the less you stood to gain. In this case, the risk was higher, but the reward was lower.

Then came the bust. If you stayed around with the crowd, you lost when the bubble finally popped.

The same thing happens in real estate. People see a shortage of condos and they start building. That's great. Then more and more people start jumping on the bandwagon. Condo projects start going up like crazy, and so do prices as more and more investors come in hoping to make a quick buck. At some point, once the crowd starts streaming in, prices go up. The buildings get overpriced and you're getting the slim pickings. You're getting the ones others have already rejected because they were really marginal economically.

And sooner or later, too many new condos get built. You have more units available than you do customers. Prices start to fall. Speculators panic and start unloading as fast as they can, or defaulting on their loans, and . . . pop! The bubble bursts.

The people who make the most money are the ones who go in early. The later you come in, the less money you are likely to make and the greater the chance that you'll end up losing money.

For example, the guy who did well speculating in the Miami condominium market is the guy who bought a condo when it was $250 a square foot, not the guys who bought in two years later at $700 a square foot. Whatever you do, always try to be at the forefront of what you're doing, because you're going to create the most value when you are there at the beginning. Everything goes in waves. You've got to catch that wave as it's going up. You can't buy it when it's peaking or at the top. You will get hurt.

If you want to be really successful in real estate, you have to get ahead of the crowd. You have to decide for yourself where you should go and what you should do. If everyone is building condos, condos, and more condos, you should be looking to build something else, or looking for places where they are not. If everyone is building luxury condos, for example, you might look and realize that what people want and need are affordable ones. If everyone is building in one place, you might determine that it's time to go someplace else—to another city or to a different area within the one you're in.

But not following the crowd doesn't mean going against the market. You can't go against the market.

For example, if every three-bedroom apartment in your area is sitting empty, and the demographics are changing so that you have young families leaving and retirees moving in, building three-bedroom condos is pretty stupid. There's no market for them. It doesn't matter if they're green or blue. It doesn't matter if you make them affordable or luxurious. There's *no market*! Building them isn't getting ahead of the crowd, it's ignoring reality.

When we started with the properties in Little Havana, it was a run-down area that nobody put any money into. If you owned a building there, you did as little as possible to it. The way to make money was by keeping your costs down, not by improving the property and pushing your rents up. We took it and said, let's build a program with the federal government in which we're going to reverse the trends we face and breathe life into those neighborhoods. That was an anti-trend. That was going against the crowd. That was going against the opinion. That was going against what was happening every day.

But it wasn't going against the market. It was discovering an opportunity in the market that others hadn't seen yet. As I'll show you in chapter 3, a thorough market analysis will serve as your guide. It will tell you where things are really going, not just where people are headed.

So whenever you do something like this, you need to get away from public opinion and do something different. Do something that, at times, bucks the trend.

CASE STUDY

The Island Club at Brickell Key—Don't Go with the Crowd

When everyone—including me—was building market-rate apartments in the suburbs of Miami-Dade County, I decided that the way to go was to build luxury apartments downtown, right by the water. I figured most people hate commuting. They hate being stuck in traffic. I thought they would be willing to pay more for a place in a premier location, close to work, with luxury touches and great water views.

But everyone told me I was crazy. Lender after lender refused to give me a loan to build them. Every lender I was speaking to in South Florida had a house in a nice residential neighborhood with a manicured lawn, in places like Coral Gables and Kendall, far from downtown. And they were saying, "Who would ever live in this location and pay twice as much in rent as they would in one of those beautiful garden apartments that you develop, Jorge, with resort-style amenities and barrel-tile roofs?"

Because that was the trend at the time. There was plenty of cheap land far from downtown, and that meant developers could offer lots of nice touches and still keep rents relatively low. The people who lived there paid in gas and time as they wrestled with traffic on their way to work in the morning and back home again in the afternoon.

And I kept trying to convince them that while that was *a* way of living, it really should not be the preferred way of living. But everyone kept saying no.

Do you think I had my doubts along the way? You bet! As lender after lender told me no, I had to ask myself if they were right and I was wrong.

But I stuck to my guns. I finally found a lender in New York to give me the money. Because it took somebody who understood urban living to say, "Wow! This is a great site. I'd live here in a second."

So now that I had my financing in place, I had to deliver.

We had a beautiful waterfront site, on a small island right next to the Brickell Avenue banking district and minutes from downtown. And I knew the apartments were going to be nice.

But I realized that the most important thing was that I wasn't offering apartments. I was offering a lifestyle. All those nos from all those lenders helped me understand that I didn't want people to think of these as just another apartment. I wanted them to think about the benefits of living here. And I wanted them to think it was exclusive and worth the price. I wasn't just selling a place to live; I was selling a new way of life.

So for the first time in rental apartment history in Miami, I said, "We're going to do this totally different. We're going to offer it before it's ready for rent. Before it's even built."

Usually with rentals you never advertise more than sixty days before the units can be delivered. Because people are making the decision to move much sooner. But I decided we would start taking reservations from day one. A whole year ahead of time.

So I developed a marketing campaign for the people I knew were commuting long distances. We sent mail-outs, and we put up huge billboards along the main route I knew they were stuck on every day, in both directions. It was perfect. While they're sitting there steaming about traffic, they see these signs that showed Joe Smart and the commuter.

The commuter: at seven in the morning he's getting up to travel half an hour to his gym. He goes back home. He has breakfast. He goes to work.

And at seven o'clock, you know what Joe Smart is doing? Snoring.

The ads showed a whole day's worth of the benefits of urban living. At five o'clock, the commuter is stuck in traffic for an hour.

Joe Smart is at the bar we had downstairs having happy hour drinks.

So we delivered the message very visually about the advantages of urban living. And it was a great success. And that really helped me transition so well later on into the condominiums, because marketing became very, very important then.

It also proved that Kierkegaard was right, even in real estate. The crowd is the untruth. The crowd at that time was all those lenders who were telling me I was wrong.

And many of them were very good friends of mine and people I really liked. So I could've either buckled under that pressure and said, "Hey, you know what, they're right. Let me just continue building my garden apartments. I'm really successful at it, I mean *really* successful. There's lots of land in suburbs all over the place. It's not like I'm going to run out of opportunities to do what I'm doing. So let me just stick with that."

But I said, "No, no, no, no, no. I'm going to do something new. I'm going to do something that hasn't been done. And by the way, because it is new, I'm the first one there. And if I hit, I'm going to be able to maximize my profits. Because profits are squeezed when everybody else comes in and then the margins become much smaller."

So we went against the current. We bucked the trend. And we were very, very successful.

Key #3: Know What You Have

On top of knowing what your goals are and what level of risk you can tolerate, to pick the best investment for you you've got to know what abilities and resources you have going in.

Those resources include any expertise or skills you might have. Are you a general contractor? Then you know construction and, most likely, what it costs to build something. That's extremely important. Are you a real estate agent? Then you probably have a pretty good idea of what sells and what doesn't in your area. You may have realized that market trends are pointing in a certain direction.

Your expertise isn't limited to your profession. If you're an architect, that's great. Someone's got to draw the plans if you're going to build something; if you know how, then you've got that covered. But if you've been living in your city for your whole life and have watched it grow, you know the geography and the trends. You've seen the roads spread out and you know the good neighborhoods, the decayed neighborhoods, and the ones that are likely to be hot spots.

In South Florida, where I live, artists moved into an area known as Coconut Grove when it was run-down and drug-infested because it was cheap. They made it cool. Soon enough, other people followed and prices started climbing. Now it's one of the most desirable—and most expensive—areas of Miami.

You may see similar trends in your hometown. That's valuable knowledge.

Another point you need to consider is your personal and financial resources. Real estate takes money. You have to know how much you can get your hands on, whether it's yours, a bank's, or somebody else's. There are a series of questions you have to answer: How much money do I have? How much money do I want to risk? What lenders and friends do I have out there that I can count on, and I'm willing to go to for financing and resources?

> The people you know are some of your most vital assets.

When you're starting off, your personal relationships, the people you know, are some of your most vital assets. Not just to help you raise money, but to help you make your project a reality. You have to ask yourself: "Who do I know in the different types of real estate who can be an asset to me? Do I know an architect? Do I know a lender? Do I know a consultant? Do I know a government employee who knows how to tap into some federal, state, or local programs?"

You also have to know what you're willing to put into your dream: How much am I really willing to work and get dirty? Not just as a thought, but as a reality. Don't kid yourself about your capacity or willingness to work. If you have to work a full-time job that requires a lot of overtime and you're not prepared to put in weekends chasing after your real estate dream, when are you going to do it? It's not enough to want it. You need to be able to make it come true.

So be honest with yourself. Look at your limits. Look at yourself in the mirror in an objective way. Don't kid yourself about your capacity or your willingness to do the work it takes. Be honest, and then pick accordingly.

If you don't think you have enough money, or if you won't be able to put too much time into it, then pick something you can do within the time frame you've allocated. It could be rehabbing a single house, or a small building. Or it could be teaming up with partners in something bigger. Whatever it is, knowing the resources you have will help you figure out what resources you need.

Key #4: Know What You Need

You have to be very honest with yourself about the resources and skills you don't have, and which ones you're not that good at, so you can surround yourself not with people who are the same as you, but who complement your weaknesses.

For example, if I am awesome at marketing, and I know I can go to lenders and investors and do a great presentation and tell them how I'm going to get this first venture off the ground, as convincing as I am, that's probably not going to be enough. I may have a great personality and be great at preparing a presentation, but doing financials is not my strength. Well then, I'd better have somebody there with the accounting knowledge that would complement my sales presentation, somebody who can explain the nuts and bolts of the numbers of why it is we are going to do this.

So surround yourself with those who make the process complete. From the beginning I knew what it took to make real estate successful. And I very rapidly developed relationships, both personal and professional, with those people who were of extreme importance.

You have to remember, I was a twenty-seven-year-old kid who had finished an urban planning master's at the University of Michigan, but the nitty-gritty was totally esoteric. Because at the University of Michigan you really don't build, you study the philosophy of urban planning. And in mathematics you really do complex statistics that ultimately have very little to do with the reality of developing.

So I knew I needed all those people around me as consultants. And in picking the brains of those consultants, I was able to develop my program.

I found real estate brokers to help me find the property, an architect to help with the plans, a general contractor to help break down the costs and oversee the construction, a financial adviser to help with the numbers, and an attorney to help with contracts and legal issues. I also needed an accounting firm to help get what's known as syndication money, where you sell tax credits from your property to people who need write-offs, thus providing you with the necessary equity and, ultimately, your profits.

And by the way, as you pick people's brains, they're going to tell you about the resources that are out there. Because the guy who knows the accounting also knows about the programs that are available. The mortgage brokers who you will use to help you get the financing also know about the programs that are available. So as you pick the brains of the people who are working with you, you learn about the programs that will help you succeed.

That's part of the research. To understand the way the federal programs worked, I also set up appointments with people in the main federal housing information office in the state, up in Jacksonville. And I spent the whole day going office to office, picking up all these little booklets, I remember, finding out what programs were available for me to be successful. It wasn't only about the project I was working on back then; it was also about finding the information that would allow me to do other government programs in the future. And in doing so, I tried to meet as many of the government officials as I could who would be reviewing and approving my projects.

So I started to read, read, read, read. And the more you read, the more questions you have, the more you go to experts to ask them to explain and give answers to the questions you have. And many times, the experts are in the agencies.

When I wanted to know, for example, how this FHA 221D3 program works, I had one of two choices. I could ask a lender who works with it, or I could call the guy who works in the FHA program, who typically is the biggest expert himself.

And you'd be surprised at how many people are willing to lend you a hand and to help you make your dreams come true. You have to be humble and nice, because nobody likes a jerk. But if you have humility you will be surprised at how many people are willing to help you.

Some of these consultants are going to become your partners. So a word of warning: I think a good deal with a bad partner tends to become a bad deal. On the other hand, sometimes deals that might not be great turn out to be okay when you have good partners. Because you don't always win. You can't. There's not a person out there who wins every time.

But when the cards are bad and the deal is not going as you expect it, what you want is to have somebody there who has the integrity, the perseverance, the loyalty that makes those hard times better. Someone who's looking out for you and not trying to stab you in the back.

I've had very good deals in which I've made money, and I've come out and I've said, "Never again. Never again will I do it with this guy." Every bit of the way was a negotiation. Every bit of the way the other person was trying to take advantage.

And I've had other deals that didn't do as well and I would say, "I will partner up with this guy anytime, anyplace."

When you're picking your partners you have to test your gut. Gut is extremely important, that first feeling you have when you meet somebody, when you talk to somebody and you get to know him and his family.

But gut only goes so far. Then you have to check the person out. You have to find out about his reputation. Has he had bad relationships with his partners in the past? Not finished the work he promised? Defaulted on loans? You have to find out about his connections—who he does business with. Are they people who can affect your deal? Is he a good citizen in his community?

You weigh all of those things together and make your decision. I've had very successful deals with partners who didn't seem like good bets. But I used their bad reputation to my advantage.

One was a guy named Thomas Kramer, who had earned a reputation as a "bad-boy developer" in South Beach. He was in trouble with a condo project known as the Portofino Tower. He had already put like $30 million into the land and construction, but he couldn't finish it. And because of his reputation, the banks wouldn't lend him the money he needed, he couldn't find investors, and there weren't too many people who wanted to risk partnering with him.

The project, though, was on one of the premier sites in all of South Florida, right on the water at the southern tip of Miami Beach. And the building was beautifully designed. You could see it was going to be an icon.

So I quietly went and found out if lenders would be willing to back me if I went in on the deal, then I went to Kramer and convinced him that if he wanted to finish his project and make any money, he had to do it with me. But I set several conditions: I had to be the 100 percent managing partner. All of the decisions would be mine. He had absolutely no say at all. And I got him right away to sign two more deals, giving me the first priority for two other choice properties he owned on the water in South Beach.

He agreed. And I didn't put in any money. He put up all the equity for the loan. And I made more money on that deal than I ever had up to that point.

The key lesson is that when you have doubts, which we did, make sure the business deal addresses those doubts and gives you all the security you need. And make sure you have the control over everything that goes on, so you're never embarrassed by the acts of a partner. He never had anything to do with anything because he had no say whatsoever and never really got involved. As a silent partner, he was an excellent partner.

But I did have bad experiences with partners early on, when I was starting out.

The Section 8 federal subsidy program, which guaranteed rent payments for low-income people, was very political. In order to get units you really had to have Washington connections. And, being a Democrat, I had lost my Washington connections, because at the time it was a Republican administration.

Some people I knew, guys who were good friends in a totally social sense, came to me and said, "We don't know how to build, but you do. We can get the Section Eight units, which is all-important." They wanted to do something under what was then called the Section 8 Moderate Rehabilitation Program. They would secure the projects, put the applications in in Washington, and use their political connections to get the subsidies. They said, "You will be the guy who gets the financing, and who is the expert at developing and managing the building. We'll be fifty-fifty partners."

I said yes. My mistake was that I confused personal friendships with business partners. And as we secured the properties we had to put them in their names, because they were the ones who had the political connections. I was taking a huge risk, but I was young, you know?

Then they called for a meeting. And they said, "Instead of this being fifty-fifty, we'll give you twenty percent. The properties are under our names. We have the subsidies and we can buy what you do for very little, without giving a partnership interest. But since you're a friend, we're going to give you twenty percent."

My attorney had to hold me back, literally had to hold me back, because I was throwing punches. My attorney sat me down and said we needed to negotiate.

But I didn't want any part of it. I figured that if I stayed in with the 20 percent, I was still partners with them, and they controlled it. But I knew they didn't have any money. I thought, why not take a chance? Instead of keeping the 20 percent, which might be worth $1 million to them, I would do a deal with them in which they'd give me $500,000 up front. It would make them happy and I'd get out of the deal.

Remember, this was a federal program—from there on they still had to enter the federal program, secure the subsidies. They had to get a contractor. They had to go to a bank and convince the lender to give them a construction loan. They needed to line up the syndication dollars. And they needed somebody to manage it. All the things I knew how to do. But they didn't.

So I took a chance. I got my $500,000 and I said, "See you guys. I don't even want to talk to you anymore."

There's a saying I really like: When they spit in my face I don't call it rain.

So I left.

And I made sure every lender they could go to knew what had happened, and every syndicator, too. I sent out the message: "Be careful with these guys. This is what happened. . . ."

And I waited.

They had a one-year holding period on the property. And I kept hearing, "They want to talk to you. They're having all kinds of problems. They can't get anybody to go in with them, because everybody knows what they did to you."

They finally called me up, just like I knew they would.

By the time they did, I had already worked the whole deal out with lenders and syndicators, but my ex-partners didn't know that. So when we met I played a game of, "Hey, you guys have shopped this everywhere. It is going to be really difficult. What makes you think if you guys couldn't do this with the lenders and the syndicators, I'm going to be able to do it?"

They said, "Oh, you know you have relationships with everybody. Everybody tells us."

Then they made a big mistake. They showed me their cards. They said, "We have gone all the way to the limit in this project. If we don't close this by next week the lenders will take all the property back. The buyers that we got to take options to hold the property will take all that land back. Because we have no money whatsoever. We have put every penny into this deal."

They said they wanted to go back to the same deal, fifty-fifty. But I said, "You know, guys, I learned my lesson. I don't want to be your partner. If, by any chance, I could secure this and work like crazy, you'd find another way to stab me in the back."

They said, "Oh, no, you're a friend. We would never do that. We are so sorry. We should've never done that." They did the whole apologetic thing. I thought violins were going to come in.

My attorney, on the other hand, was telling me, "That's not so bad. Take the fifty-fifty."

I said, "You know what? Let me negotiate. I'm going to do exactly what they did to me. I'm going to buy them out."

It took a lot of negotiation. I left the table. They called back and said they were going to lose all their money. Finally, I bought their position for the same $500,000 they had given me the year before.

And the next day, the whole deal was put together with the lenders and the syndicators and we made $5 million in cash. The next day. And what I did was I sent them all copies of the closing statements, so they would know how much money was made in the transaction. I just had to let them know they messed with the wrong guy.

The lesson: Be careful picking partners. You have to know when you need partners who will bring skills or resources that complement yours, but you never need bad ones.

CASE STUDY

My Very First Deal—Getting Advice

Little Havana was an area of the city that was derelict and had a concentration of the oldest buildings in the city. They were typically three stories high, walk-ups, without an elevator. Little Havana was one of the lowest-income areas and was also filled with elderly, Cuban elderly, who stayed there because of all the social services.

The city had set up a "neighborhood strategy area" and was offering incentives to developers to revitalize it. And I knew there was a federal program that would provide subsidies to developers who rented to low-income people, and I knew I could use that guaranteed subsidized income as equity in applying for a loan.

But I knew I needed help finding the right building to rehab. Little Havana is a large area. Me going door-to-door alone would've taken me way too long. I did go door-to-door, so the sweat equity was there, but I didn't do it alone. I enlisted two or three of the best brokers in the Little Havana area to help me out.

How did I know they were the best brokers in the area? I got in my car and I started driving around and I saw that they were the ones with the most FOR SALE signs in front of buildings. So I figured they were the ones doing the most work in Little Havana.

I told them what I was looking for. Then I used them as my first consultants. I said, "You know this area better than I do. How much do you think these buildings are worth?"

So with their knowledge—here it is, taking advice—we established the most important component of the cost structure, which was the acquisition of the building.

Then, with their knowledge, I got to know the people who owned the properties in the Little Havana area. So getting the advice of these people saved me a huge amount of time and gave me instant knowledge that would've taken me a long time to get if I was going to try to do it by myself.

Instead, we broke it up with two or three brokers and we covered the whole area. We did it rapidly, so that other people wouldn't come and get the best buildings away from me and in order to avoid a bidding competition.

And once I found the properties, I used the brokers' knowledge on how to really negotiate with the owners. Because we didn't want to flat-out buy the property, the way most people do. To get the incentives and the federal subsidies, we had to compete and be selected by the city. So I had no guarantee that after doing all that I was going to get anything. And I sure as hell didn't want to end up owning some poorly kept building with no chance of getting the federal dollars.

Typically, when somebody is interested in buying a building, they do just that: they buy it. But not me. I was telling them, "Hey, I'm going to buy your building. Here's a five-thousand-dollar deposit. I need you to hold it for me six months while I go and present this thing to the city and see if I get it approved. If I do, you'll get paid. If I don't, I want all my money back, plus interest."

The fortunate part was that because it was a ghetto it wasn't a high-demand area. So I was able to convince them to hold, because in many cases I was going to bail them out of having this run-down apartment building, at a very attractive price.

Then I got an architect to draw the plans and explained to him that he would only get paid if I was able to get the project up and running. I got him to take a chance on me because I convinced him that if this deal went through, there would be more like it and he'd make lots of money.

Then I got a contractor to do the takeoffs the same way, for nothing up front, because I had no idea what it cost to rehabilitate such buildings. He had to break down what it would take to put new windows in, do inspections of the floor, see what part of the plumbing worked and what didn't, see how we could put an elevator in so that the federal program would approve the building for the elderly, and see if the old electrical system could be updated to handle that elevator and the new appliances and fixtures.

So there was a lot of convincing to do, but I got all of them to do all this work for nothing.

And then I got a financial broker, an accountant, as a consultant. This was very important because I had never actually sold the tax credits on one of these jobs to people who need the write-offs. I had no idea which New York syndicators or Boston syndicators would be interested in this project. So what I did was I went to the federal Department of Housing and Urban Development and asked for a list of the people who do these kinds of deals. And I found that there were a few accounting firms that specialize just in these programs. And they, in turn, worked with the syndicators that were the buyers of these tax shelters.

I figured I was going to have to have an accounting firm anyway. So I hired the one that had the most knowledge in syndication. And I picked their brains, even before I hired them. I told them I was looking to pick an accounting firm and I asked them to tell me how all the syndication numbers work, and how the accounting for syndication is done. Because remember, I am not an accountant. And I'm not a tax expert.

So I got an expert in another very important function to give me advice on how to run the numbers to make it the most sellable to the end user as a tax credit. The accounting firm helped me find the most active and aggressive syndicators, because I wanted to know which ones would pay me the most.

They gave me a list of those and I did the same thing. I called them up, and before I gave them a contract I picked their brains. I asked them not only, "How much will you give me?" but, "Why will you give it to me?" Because I wanted to learn.

So they taught me about syndication and the relationship between losses and money coming in. For example, I found that they would give you so much for the shell of the building, but you can get more money for the rehabilitation of the building. Because the building was depreciated over fifteen years and the construction cost could be deducted over five. And if I found a building that was somehow declared historic by the city or that I could get declared historic, it was worth more.

So now that I had a whole team on board, I needed to get the investors. Problem was, I didn't know any. That's when Steve Ross, who is now my partner, came in. He was an expert in syndicating tax shelters to people who have a lot of money and who need tax deductions. And we formed partnerships where we were the 1 percent general partners, and 99 percent of the ownership went to the limited partners. But that 1 percent gave me full authority to manage everything, and all the money I took in from them to participate gave me my profit up front. And I didn't have to wait until I finished the job for them to give me the money. I used part of it to make the down payment on the building and construction, so I never had to lay out a penny. The first deals we did were with absolutely no cash.

In putting that first deal together, I knew my strengths; and I knew what I didn't know. To succeed, I realized I needed help from a whole host of advisers. By the time it was done, I had consulted real estate brokers, an architect, a contractor, tax advisers, the federal government, and the man who would become my partner from that day forward, Steve Ross.

KEY PRINCIPLES

- Start small. Pick an achievable goal, then be unwavering in your pursuit of it.

- Only you know what's right for you.

- Learn the difference between the things you can do something about and the things you can't do anything about.

- The only way to succeed is to take smart chances.

- Reducing risks is not the same as not taking risks.

- Prepare and plan, learn and get advice—but you'll never know for certain. You just have to do it.

- The people you know are some of your most vital assets.

LAS RAMBLAS,
Las Vegas, Nevada
Arquitectonica

3 ▪ THE FOUR CARDINAL RULES FOR PICKING PROPERTY

"You've got to kiss a lot of frogs

before you find a prince."

Afer you've picked the right type of investment for you, it's time to find the right property. But that doesn't mean you jump in your car and start looking. Before you even go looking for the property, you have to know exactly what your plan for it is.

What are you buying the property *for*? What are you going to *do* with it?

Your plan will lead you to the right property.

My plan, as I've told you before, was subsidized housing. Before I looked at the very first piece of property, I knew where I was headed. Now I had to draw the road map that would take me to the light at the end of the tunnel. I had to build the whole plan, in all its different aspects: Where do I get the money? Where do I get the partners? How do I do it with the resources I have available? How do I get the consultants? How do I build the pro formas that say the cost is this, my revenues are that, and show me what my bottom line is?

I also had to look at the market and trends to determine what the need was. You have to know your market. And, most important, you have to know what the market is missing. Remember? Where is the crowd heading? The way to make money is by getting there first. You have to find the holes and fill them.

Rule #1: Have a Plan

The first step toward making your detailed plan is to know what the market wants.

The market will always tell you what it wants, if you learn to read the signs. It will tell you what it wants whether you know it or not, but you'll only make money if you deliver the product people want. If you don't pay attention to the signs and listen to what people tell you, you won't. At least not in the long run. You might get lucky a few times. Or the market might be so hot that you'd have to be a total idiot not to make money.

But for long-term success, you can't succeed without learning how to analyze market trends and data.

It's part science and part art, sort of like the way a violinist converts what he sees written on a score into beautiful music. Even a beginner can learn how to read the notes and play the music. But the more practice you get, the better it will be. It's the same thing with market data. Even if you've never done it before, you can learn to read the market and know what product will be successful. Then, the more you do it, the more you'll be able to see subtleties in it that will shape your decisions.

When I do a job, I break the market analysis into two main components. One is macroanalysis. The other is micro–market analysis. On the macro level, I look at overall market forces; on the micro level, I zero in on the competition in the specific area around my project.

For example, when I would embark on an apartment project, we would start with the macro trends to determine: What are the trends for the region? How many households are coming in? What is the income of those households? I look at the economic trends. I look at employment. I look at all those things. Those are the macro trends you look at. They give me what I can expect over time for that population.

That data would tell me, yes, you're in a growing place. Yes, you're going to have this many households to choose from in the future. So from an overall point of view, that is very good.

The macroanalysis takes in information from a larger area that includes the market area where I want to do my thing. I'm looking for the overall patterns that affect my immediate area. So if I'm looking at doing a project in one neighborhood, I'm not just looking at houses in that neighborhood, because the decision to live in that area is not made only by households there. It's for people who are moving into the county, for example, from someplace else. When you get a job and move to the county, you select between alternatives around a radius of how far you're willing to travel to work.

So if I'm building rentals, I'm looking to see what the household growth is, and whether it is going to bring me tenants. And I want to know what the incomes of those tenants are, so I can break it down by the amount of money they can pay toward housing. I also ask, What are the choices of those tenants? What percent of them are picking rental versus home ownership?

Now, once you finish doing that market analysis and you feel that the macro trends are there for you to make this investment, then you go down and you study the micro trends. The microanalysis is one in which you study the immediate area you're in. You study the competition. You go and see how many building permits are being pulled. What is the existing competition today? How many apartments are there? What are the rents? What are the sizes? What is the occupancy? What amenities are being offered? Are they giving discounts on their units because there is an oversupply? You can always tell when there's an oversupply because you'll see signs that say one month free rent, come in and no deposit down. Whenever you're seeing that, it means the market is imbalanced.

When I was doing market-rate apartments, we would go to every property in the market area we were in and ask: "Who's doing well? Who's not doing well? And why?"

What you try to find is, What is there not enough of in the market? What is there in the market that people really like? And when you find what it is that people really like, really need, and that there's not enough of, how do you react to it in the product that you're building? And how do you actually make it better?

So the macroanalysis may tell you, "Okay, over the next few years I'm going to have five thousand households that are going to choose being renters who can afford my property and are going to live within the radius that I'm in." Now, you have to look at the competition in the specific area you're thinking of building in. Because all of a sudden, when you do that narrower analysis, you may find that there are twenty thousand units being built. Then you go and say, "Whoa! We're going to have problems in this market."

The microanalysis helps you determine if the product you're putting on the market is going to be consumed or not and at what rate and price it's going to be consumed. You look at the demand side, household formation, and income, and from the supply side, the number of building permits and the number of units that are being done. From that you'll be able to see if there are enough buyers and if the demand exceeds the supply. If that's the case, then the imbalance is in your favor and you should definitely move forward with the project.

Basically, the microanalysis is a nitty-gritty market feasibility study that answers the question: What type of product do I build and at what rents?

Of course, the most important thing is finding out how you should price your product. So the market study will tell you that B-class apartments, that have certain types of amenities, certain types of finishes, rent for $1 a foot. A-class apartments in the market area that have better amenities, that are roomier, that have better finishes, better and better locations in the market and the submarkets and so forth, get $1.50 a foot.

So the question you have to ask yourself is, What is there more demand for? Is there more demand for the higher end or the lower end? You find out. Should you build more one-bedrooms or two-bedrooms?

You might find out, for example, that they're giving concessions on all the two-bedrooms. Just because the sign in front of an apartment complex says ONE MONTH FREE RENT doesn't mean they're all being discounted. It could be just one month free rent on a specific unit type. For example, they might be having trouble renting their three-bedrooms because they overbuilt that size and it's a market for young people with one baby or no babies at all. These are the things the microanalysis will tell you.

In some other markets, you might find totally the opposite. You might say, "My God, there isn't a three-bedroom available in the whole market." You've got to figure out why.

Sometimes there isn't a three-bedroom in the whole market because there are no families with children in that market. And sometimes they aren't there because developers don't like to build for families because children tend to destroy things. But if that's true—and there are families that need three-bedroom units but there are none being built—you've discovered a hole in the market that you may want to fill. Maybe then you go and do what we've done before: you say, "What if we build town houses? That way the children can't destroy hallways in common areas and things like that, because they're all their own separate units."

We were the first ones to build town houses for rent in western Miami-Dade County. We saw a hole and filled it. It was a *tremendous* success! Families came in and we could command whatever price we wanted for those, because there were no alternatives for the family that had two or three kids.

So the nitty-gritty market study is going to tell you what to build. It's going to tell you how to do your kitchen and your bathrooms, and what amenities people want. Do they use tennis courts? Is that something you need to have? A pool? What type of pool?

Use that total knowledge of the market to make sure your project doesn't fail. Don't be one of those people who says, "I want to be a rental player," and they only go to a couple of places and think, "Okay, now I know what to build." Invariably, they're not going to do well.

The way to succeed is by doing your homework. Do a detailed market analysis that looks at both the macro and the micro trends, that examines the feasibility of what you want to do where you want to do it, and gives you the armor you need to go into this battle.

> **The way to succeed is by doing your homework.**

A good macro- and microanalysis also helps you see where the market is headed, so you can get ahead of the crowd. Remember, the people who make the most money are the ones who go in early. I said it before: You've got to catch that wave as it's going up. You can't buy when it's peaking or at the top. If you do, you will get hurt.

The market analysis gives you the information you need to refine your plan, to build the detailed road map you need to succeed.

Maybe you say to yourself, "What if I buy an office building? And what if I run the numbers and do the pro forma on that office building and I make it look better and increase the rent and increase the cap rate at which somebody else will buy it from me?"

Let's say I can buy a building that produces $100 for me and I buy it at ten times that, for $1,000. The percent of what the income is to the price is called the capitalization, or cap, rate. Paying $1,000 for a building that produces $100 is a ten percent cap rate. Now, if I find that by giving it a paint job and making it nicer and doing certain things to it I can raise the rent to $150, I've increased the value. If I go to sell, at the cap rate of ten, then the building is now worth $1,500. But, I may also find that the cap rate is lower in better buildings, thus producing a higher multiple. So after I've improved my building, I may be able to sell it at a cap rate of eight. Dividing $150 by .08 is $1,875. So my $1,000 building is now worth $1,875.

Once you set that in your mind, that's the plan. That's the vision you've got to have. You can find anything in real estate and it works just the same. The plan has to answer the question, How do I create value? What am I going to do that will make this property worth more?

It's pretty simple. You're in this to make money, right? Well, you make money in real estate by creating value.

So now your job becomes: How do I find the building that meets the characteristics of my plan? That's when the sweat equity comes in.

You've got to kiss a lot of frogs before you find the one that turns into a prince. Your lips are going to be sore.

You're also going to have to find the consultants you need to be a successful investor. Continuing with our office building example, who do you need? Who are the best brokers who know about the office market? I establish certain parameters—I'm looking for a building that costs $500 or less, that's a bit run-down and charging lower rents in an area where better buildings charge more, and so on. Who do I contact so I don't have to go and look at every building in Miami?

Now, if the brokers find a building that has more vacancy than it should have because the owner is in Australia and he's really not managing hands-on, that needs a paint job, and that has tenants that are really bad, but I can see myself replacing them or increasing the rents, that fits the bill. Then I would say, "Okay, the guy wants to sell it. I can get a pretty good buy." Next part of the plan: How do I buy it? Where do I get the money? How do I structure the deal to make it profitable, with the least amount of out-of-pocket costs?

Building your plan

1. Do the research.

2. Find the property.

3. Find the money.

No matter what area of real estate you go into, it will still require a plan. For example, you can say to yourself:

"I've saved enough that I can buy one house at twenty thousand dollars and I know I can rehab this house. I can rent it and it will provide me a fifteen percent cash-on-cash return on my money. Or I can sell it and make so much more money and then buy two houses."

You can start small and grow within the time limits and the resources, both human and financial, you have available.

Starting small only means your plan could take longer. Just because you start by doing one or two houses doesn't mean you can't become the king of real estate; it just means that first you will become better acquainted with federal programs, with making the money, with managing the money, with renting the houses, with finding buyers, and reselling them with the people that are in the business. Then, after you learn, you can do four or five at a time.

You set your goal and you can measure your progress.

And then, after a while, after you feel sure with it, you say, "Honey, you know what? I'm making seventy-five thousand dollars in my present job. And I'm already making a hundred and twenty thousand in this one."

So you have enough confidence and enough money that you can take that plunge. You learned about that in the last chapter, right? Sooner or later, you've got to take the leap of faith.

Well, now that you're dedicating yourself, maybe instead of buying single-family FHA abandoned homes in the worst neighborhoods you can buy FHA quadruplexes or small apartments. And since you've already been doing this for a while you have built up some relationships. You have better sources of money from lenders. You already know more people who can become your partners. You can convince somebody who has a not-so-nice building to put that in and you will do the hard work. So all the things you learn as you're getting involved in the business are what will help you grow.

You've got to remember I've been in this business for twenty-nine years. So plans for a site are in my head, regardless of where the site is. I've got plans in my head waiting for me to find the right piece of property to make them work. So it may seem like I see a piece of land for the first time, fall in love with it, and then come up with a plan to make it work, but I don't. The plan was already there. And just like I did when I started and I was looking for a piece of property that fit my plan, just like you'll do now, I've got a plan and I'm looking for the property. Not the other way around. I just have more plans going at the same time than I did when I started.

> The plan comes before the property. Always.

I don't buy any land without a very good idea of what I'm doing. We've never played the game of, "Let's just buy cheap product, because the market is collapsing, and wait until the market gets better." I'm not saying that people don't make a lot of money in that. That's just not what we do. Wherever I buy, there's always a project in mind. We don't speculate in land and resell. We don't speculate in buildings and resell.

We take our game plan and we find sites that meet our game plan.

We started expanding into Mexico last year, building resort condominiums for international tourists. It may be a different country, but the rules don't change. As my people look at sites, they automatically ask the question: "Does it fit our game plan?"

People will show up and say, "Hey, look at this great site." And they're right. It *looks* great.

But then I ask, "Where's the international airport?"

They say there is none.

And I ask, "Where do you see the tourists going when they're here? What's the local flavor?"

They don't have any.

"What's the development around it?" I ask.

"Oh," they tell me, "it's middle-class Mexican tourist."

"Is that what we're going after?"

The answer to that is, No—at least not for this particular project.

So it can be a great site for somebody else. But it isn't what we do.

You have to visualize your plan. In detail. Then write it down.

You can't just say, "I'm going to build a condo project." Or even, "I'm going to build a luxury condo project." You have to say: "I'm going to build a luxury condo project in a premier oceanfront location that offers restaurants and shops and recreation within walking distance, and allows the people who live there to commute to downtown offices in ten minutes or less."

It's a question of honing your plan until you have a very specific concept that will work.

Write down your vision and the plan for achieving it. And don't deviate from that road map. In any aspect.

And the plan isn't only about how and where you're going to build; it involves every aspect of the project along the way. As I'll show you later, my plans include the way we sell. We establish a strict, reservation-first process. And we stick to it. It's not like a salesperson comes to me and says, "Hey, I've got this unit and I've got to sell it because the customer doesn't want to do a reservation. He wants to buy right now."

The answer is no. No. Stay with your process. Stay focused on the end goal.

And don't get lost in the meaningless details. Details are extremely important. Critical, even. But meaningless details are just that: they're meaningless. Don't waste time on them. The color of the lobby matters. The color of the plumbing inside the walls doesn't. If you want to build a beachside condo in a nice tourist destination that will attract buyers from other places, the beach and the restaurants and the local flavor matter. The color of the maracas doesn't.

I've got a banker who says it perfectly: "The main thing is the main thing."

The big picture is what matters. Keep your eye on the details, but only the ones that affect the ultimate goal.

> The main thing is the main thing. The big picture is what matters.

Ask yourself, "What is my goal?" You start from there, and based on the goal you let the plan flow, always keeping the goal in mind.

Work backward to determine what you have to do, never forgetting your goal. Because if you forget it you'll get sidetracked with issues that have nothing to do with your goal and you'll get distracted. And it's so easy to get distracted. I see it, because it happens to all my young people in the company all the time. I have to go and say, "Hey, wait a second. What are you doing?" They start telling me about the color of the tiles by the rooftop pool deck, instead of telling me that the engineer has determined that the size of the pool has to change because of the load considerations. That's what they should've started with. That's what we should be concentrating on, and they start by worrying about what the new tiles are going to look like.

So I tell them the same thing I'm telling you: Don't get caught up in all the meaningless details. Go to the main thing. Stick to your plan. Everything else will flow from there.

Rule #2: Have Vision

You make money in real estate by creating value. The more value you can create, the more money you make.

Example: A piece of land is only worth so much. Put a house on it and it's worth more.

Simple enough. And that's what most people do. But if you want to make even more money, go to the city, get the property split into two parcels, and build two houses. The piece of land you started with is now worth a whole lot more.

Smarter, right? But what if you take the two parcels and get them rezoned for town houses? You build two rows of four, facing each other across a lushly landscaped common courtyard, with small, private gardens in back. Put a fence around the whole thing, with an automatic gate at the entrance. Add some upscale touches in the kitchens and upgrade the bathrooms and you've got eight "affordable luxury homes in an exclusive, gated community."

That's vision. And that's what you need to *really* make money in real estate.

It's all about creating a better concept that will fully cater to what the consumer needs.

One of the best ways to create the maximum value on any property is to see things in ways that nobody else has thought of, at a time when no one else has thought that something of that nature could be done. So it's both the visualization and the timing.

You have to have a plan, and your plan will lead you to the right property. But don't let your plan limit what you see when you're looking at a piece of property. For example, if you want to build market-rate apartments for active singles and young families, within ten minutes of the downtown offices where they work, you have a good plan. But that plan doesn't necessarily mean that you must absolutely find a *vacant* piece of land, next to a major road. And it doesn't mean they have to be cheap market-rate apartments.

What happens if you find a small old boatyard sitting on the water? Let's say it doesn't have easy access; it's only got a winding dirt road leading in off some narrow streets behind some warehouses. The owner wants to retire, business is eroding, so he's willing to sell cheap.

Do you reject it? Maybe.

Or, you might look at it and say: "What if I build a bridge in that other direction, and connect directly with downtown? I can tear down the boatyard, build apartments facing out toward the water, maybe leave a small area for a private beach. On the side facing shore, I'll put up a small retail plaza, offer some commercial space for a restaurant, a small deli and market, possibly a boutique or two. Behind them, we line the shore with trees that block the view of the crappy warehouses."

Toss in some Jet Skis and a couple of boats for the residents to rent (I did with a project I'll tell you about in chapter 6) and you're still offering market-rate apartments for active singles, and so forth. You've just turned them into "*luxury* market-rate apartments on a *secluded* private island just minutes from downtown, with *select* shops and gourmet restaurants, and an *exclusive* beach club for residents."

What can you charge for that? Think you'll have customers?

The lesson: When you're looking at properties, work backward. Look at a piece of property and see what it can be. You have to visualize how your ideas can become reality, but not be so rigid that you can't see possibilities. Be ready to modify your vision and ways to get there. Everybody has dreams of greatness; few put them into an achievable format.

> Visualize how your ideas can become a reality, but remain flexible when considering other possibilities.

CASE STUDY

The Lofts

Vision allows you to find a special niche. It allows you to find places and ways to make money that others don't see.

We did that with a project called the Lofts. In a market where nobody was selling, I sold 450 units in a month—in the worst market you could imagine!

How? I found a niche. I found something that defied the regular market.

In 2002, in the midst of one of the largest real estate booms in South Florida, we realized that it wouldn't last forever. We looked at the market trends and we saw an oversupply of condominiums. We also noticed that one of the side effects of the boom, the skyrocketing price of real estate, was pricing the middle class out of urban areas.

But the middle-class market is extremely deep in South Florida. And I figured that we could do extremely well with a market others were ignoring, if we could come up with a product that would be attractive to them, at a price they could afford.

We'd already discovered that there was a market for the upper middle class and the upper class—they would buy attractive luxury condominiums in an urban setting. So I felt that if I could attract the wealthier customers to come to an urban environment, we'd also be able to attract all the moderate and middle-income people who work downtown—the policemen, the secretaries, the Miami college professors, the public employees, and so on. They couldn't afford your $400,000, $500,000, or $600,000 condominium. But I figured that if they were given the option they would probably also want to live in an urban environment.

So we came up with a plan to build attainable, affordable housing in downtown.

The problem was that prices had skyrocketed for developers, too. Demand had pushed land prices up. Construction costs were going through the roof.

If we wanted to bring our selling price down, we were going to have to be exceptionally creative.

We started with a very detailed plan of what we wanted and what, with the needs of the population, were the needs of the job. In order to make it successful, we had to find a site we could get for very, very, very cheap. We needed a parcel of land that was tiny, that would have absolutely no value for the normal developer. Because when you're going to get density, normally a parcel has to be large enough to allow for a garage to be built under the building for the residents to park in. Traditionally in Miami, no one would even think of building a building without parking. So the challenge for this project was that we had to find parking without having to build it. We also wanted the government to help subsidize the building.

We wondered if we could work with the city and find an existing, underused parking structure where the residents of our building could park. Then we'd only need a very small piece of land that could otherwise not be built on because of the parking requirement. We'd put a very skinny high-rise building on it, with a footprint that would be extremely cheap to build. With no on-site parking, we could build enough units to make it profitable and still sell at a low price.

We had to convince the city that if they were ever going to get a walkable city, with fewer cars, they had to start doing buildings like they do in Chicago and New York and other large, urban places. In New York, you still don't park in the building. So we actually worked with them to change the city ordinance so it would allow buildings to be built without parking as long as they were very close to the city parking or a mass transit station.

Then we found a very small site, across the street from an underused parking garage. We convinced the owner to sell us the site for what ended up being, on a per-unit basis, an extremely cheap price. But in reality—since we were able to build even more units because now we didn't need the parking—it was a good price for the seller, and a great price for us.

For example, on the same site with parking, you might've gotten twenty units. Maybe. We got two hundred. So the per-unit value of the land became extremely cheap. And because I didn't have to pay for building the parking, which can run $30,000 per space and add millions to the bottom line, my land costs and my construction costs became unbelievably low.

We also convinced the city that they needed affordable housing, and that they should give us a grant to help build it. So altogether— with higher density than anyone would have expected from the site, extremely cheap land costs, not having the cost of building parking, and receiving money from the city—at a time when condominiums were selling downtown at $500,000 and up, we were able to make a profit selling condominiums in the Lofts starting at $99,000 and going to $200,000.

As logical as that seemed, we still didn't just rush forward. I wanted to know if they would sell or not. I had already put the property under contract; now the question was how much more money I had to risk to find out if my concept was valid.

What I did was this: I told my vice president of attainable housing, Oscar Rodriguez, "This is what you've got. We're going to pay the architect only ten thousand dollars to do the preliminaries. And he is going to get the job if we get it. And we're going to spend two hundred thousand dollars on a marketing campaign to see if people react to this, to thoroughly test the market."

This goes beyond the market studies. We had done those. But research can tell you things should work. The proof comes when you sell it. I wanted to know if, after we did all this for three months and spent $200,000, people were going to come and give us deposits. And they did. If I had done that and found myself with only 30 percent sold at the end of that time, I would've said good-bye to my $200,000 and left it for another time when the market was better. But that wasn't the case.

So far, there's been an almost never-ending demand. Providing that kind of product in downtown became another one of our great successes. Now we are up to Lofts IV. The program has been so successful that we are getting calls now from cities around the country asking us to help them build affordable housing through a similar program.

So again, it's the vision of taking a site and visualizing a use for that site that no one had envisioned. And by doing so, we were able to create value—out of nothing, really.

Rule #3: Execute Perfectly

No matter how perfect your plan is, it's worthless if you don't execute it perfectly. A detailed plan may require having all kinds of separate pieces come together to make it work. You may need a zoning or ordinance change from the city, neighborhood support, federal or local government subsidies, two or more loans for buying the land and financing the construction, and, the linchpin of it all, the perfect property.

Failing to get any one of those components could seriously hurt, or completely cripple, your plan. So you want to minimize your risks as much as possible until you get everything set.

The first concern is the property. But just because you've found the perfect property doesn't mean you rush forward and buy it.

What would have happened if I had plunked down the money for the site where the Lofts ended up being built, but the city hadn't changed the ordinance to allow off-site parking? I would have gotten it cheap, yes, but what was I going to do with it? I couldn't build enough condos at a low enough per-unit cost to be able to sell them for much cheaper than the price I already knew my target market couldn't afford. And as I mentioned before, at the time there was already an oversupply of those.

That's why you don't buy right away. You tie it up. You don't want to go on with your plan without tying it up. But you don't want to risk money, either. What you do is, you put some money down to hold it, for what is called the due diligence period.

This happens all the time in real estate, and you won't be asking for anything unusual. Everybody who has bought a home has done the same thing, they just call it "getting the inspections done" and "getting the bank's approval for the mortgage loan."

You say to the owner, "I'm going to buy your building for five dollars, but I need ninety days to do my due diligence. If I find anything wrong with the building in that time period, you just give me my money back."

Typically, people ask for 90 days, 120 days, or 180 days, but you can ask for whatever you think you need. Then you put the money in an interest-earning escrow account with your attorney.

It's like putting it in a savings account, because you know you're not going to lose it. It comes back to you if the deal doesn't go through.

The due diligence period gives you time to put your deal together: to check out the land or building thoroughly, get your architectural plans, find out how much refurbishing or construction will cost, make sure you can get city approval to do what you want to do, run the numbers, and get the money you need from investors and lenders.

When everything comes together and you know the deal will work, then you close on the property. Not before.

The difficult part comes after you close. You've got to produce. You have to make your plan a reality. What does that mean? It means I hope you have really done your due diligence. I hope you've run your pro formas with a realistic idea of how much it's going to cost to get somebody to go paint the building, change the carpets, and do those things. So that when you said you're going to spend $50,000 rehabbing this building, the $50,000 doesn't turn out to be $200,000.

Lenders and investors don't like surprises. So make sure you're giving them the right numbers, and that you put contingencies in there. The worst thing you can do when you're trying to build relationships is go back to people and say, "I messed up. Turns out we're not going to make any money."

Do that and you've lost your relationship.

That's why, before you close, you run and test the numbers. You need them to get the bank to lend you money and to attract investors. It's not enough to say you have a good program that's going to be profitable.

You have to show them how it is that they are going to make the money. You have to tell them which building you're going to buy, and for what amount. They need to know how much money is going to go into rehabilitation, how much you're going to pay the contractors, and how much you're going to get from the government and the tax shelters you're going to sell to syndication groups.

Then you set up a set of variables that shows them various scenarios. What could go wrong if this or that did not work the way we anticipated? They'll ask you what happens if . . . ? What happens if you get it at a better price? What happens if you raise your rents? So you have to play with the numbers under different types of scenarios. You have to be able to project. Typically, we run at least three scenarios and call them Worst Case, Most Probable, and Best Case.

When I was running the numbers on my very first job, I didn't know what price I was going to get the building for, because I didn't have it yet. So I had to build different models that said, "If I pay twenty thousand dollars a unit, I'm going to do so much rehabilitation," so it would end up with a number low enough that the whole thing would work. If the total amount I could spend was $40,000 and still make the profit I wanted to make, then I could either buy the building for $10,000 and put $30,000 in the rehabilitation, or I could buy the building for $20,000 and put $20,000 into rehabilitation.

And then, as the syndication numbers came in, I had to run loss scenarios. Because what you are selling is losses. That's how the syndicators got the tax credits. The project didn't really lose money. But even though most property tends to go up in value over time, the federal government allows investors to treat the building like a car or a piece of equipment—as something that depreciates over time. They're called paper losses. The syndicators then get to use these as tax write-offs. So I would project a depreciation of the building so I could then sell the tax credit to a syndicator.

So here I was, twenty-seven years old, and I prepared this whole package for these people and convinced them that it was going to be very profitable.

It's no different today. Knowledge of financing and numbers is of extreme importance. But the main thing you should know is that it's not impossible. This is not high math. It's really just adding and subtracting. People want to know what their return is going to be. You have to be very, very clear with both lenders and investors to show them numerically why it is that they're lending you money or becoming your partner.

How do you figure out how much everything is going to cost? That's where those advisers you gathered around you come in. You get the architect to draw up very detailed plans. Then you get the contractor to say how much it's going to cost to do all of this. Usually, the general contractor goes to the painter and the electrician and the plumber and the carpenter and all the rest of the subcontractors and prices it out with them. And he adds in the materials, his labor, overhead and profit, and gives you a price. But if you're small, if you're starting off with a house or a small office building, you're probably going to go directly to A&A Painting or G&G Carpet and ask them how much it costs. All the contractor does is coordinate the subcontractors and guarantee your price.

Then you're going to add all that up. And you're going to put in a contingency. There will always be a problem, believe me. Construction always takes a little longer than you expected and it's always a little more expensive than what you think. So put an adequate contingency in there. We always use 5 percent of the construction cost as our hard cost contingency, plus another 5 percent of soft costs (nonconstruction and land) for our soft cost contingency.

> Construction always takes a little longer than you expected and it's always a little more expensive than what you think. Put in a contingency.

And that's why I take a look at my numbers before the end of my 180-day due diligence period and I go to my investors and I tell them exactly how much it's going to cost, how much money we're going to need, and how much we're going to make.

Then I go back to the owner and I say, "We're going to go through with this."

Or I look at those numbers and I say, "No." And I either reduce the price or walk away.

At this point, it hasn't cost you anything except your time. Because if the numbers don't work, you go to the seller and ask him for your money back. The broker is working on commission. He only gets paid if it sells. With the architect, hopefully you've convinced him to do his work for free.

As a matter of fact, the deposit you put in is getting interest on your money for you, not for the seller. The deals are structured so that if the deal goes through the seller gets the interest, and if the deal doesn't go through you get the interest.

Now, in the same way that you can't let your plan blind you to the potential of a piece of property, you can't let yourself get so locked into the plan after you have the property that you ignore the market. Things change. And when they do, you have to be nimble. You have to be ready to modify your plan to adapt to market conditions.

You do that by doing constant market analyses, and keeping an eye on the competition and on trends. That will help shield you against sudden moves by your competition and against downturns in the market. Like I said in chapter 2, things come in waves. Real estate goes in cycles. You never know when your downside is coming and you've got to be prepared.

If you look at our history, the first year we made $1 million. And since then, we've gone through maybe four or five down cycles—serious down cycles—but in our history we have never had a year when we made less than the first year. We have never had a negative year in the history of the company. And that's because we have been very nimble at reacting to what the market gives us.

You don't go against the market. You use the market.

I find openings. I find pockets that will allow me to swim. I find the gaps in the market that are not being met or covered, like with the Lofts project.

To do that, you have to be able to make real tough decisions and not look back. You can't look back and regret the times when you could have made more money. You make what you make, and as long as there's a profit, you shouldn't look back.

Take One Miami, for example. I sold at $250 a square foot. Yes, I could have sold for more, but the bottom line is I made a profit and that's what matters. My business is to build it, sell it, make the people as happy as I can so I have future customers, and to build the Related brand. And to not be caught when the market goes down.

Right now, as I'm writing this, there's a ton of new condominium product coming online in Miami, all new stuff that's being completed, and people who were speculating and got in over their heads are being foreclosed on left and right. We saw it coming. We are adapting, getting ahead of the crowd and preparing for the next wave.

It's like the stock market, like those guys who were looking to get a deal when it was at the lowest—but who really knows when it's the lowest? You just play the trends in general ways. So if my condominiums in One Miami were bought at $250 a square foot, and are now selling at $600, what's a good buy?

As prices rise over time, I think a good buy is anything below the replacement cost. That's a key thing: Can I build a new one at that price? And if I can't build a new one at that price and I believe in the future of the area I'm in, then typically I'm getting a good buy.

I've been around long enough that I see the light at the end of the tunnel in every downturn. Now, I can't tell you if it's a year. I can't tell you if it's two. I can't tell you if it's three. I'm telling you the trend of real estate in most places is up.

Don't get caught going only one way. Always be looking at changes and things to do, opportunities.

Watch the numbers. Watch the details. Execute your plan perfectly. And give yourself some wiggle room with a contingency built in to your budgeting. As long as you're on top of your projects, you'll have a better chance of succeeding.

RULE #4: ALWAYS HAVE AN EXIT STRATEGY

One of the first projects I built on Miami Beach was the Yacht Club at Portofino. We built that as a rental. But while we were building it, I was finishing the Portofino Tower, which was a condominium project on South Beach, and I saw the successes we had with that one. I realized that the condo market was going to be strong for a while. So I looked at my profits in Portofino and I compared them to what my profits would have been if I sold the whole building as a rental—and they were three times as much.

Now, as a rental you give a product that has different finishes than you do in a condominium. You don't want to spend the money putting the most expensive touches in units you're going to rent. Renters tend to not take as good care of the units, and even normal wear and tear means you'll have to replace the finishes periodically. The more expensive they are, the more you spend on replacement costs.

For example, the bathrooms. In many of the condominiums we did oversized garden tubs, as opposed to the regular tubs you had in your rental apartments. We used marble sills in the bathroom. We used much better marble or tiles on the floors and took it all the way up the walls. In the kitchen we used Italian kitchen cabinets that were much better, and granite countertops. The upgrades make them more attractive to buyers.

For the Yacht Club at Portofino, I had gotten a loan from the lender to do a new rental. But I thought, "If I turn this into a condominium, it could be unbelievable!" It was on the water. The location was spectacular, as good as any. It had incredible condominium potential.

But I had my loan set up in a way that did not allow me to do that. It had been structured as a rental property. It didn't give me releases to do it as a condominium loan.

The difference is that when you do a condominium loan, it gives you the right to pay the loan off individually by apartment. So when I asked the lender about going condo with it, he said, "Wait a second. I don't want to do that. What happens if you sell a quarter of them, but not the rest? My protection is a lot less."

The contractor said to me also, "Hey, I didn't sign up for a condominium. There's a lot more risk in a condominium." Because remember, when I do a rental, he finishes and he's only dealing with me. When it's a condominium, he has to deal with 350 unit owners who are going to be much more demanding. So the risk levels for the contractor are much greater.

So, what did I do? I went to the contractor and told him the contract didn't stipulate rental or condominium. But I understood his concerns about the added risk and I wanted him to be happy. So I gave him something like another $200,000 so he would be happy, and he went along.

Then I had to convince the lender that it was going to be a success. So I told him we had some savings in the building cost that I put back in the construction contingency fund. I asked him to let me use that contingency to establish a presales office and go out and market it to prove there was a demand for condominiums, that we weren't going to be stuck with a building that was half sold.

He said yes. And we did exactly that. The building was a huge success. All because we were watching the market closely.

Now, if our sales hadn't gone that way, we could always go back to finishing the building as a rental. But you don't always have that option. That only works as a backup plan for lower-price condominiums. When you build condominiums to sell for $500,000 to $1,000,000, say, it doesn't work as a rental. The returns are so, so minimal it just doesn't work. You can always rent them and get some money, but it's not really an alternative exit strategy.

You always want to have a viable exit strategy. What I usually try to do is make real sure that the land I buy is so well priced that if the job is not successful and does not go forward as planned, the land itself will cover my costs.

> Make sure the land you buy is well priced enough to cover your costs in case the project is not successful and does not go forward.

In addition to location, location, location, there's another equally important factor in selecting great properties: price, price, price. Never overpay for land, particularly in an uncertain market.

It's not just the price of the land that will determine how much it costs you. Additionally, design, site conditions, and dimensions play a huge role. For example, a site could be in a great location strategically, but could be irregular in shape and might require more expensive architecture and construction. So in essence, an irregular site is an added land cost that would not otherwise be there.

Sometimes sellers come to me with what they say is an incredible piece of land. It's only $1,000 an acre. And they've got one thousand acres to sell.

It sounds great. But then I look at it and ask if they realize what the off-site improvements are going to cost to take this mountain and put water and sewer in.

So while the land price might look cheap, the associated development costs make it impossible.

Once I was offered all this land in the north end of the county that was selling for one-fourth what I paid where I usually built in the southwest. But when we studied the soil conditions, it was both very low and had a lot of muck. You had to remove all the muck and fill it back up. By the time you were done you were at a higher price than the average sales price of a normal piece of land.

So land in itself is not what sets its worth. To know what does set the value, ask, What does the land mean? What will I be able to do with it?

The same goes for buildings. Cheap, by itself, can wind up being more trouble than it's worth.

Take condo conversions, for example. Finding an apartment building and turning it into condos for sale seems like a quick and easy way to make money. And it can be, if you're in a hot condo market and everything goes smoothly.

A condo conversion can be very simple, but you need to know the rules. You need to know the rights of the tenants. You can't just kick them out. So when you do a conversion, you better know the leases. You better know when those leases expire. You better know the rights of first purchase that you have to give to the existing renters.

And rehabilitation can be the toughest thing, because you don't know what's inside the walls. It's not like the seller or his tenants are going to say, "Come on in and destroy all my drywall to find out what's inside the pipes. No problem."

So it's full of surprises. You might think you're going to only change cabinets, and then you go into the bathrooms and find out there has been water penetration and all the tiling is bad. Then you have to take all the tiles off the bathroom walls. So the difficulty is knowing how much work you're going to have to put into it.

The other problem with condo conversions, and that's why we haven't done too many, is the following: By definition, rental jobs are in less-desirable places than condominiums. Why? Because in order for you to build rental jobs you have to go to where the land values financially allow you to build a rental job. So typically you're dealing with a secondary location, as opposed to the condominiums, where you're going to pay top dollar for the land.

It also tends to be an older product. And you can do whatever you want—you can paint it, change the carpeting or the tiles, put in new kitchen cabinets, whatever—it's still old. And because of its age, when people are buying, they go, "Yikes! What am I buying? This was built twenty years ago. What do I not know about?"

In a normal real estate cycle, you'll see that condo conversions happen at the end of the cycle. First you have all the condominiums they add. Then, when you're running out of land and everything is becoming very expensive, people turn to buying old apartment buildings and offering a less expensive alternative to the new-construction condominiums.

The problem is that condo conversions are more difficult to sell because of the location and how old they are, and also, because they typically come at the end of the cycle, they're typically the first market that drops. It's the last one to be there and it's the first one to collapse, because it's a secondary product. So you can get stuck with a rental property where the rents don't justify the investment.

Right now, for example, there are all these apartments in Florida that because they couldn't take the tenants out, because they delayed the start of sales or the delivery of sales, took longer than they thought, and now the cycle is going down. So all these people paid top dollar for apartments they can't sell. They're too expensive to hold, and too high priced to sell.

That works okay if you're converting and selling them as condos. But as we mentioned in chapter 2, you should really buy an apartment as an investment that gives you a steady return. Say it gives you an 8 percent return. That's better than your average certificate of deposit. And typically you value it based on that rate of return.

But the condo converters said, "I don't care what return it gives me. I'm not buying it for economic return as a rental, I'm buying it to convert it."

So they took it out of its natural economic function. For a building that is worth $120,000 a unit as a rental, condo converters were paying $200,000 a unit. Not because of its income potential, but because of its conversion potential.

But as soon as the market for conversion drops, here you are sitting, owning an apartment building you paid $200,000 a unit for, as opposed to $120,000. Many times you've had to put another $20,000 a unit into it because of rehabilitation. So now you've got $220,000 a unit in it. From an economic point of view, you can't convert it, but it's giving you, maybe, a 3 percent return. Meanwhile, you're paying a bank loan of 7 or 8 percent. So now you've got negative leverage. You're putting out more than what's coming in. And that's where the foreclosures come in.

But somebody's problem can be somebody else's opportunity. Other people's foreclosures can open up opportunities for you to pick up buildings from lenders who have taken them back, at good enough prices to provide you with an exit strategy.

Banks are not in the business of either managing or selling apartments. And the bank regulators hate to see REOs—real estate owned by the bank—on the bank's books. Banks have special departments—REO departments—that are just sellers, with strong commands to get rid of what they have, even if they have to write it down. What that means is that they've already taken a loss. Now they just want to get it off the books to make the regulators happy.

As the market gets bad, one of the investment strategies can be to go and see the banks that were active in condo conversion lending and see if they have this product that was given back to them. Because at some point the bank is going to get pretty desperate to get rid of it and they'll be willing to sell at very low prices—just to get it off their books.

That gives you a chance to buy it at a real good price and leave it as an apartment, or maybe hold it until the market gets better and sell it as a condominium. While you're holding, you might be able to increase the rents and better your returns.

So in a bad market, you can go to the bank and make a deal to help them get rid of all the REOs and at the same time be able to come in with very little money.

Knowing about REOs, and applying a little vision, we were able to turn a foreclosed office site into an extremely successful—and completely unexpected—apartment project called Lakes of Deerfield.

The site sat right on the border between two well-to-do cities, Deerfield Beach and Boca Raton, next to the interstate—a tremendous location. It was zoned for offices, and would have been a great site for an office considering where it sat, but the office market collapsed. The lender got it back from somebody who was going to build an office but couldn't when the office market died.

When I heard about it I thought, "That's a fantastic location. But I'm not into offices. And that market's in a coma anyway."

But it was such a great site, I kept thinking about it. And the lender kept advertising it as office land.

Well, I knew the people at this bank (the importance of relationships, again). So I went to see the REO officer and asked him what he was going to do with it. He told me, "I don't know, Jorge. But it's got to go. I've got to get rid of it before the end of the fiscal year. Even if it's for one dollar, I've got to get it off our books."

The original purchaser had bought this land for like $8 million, and placed a $6 million mortgage on it. I ended up buying it from them for less than $1 million, knowing—and here's your exit strategy—that even if I couldn't get it rezoned, at that price I could turn around and sell it to an office developer for $2 million right then. He'd get it at a bargain price and I'd double my money.

But here's where the vision comes in. Nobody would touch that site since it was zoned for offices. My plan was to get it rezoned to multi-family. I went to the city and I said, "Hey, multifamily is going to be lower density. It'll have less traffic than those big office buildings that you guys were planning. And we're going to set at least twenty percent of the apartments aside for moderate-income families."

Reserving for moderate income actually worked in my favor as well, because we were able to get tax-exempt bond financing for doing it.

And the city agreed. They wanted it to become a Mediterranean-style garden apartment project.

So I bought it for a steal. And instead of letting the land sit there empty waiting for someone to put up an office building, I proceeded to get it rezoned for close to three hundred apartments. That made it usable immediately, which increased the land value to over $5 million. The increase in the land value provided all the equity I needed for the construction and property loan. So I put no money in, and it allowed me to do apartments and to get a huge return. We kept the apartments and it's still giving us a huge return. As a matter of fact, we have been able to steadily increase the rents and have increased the financing on the property, enabling us to take out millions of tax-deferred dollars while still receiving a substantial cash flow.

But I had to look at the property with different eyes than everybody else in order to create that return. Everybody else was looking at it and seeing offices. And if my plan didn't work, I still had bought the land for cheap enough that it gave me an exit strategy that would make me money: I could always hold it for a while and then, when the office market started to come back, sell it to someone who wanted to build offices for more than I paid.

You always look to buy properties that have a great location and that you're buying at a price that is good enough for you not to get hurt by holding the land.

When I'm buying premium-priced land for condominiums, I'm still looking for exit strategies. I'm looking for it to be in such a choice location that it can't go down in the long run. If you buy on a golf course, they can always build another golf course. There's only so much ocean-front or bayfront, no matter where you are. Be sure the land is so unique that the value can never go down in the long run. All you might have to do is wait it out.

> There's only so much oceanfront or bayfront, no matter where you are. Look for a location whose value can't go down in the long run.

If the location or land conditions are special enough that it won't go down in value, then I'm not worried. As long as I have the zoning in place to build something profitable, I have a gold mine. What you can't do is buy something without the zoning in place, because if all of a sudden the city decides it won't allow anything more dense than what already exists there, you're in deep trouble.

Buying well gives you an exit strategy. You may have to hold for a while, or you may end up turning your condominium project into a rental building, but if you buy at a low enough price, you can always come out ahead—even if your plan falls through.

Las Ramblas—Moneymaking Exit Strategies

The perfect example of a good exit strategy is what happened to us in Las Vegas. Even when the market collapsed, we were still able to make a profit by disposing of the land as an exit strategy.

Las Ramblas was a huge project. There was going to be a casino and, at one point, nine buildings with restaurants, nightclubs, a spa, and forty-four hundred hotel, condominium, and condo-hotel units. At the time, in a city of huge projects, this was one of the biggest projects there was.

It was a project of a scope that was scary, even to me. It was a very, very massive project. Because of the fact that it was so scary, from day one I wanted to make sure that if something happened we would not be financially hurt. And the reason we loved that site is because it was located where the value of the land was very similar to the economic value of the existing old apartments that were already there. The apartments were producing enough income to support the mortgage.

Because it was such a big project, I'm going to use some big numbers here, but the same holds true when you buy a single house or a single small apartment building.

When you buy a piece of land and you have to hold it for a long period of time, the interest on the financing can kill you. If you buy a big piece of land for, say, $100 million, the interest on that could be over $10 million a year. And not only do you have the interest to carry, but your taxes, insurance, and so on. There's no money coming in. If your market goes sour and you have to hold the land for five or six years, you end up paying double the price on the land.

In this case, the existing old apartments covered the debt service. So if I would've bought it for $100 million, and borrowed all the money to pay for it, ten years from now my debt would not have increased because the building was producing enough to cover my debt service on the property.

So that was one part of why I liked that particular large site. It had an existing use to pay my mortgage and my carrying costs.

Two, as I saw the development of Las Vegas, I was looking at people on the Strip paying five, six, seven times the amount on a per-unit basis that I was paying in this location, which was very close to the Strip, on what was called the Harmon Corridor. It's next to the Hard Rock, one of the most successful hotels in Las Vegas. And then, as I was doing my due diligence, W, the luxury hotel chain, started investigating the site on my other side. So on either side of my site I could have ended up with two of the most popular, hip hotels in the world. Clearly, if these hotels worked, this would be the next Strip. It's right there. We'd be on the young, hip Strip with the W and Hard Rock.

What we wanted to do, though, was get it rezoned to allow a casino and a mixed-use project containing several buildings, a hotel and condominiums. Getting the zoning would create even more land value, even if we never built it.

So I was thinking:

"If my zoning comes through, I'm going to double or triple the value of that land just because of the effort of visualizing that and convincing the city to give us this new zoning in Las Vegas. That's a triple.

"If everything does go through, and the market stays strong and I can build and create Las Ramblas, then that's a home run.

"But even if this doesn't go, and I can't get it rezoned, I still have a solid hit with the land, because of the location and the existing income-producing rental."

From the very beginning, I wasn't losing money.

Now, the home run didn't happen. But the triple happened.

We got our first victory when we got the project zoned for all the buildings we wanted. We got a casino permit. So we created value.

Then came trouble.

There was a combination of things—lower demand, higher construction costs, shortages of labor and contractors—that made us rethink such a huge commitment. And since I was the new guy in town, I didn't have the relationships with the contractors and subcontractors to ask them to make my project a priority, or to give me a break on the price.

It isn't that we just gave up. We looked and looked and looked, and you know what? It just couldn't be done. The difference was, I keep on saying: Know your market. Know what you do well.

All those things contributed to me realizing I couldn't handle it well there. And then the market also suffered a serious downturn in which demand greatly diminished.

So it was a perfect storm: Management. Long distance. Not enough knowledge of the market. No relationships. Everybody wants to be building in Las Vegas at the same time. And, boom! The economy tanks.

Looking at all that, at one point I looked deep inside and thought, "Having pride is a good thing, but you can't let pride stand in the way of the right decision." The fact that I had never walked away from a job that I had announced was a big shock to my system, something that didn't make me feel good, but there are times when you have to look at the alternatives very coldly. I had to figure out which was better for my reputation in the long run: that I started a condominium that goes sour, or that does not deliver, or that makes us lose money for the first time? Or, should I take my losses and let the press and people criticize me for having a failure?

I consulted with numerous people—not with numerous people in the business; I knew what the business deal was. I talked with lenders who for many years had been my friends and I told them exactly what the situation was. I talked to my attorney. I talked to my business partner, Steve Ross. And after all those discussions, the right decision was to abandon it. And it hurt.

But it's a lesson. This goes back to when you take that first loss. It's a reminder not to get consumed by negative thoughts. Because Las Vegas became my albatross.

So I said, "Enough is enough." And we exited as cavalierly as possible. We still kept excellent relationships with the mayor, and with the contractors who we did talk to, and with George Clooney and Rande Gerber and the other partners we were going to have there. So making sure we didn't damage our relationships was still very important in the exit strategy.

And even though I wasn't happy about having to pull out of a project I had announced for the very first time in my career, when we left we sold the land to the people next door, and we made $100 million profit.

I guess that's the importance of buying correctly. Of location, location, location. The condo market may have died, but people were still going in and speculating on land and we thought we were going to get the greatest price for that land at that point. Others, apparently, had not seen the market retrenching as we had.

KEY PRINCIPLES

- The way to succeed is by doing your homework.

- The plan comes before the property. Always.

- The main thing is the main thing. The big picture is what matters.

- Visualize how your ideas can become a reality, but remain flexible when considering other possibilities.

- Construction always takes a little longer than you expected and it's always a little more expensive than what you think. Put in a contingency.

- Make sure the land you buy is well priced enough to cover your costs in case the project is not successful and does not go forward.

- There's only so much oceanfront or bayfront, no matter where you are. Look for a location whose value can't go down in the long run.

ST. REGIS RESORT AND RESIDENCES, Bal Harbour, Florida
Rendering developed by BridgerConway

4 · THE TEN COMMANDMENTS OF NEGOTIATION

"Always leave money on the table. Building
a relationship is more important than
making one deal."

Negotiations are like playing poker. You have to know what cards you're holding, read the cards your opponent is showing, and try to learn as much as you can about the ones he's holding without letting him know what you've got in your hand.

You also have to know as much as you can about him as a player—what his style is, and what his strengths and weaknesses are.

End of analogy. After that, it's completely different. Because in real estate, every negotiation is unique, and the goal changes every time. There's no such thing as a single winning hand that beats all the others. You want both of you to win.

COMMANDMENT #1: KNOW YOUR OPPONENT

Let's say you've found a piece of property that fits your plan perfectly. When you approach the owner, you need to understand what your position is: Not only is it the greatest site in the world, but the owner is filthy rich and he's got twenty offers to buy the land. If you really want that land, you're going to have to beat everybody else. You're going to have to pay the most, or show him that if he partners with you he'll make more than he can with anybody else.

But let's say you're looking at the same piece of property and this time the owner has been trying to sell it for a year and has had no offers whatsoever, he can't afford to keep up the loan payments, and he's facing foreclosure by the end of next month. Everything I just told you is totally different.

In every negotiation, you have to understand what the conditions are on the other side in order for you to squeeze the most out. You have to know if your opponent is strong or if he's weak. You need to get into his shoes.

The only way to know that is to do your research beforehand and to keep your ears open for clues. People will show you their cards, if you pay attention. What you want to know is if they're holding a pair of aces or a three and a five.

We got involved in a deal once for some beachfront land in Cartagena, Colombia. The owners had come to us. They were looking for someone to help them put up a hotel and build a resort overlooking the Caribbean on the country's north coast.

As we investigated, we found out that the owners had power in Colombia, in Cartagena particularly, because they knew a judge and had been there for many years. We also found out they were in a money squeeze. And they even told us they had been unsuccessful in recruiting hotel groups and other potential partners that would allow them to start a project. So we knew some things to watch out for, along with some things we could use to get the upper hand at the negotiating table.

A person who didn't do his research might have thought they could go see hotels by themselves and probably do it. So if you don't do your research it looks like they have all the cards.

What you want to be able to do is get into your opponent's head. You have to try to figure out what they really want, and why. They may say they want one thing, but in reality they want something totally different.

Maybe a neighborhood group will say they don't want you to build your condominium so tall because they don't want all the traffic it will bring to clog up the roads. But when you keep talking to them you discover that the real reason they're so worried about how tall it is is because they don't want it to block their view. If you offer to move it over a few feet, suddenly it's okay.

So again, know the people you're working with. Know what the hot buttons are for them. What are their needs? What is it they really want?

When I was doing that deal in Colombia, I knew it was very different than if I had a deal in New York in which they send me a bureaucrat and all we do is hammer everything out and get the deal done. In Colombia, much more than here, a relationship needs to be built. So before we could even actually begin negotiations, we had dinner together, we went to the beach with their wives. They took us to a resort island for a day. We built a relationship. All so we could start talking to each other in a better way.

So it's not only that you know him, you also know the way he lives, the way he operates. And you don't push. You have to know the idiosyncrasies of the people you're dealing with.

The amount of experience the other guy has makes a huge difference. It's more difficult when you're dealing with inexperienced negotiators than it is when you're dealing with people who know what they're doing—particularly people who are fanatical about things. They have no sense of reality. There is no give-and-take. You go in and you give and you give and you give. You say, "Yes, we'll do all that." Then they come back and say, "Forget it." Out of the blue.

People think that when you're dealing with someone inexperienced you can take advantage of them. I say, "No, no, no, no."

I want to buy from people who know a lot and I want to sell to people who know a lot.

> Buy and sell from people who know what they're doing.

Sometimes people are emotionally tied to a piece of property. Or they're resistant to change. Maybe they're heirs fighting over an office their father built. That complicates the negotiations. When you're dealing with people who are more fanatical and emotional in nature it is very, very, very difficult to negotiate. It's almost like a jihad.

I've gotten tangled in talks with neighborhood groups where we've held meeting after meeting. We've given compromise after compromise. Then, finally, we come out of a meeting thinking it's a done deal because we came up with solutions. We met with two or three members of the board. They said yes.

Then they go and meet with the rest of the group and they come back and it's like we have not talked at all. Other members will disagree and they'll carry the day.

Usually the ones who are disagreeing are much more passionate than the ones who were willing to negotiate. There's no way of budging them. Why should they want to compromise? What they really want is to keep things exactly the way they are. They win by standing fast. And as the fight drags on, the ones who were willing to reason start dropping out. They disappear—because when they go back and they say, "This sounds like a reasonable compromise," the fanatics come in and lynch them. Then the less fanatical ones get tired of getting beat up for trying to be conciliatory and work out a solution both sides can be satisfied with. And they leave. The passionate ones are the ones that stay. And as time goes by, you end up with only the entrenched ones left.

You've got to know what your opponent stands to lose, and when he's got nothing to lose. If the other person negotiating has no downside, then you've got a lot less negotiating power. If you can just say no to me and you have no consequences and I can't do anything to you, then it's very easy for you to say no. And I have to understand that.

Never underestimate your opponent. Never. Under any circumstances. Don't think that they're stupider than you are. You've got to think they're trying to get to know you exactly the same way you're trying to get to know them.

Keep quiet and listen as much as possible. Negotiation is not just talking and salesmanship; it is to a large extent, but it's much more about listening. If you listen you can see exactly where they're coming from, what their key issues are, and what their weaknesses are.

> Negotiation is not just talking and salesmanship.
> It's much more about listening.

COMMANDMENT #2: KNOW YOURSELF

Everything you need to know about your opponent—strengths and weaknesses, his position, what he really wants—you have to know about yourself.

I've done a lot of deals over the years. That gives me a lot of experience and a lot of credibility. The Related brand is worth something, in terms of what we can get done and the relationships we have—with lenders, investors, government officials, and customers.

Those are some of my strengths going into a negotiation. I know it. And I make sure the other guy knows it, too. If the other person has never heard of me or Related, that's fine. But we're not going to negotiate without me telling him what I bring to the table.

In the Colombian deal I mentioned earlier, I wanted to partner with the guys who had the land for a variety of reasons. They knew people there. They knew the system there. They understood how things worked.

But while we were talking about how the partnership would work, what we would each put in, they said they didn't want to put the land in at what it cost them.

I explained to them that if all they wanted was a financial partner, they should go ahead and get a bank. They added value by getting a great piece of land at a good price and by knowing local people. But we brought huge value that counteracted what they brought into this deal. Most people have to pay dearly to be in partnership with us. That's the truth. We were giving them a partnership without asking for anything extra in exchange.

We brought expertise and relationships that would make them even more money. Because instead of selling to the local market for $200 a square foot, we were going to sell internationally too and put a brand in that was going to allow them to sell it at $300 a square foot. So while they might not get the $3 million they thought was the imputed value of what they had done, the pro formas have us making $20 million or $30 million on this project. And if they took 50 percent of that they would make, instead of $3 million, $15 million.

So to counter their argument, we talked about us and the value we brought to the table. We had to convince them that we were the greatest thing since sliced bread when it comes to development, and particularly in international development.

Again, that has to do with knowing who you are. Not just your opponent, but who you are. What do you really bring to the table? What do you bring to the table that they don't have? You've got to spell it out.

> Ask yourself: What do you bring to the table that they don't have?

And when you're starting out it's the same thing. What are you bringing here that the other people don't have? If you're starting a business and you're looking for partners and you're negotiating, well, what you are bringing is your time and expertise. These are going to be passive public or private investors who don't know development. What you bring to the table is the ability to get the deal done and produce a greater profit. They can't do it without you. That's what you have to tell them you do.

You negotiate to bring their points down and to put your points on top.

Now, to do that, the power of personality is very important. In my case, I must say, I am foremost a salesman. I have a strong personality. That's why attorneys want me to go before city councils and want me to speak: because I speak with passion whether I'm negotiating or not. They know that I'm right, and I bring substance. It's not just like an empty suit trying to sell.

It's the same when I'm negotiating to partner with someone, to get a bank to lend me money, or to get an investor to put his money in. I tend to go in, and before we do the selling I'm going to sell myself.

They are going to feel I have a huge capacity not only to design the best product they've ever seen but to get it done. I will show them in graphics and videos and photos all the incredible projects we have developed and our relationships with powerful business and government leaders.

So I've got to get them to believe in me. That's the personality. And I've got to get them to respect me and like me and trust me. Because in effect they're going to give me everything on a silver platter and say, "We're putting our faith in you."

You may not be able to show them a lengthy list of successful projects (yet), but you have other unique assets that will make you the ideal partner. Know what they are. Flaunt them.

That's when your personality needs to shine. That's when you need to be very forceful. So all the characteristics they want in a partner, they see. They're thinking, "He's going to take us to the finish line. He thinks about everything."

COMMANDMENT #3: KNOW THE GOAL

Always know the strength or the weakness of your position to know at what point you're going to settle in the negotiations. You always go into negotiations knowing what you want to end up with.

> Always go into negotiations knowing what you want to end up with.

It's like when you go to an auction. When I go buy Latin American art, I know what the maximum is I'm willing to spend. My rule is simple: Don't get enamored with the painting and pay more than what you really think it's worth—even if you love it. That's my philosophy. Other people can do whatever they want, but when I go to an auction I write down a number—the most I'm going to pay. And I don't deviate. If somebody else gets it, somebody else gets it.

Same thing here. You need to know when to stop. And you have to know what's crucial to you and what isn't. That way you can give in on the noncrucial points, the ones that don't really matter to you anyway, but not on the ones that are essential. What is the ultimate goal? What little battles can we lose? What can we give? Not that we want to give it, but what can we give and still achieve the end result?

Lose the skirmishes; win the war.

We will lose skirmishes. We will give them things they think they have won. But we are always aware that the main thing is the main thing. What matters is whether we reach our goal. We toss a little bit of bread crumbs in there to reach it, always. But did we reach our goal?

When I went into that partnership with Thomas Kramer that I mentioned in chapter 2, I knew my goal. I saw an opportunity for me to enter into what was quite possibly the premier site not only in South Beach but probably in all South Florida; in a beautifully designed building that you could see was going to be an icon; in which he'd already put like $30 million into land and building. And he couldn't do it. So it was an opportunity for me, with very little money, to get in on this fantastic deal.

I was also very aware of his reputation. I had heard all the stories about how he got the money from his father-in-law, that he could spread it around but not make it for himself. So I had to balance what I thought was a great real estate opportunity with the problems I could see myself having with him.

So that made my goals in our negotiations clear. One thing that was extremely important to me was that I had to be the managing partner so that all of the significant day-to-day decisions were mine.

The other thing that was very important to me was that he had to give me the first priority on these other two waterfront sites he owned on South Beach.

Those were the two points I knew I wouldn't give up in the negotiations. Those were the deal-breakers. But he agreed on both and we went on to make more money on the Portofino Tower than we ever had up to that point. Then we went on to repeat that success on the other two sites.

When I went to Colombia, my goal was to secure a piece of land in Cartagena that was the best location there at under the market price. So if the Cartagena market fell apart completely and I had to sell the land as an exit strategy, I'd be safe. That was my goal. Everything else I used as a strategy to get to that goal. And whatever concessions I gave did not detract from that goal.

You learned about exit strategies in the last chapter. When you go into negotiations, the exit strategy has to be part of the ultimate goal. You can't pay so much for the land that you lose if your project doesn't go through.

> When you negotiate, the exit strategy needs to be part of the ultimate goal.

So, what have I accomplished in that particular negotiation? Exactly what I wanted. I wanted the land base to be fantastic. I wanted to get into their heads and know what they wanted, so I could persuade them that what they really wanted was what we envisioned. And the only way to achieve that was with us. We convinced them that our value was worth more than twice as much as they could get by selling the site. By staying with us and developing it together they would make much more money. And we were right. Today this land in Cartagena is worth probably twice as much—eighteen months after we started negotiations.

Thanks to that increased land value, if something were to happen in Cartagena, if I could not get the international market to buy into this, I have my exit strategy. I can sell it to a developer over there and make more money than we paid for it.

And that was the whole intent from the very beginning in the negotiation.

COMMANDMENT #4: BE 100 PERCENT PREPARED

Do your research before you go into the first meeting. You have to know your opponent, right? Well, how are you going to know if you haven't taken the time to find out? Who is this person across the table from you? Is this their first deal or their fiftieth? Do they have twenty offers already or none?

You need to know everything you can about the property—what the hidden development costs might be, how it's zoned. Have they tried to change the zoning before? What kind of opposition did they run into? You may have a wonderful plan to come into this property that faces a major road on the edge of a suburban neighborhood and put up a condo—why wouldn't you? The roads are there; traffic won't come through the neighborhood; it acts as a boundary between the subdivision's single-family homes and the thoroughfare. It all makes sense. But you may not be the first to have that idea. The present owner may have tried the same thing and run into so much resistance from the neighborhood residents that after five years of battling in court and in front of the planning and zoning board, he just wants to cut his losses and get rid of it.

What would that make the land worth to you? Nothing. You wouldn't even be at the table. But if you haven't done your research, you won't know. You'll show up thinking your grand plan will be a breeze. And when he offers the property for what seems like a song compared to what you think it's worth with your high-rise on it, you'll be left wondering why he was the one who walked away whistling. And five years and God only knows how much money later, you'll be the one trying to pass it off to some other poor schmuck with a grand plan.

Find out what the property means to the sellers. What was their plan for it? When did they get it? From who? What did they pay for it? That's often pretty easy to find out. Most property appraisers' offices have sales amounts in their records. There may be compensation that doesn't show up there, especially if the new owners joined into a partnership with the original owner, but you can often get a good idea. And do your comps—what have similar properties around it sold for recently?

Do your research.

Find out everything you can about the people you're negotiating with. What other deals have they been involved in? How did those turn out? Are they considered honest? Trustworthy? Or is every word out of their mouths a lie that you'll have to confirm separately? Are they litigious? In short, what is their reputation? There are very few people who are going to say, "You know, I'm a bad guy and I'm going to take advantage of you." They all tell you, "I'm the Mother Teresa of real estate. I'm as honest as the day is long and I'm going to always be fair with you." Check them out. The way someone has handled their business dealings in the past is a very good indicator of how they'll handle this one. A crook may not steal every time, and an honest man may lie, but generally you can expect them to be true to the nature they've shown over the long haul. The project may be so attractive that it still may be worth it to you to deal with a possible bad partner, but if you know his reputation you know that after you shake hands with him you're going to have to count your fingers to make sure they're all there. Only do it, if you *must*, if you become the general partner, in charge of all decisions.

And once you think you know all there is to know about the people at the table, you have to remember that birds of a feather really do flock together. Find out who their associates are. And what *their* reputation is.

Trust me, if they're any good at what they're doing, they're going to know everything about you.

Be 100 percent prepared. Play out the negotiations if possible. I sit down before and I practice what I'm going to say, what the points I want to make are, what I expect them to say and how I'll respond.

Generally, I don't go into a negotiation alone. So before we get to the meeting, my associates and I practice together. We do different role-playing. Who speaks about what and when? Who doesn't? Let different people on your team handle certain parts.

I sit with my vice president, for example, and I say, "This is the goal. This is what we need to get to." And we negotiate as if I was them. We go through the points I think they'll bring up and the objections they'll have to ours. We plan our strategy and our tactics.

Typically the way I do it is to play good guy–bad guy. My partner in the negotiations, my vice president or whoever, acts like a good guy in a particular case. And I become the bad guy. I say, "No way, I will not accept this. You've given too much."

And my vice president will say, "But I am trying to go out of my way to make these concessions to make the deal."

And we'll do a little prearranged show of good guy–bad guy.

Other times we switch roles, particularly when I think it's going to be a tough negotiation. I'll send my partner to play the bad guy, so they go through the shock of facing a partner who says, "No. No. No." To everything. He takes a very, very strong position. Now, while he does that, I play the good guy and say, "Hey, Federico, you've been too tough. Let them have this. Let them do it this way." All of which already had been thought out way before we got into the meeting. We had established our goal.

That way, not only do I get most of the concessions I wanted, but I have a relationship that's a positive one going into the future with the other side. I've built a relationship with them in which they realize I've also been paying attention to their needs and looking out for their interests. Which is very important, especially if it's someone we've brought in as a partner on that deal.

Often enough, negotiations take more than one meeting. Usually, in fact, they take multiple meetings. You agree on certain things, disagree on others, say, "Let's think about it," and take a break.

After the meeting ends, you review what happened to prepare for the next one. Did you find out something you didn't know? What points did they not seem willing to bend on? What concessions did you make, and which ones did you win? What's next?

You prepare for the next meeting the same way you prepared for the first, taking into account the new position you're starting from. What might have changed to affect the outcome or the tactics you employ to get you there. You do more research if you have to. Then you practice again and you role-play again from your new position.

You have to be 100 percent prepared every time you go back into negotiations—no matter how many times that is. After every meeting, you review what you've learned, what you've gained, and develop your strategies for getting the rest of the way to where you want to go.

COMMANDMENT #5: DEAL WITH DECISION MAKERS

Whether you're dealing with one person, a board, or the representatives of a neighborhood group, know the decision makers. Who are the people that you really need to convince? Who are the ones that when they say this, the rest of the people will follow?

Try never to negotiate with a proxy. You don't want to deal with someone they send who is only going to go back to the decision maker, because then you're negotiating against yourself. You will always have another bite taken from you.

Let's say the landowner sends an attorney in his place. The attorney will get most of what the landowner wants, we'll arrive at some kind of compromise. Then the attorney's going to go to the decision maker and show him where he got us to already.

Then the landowner will send him back to ask for more.

The property owner would have agreed just fine if he had been there himself. But since he already got everything he wanted, he has nothing to lose by sending the attorney back to ask for more. You just set the new baseline. From there the only way to go is up.

So that's why when I'm the one doing the negotiating, I always say, "Subject to board approval," or our partners or whatever. Do it, even if you *are* the board, or the only partner. There doesn't have to be a board to go back to. When you say that, it gives you a chance to go back, think, and come back to ask for more if you want to or need to.

Because, believe me, when it happens on the other side, and their attorney comes back with the concessions he's won from you, they're always going to say they never would have agreed to that.

It doesn't matter that you know that their attorney was really well versed in everything they wanted. It won't help to tell them that. You give them another chance at you.

So always try to negotiate from the start with the person who is going to be making the ultimate decision, so that he can't come into the room fresh later and say he would never have agreed to this.

How do I know that? Because many times I do exactly that. Because I will be negotiating on a piece of land, and I tell my partner or my vice president or whoever what I think the goal is and what we need to do to reach it. And I will send him in to get the best deal he can. If I feel when he gets back that it's not the best deal and did not meet what I wanted, then at that point it gives me a chance of now meeting with them. Having not been part of the original negotiations, I can come in and be the one who says, "No way! This is crazy. I need this and this and this."

When the other side sends a proxy, I immediately try to get him out of the way and set up a meeting with the real decision makers, or I send my own proxy to negotiate. Going back to that Colombia deal again, that's what happened in the beginning. They sent their consultant to Miami, the one who had done all the studies, had helped them get the site, had done the analysis to try to secure a hotel, and who was going to help in all those things.

He came in and did a fabulous presentation for me and told me what they wanted.

I immediately knew not to give the guy a specific offer, because he wasn't going to agree or disagree with me. All he was going to do was go back to them with it. And whatever I gave him, they were going to come back and take another bite. So what I did when the guy came and made his presentation was, I listened. I told him the problems of Colombia. And I said, yes, I'm interested, but it would take a lot to take me away from all this stuff I'm doing here to go to Colombia to do this deal.

And then I said to him, "If, based on all that, the people there are interested, I would expect all of the principles to come over here to talk with me directly."

And the next trip all three of them came to Miami. That showed me they were very keen on making the deal. We did the first negotiations here and then we went to Cartagena after there was a framework for a deal.

That was a good start. But like I said before, expect more meetings. That was just the start. We had at least ten meetings before we got to the point that a letter of intent was signed. And that's just the letter of intent; the contract comes later.

So even when you deal with decision makers, things can drag on. But if you don't deal with the decision makers, you waste even more time, or you can end up giving up more than you wanted to.

COMMANDMENT #6: TAKE YOUR TIME

In negotiations, the tortoise wins.

That doesn't mean talks have to take a long time, in the overall scheme of things. But the person who takes his time generally wins.

In negotiations, time is a tool. Time can also be a weapon.

Never be in such a hurry that you make the first offer. You always want them to. Why? Because the first offer is just that, it's a starting point. It's rarely the end. When you go to the car dealer, the sticker price is the dealer's starting point. It's the first offer. You don't expect to pay it, and he doesn't really expect you to. From there, you're both going to negotiate a lower price.

> If at all possible, don't be the first to make an offer.

But in real estate, sometimes you're going to talk with the owner of a property that wasn't even for sale. Or that the owner has let you know could be for sale, at the right price, but it isn't listed with a broker the way a family home might be—there's no "asking price" to start from. Remember that boatyard you found in chapter 3 that you envisioned becoming a private island with luxury apartment rentals, an exclusive beach club, restaurants, and boutiques? Well, the owner has some idea of what the boatyard is worth to him. If you walk up and blurt out a price, you might be offering more than he had expected. It doesn't matter what the number is. If you say, "I'll pay you $1 million," and he says yes, you'll never know if he would have sold it for $500,000 or $800,000 or $50,000. If he says yes, you may be throwing away $950,000.

Or, if he's shrewd, he'll take your number as what it is—a lowball figure to work up from. You say $750,000; he counters with $1 million. He may have been perfectly happy to take $500,000, but now that you've offered more, he knows you're willing to pay more. And, trust me, he'll let you.

All because you went first.

If you get him to throw out the first number, then you've got a place to work down from. This isn't a grocery store, where a gallon of milk costs $3 and you pay $3. This is the farm. If the farmer says $3, you get to counter with $2. Or get him to toss in a couple of eggs.

Take your time.

If you do somehow wind up making the first offer, always leave room to go up. You should have a maximum price in mind that you're willing to pay when you open negotiations. It's that number I write down before I go into an art auction. That's not going to be my first bid. I start low and work up. I take my time. Even in a fast-paced auction, I'm willing to invest a few minutes to see if I can get it for less. I do the same thing in real estate. You should, too.

And you should never look anxious or desperate. Don't let the other side see how much you want a piece of property, or how important it is to you. You're playing high-stakes poker; you can't show your cards and you can't give any tells. You can't let them read a word or an expression that lets them know what your real position is. There may be one tiny sliver of land that splits a parcel and has the potential to stop you from putting together the whole giant project you have in mind. Without it, you got nothing.

No one can know that but you.

When Walt Disney was putting Disney World together outside Orlando, he sent people in to quietly and slowly buy up all the cow pastures and farms in the area. If anyone caught on to what was happening, he knew prices would skyrocket and possibly ruin his plan. There must have been several moments along the way when some recalcitrant rancher didn't want to sell and threatened the entire project. I doubt seriously that Disney's response was to get down on his knees and beg. His people had to play it cool. You do, too.

It is not unusual for us to walk away from discussions several times over the course of negotiations. You shouldn't be afraid to break off talks if you're not getting the deal you want. If the other party is really interested, they will find a way to come back to you.

It's a question of waiting. If the other side approaches again, we know we've gained an advantage. We have a much better idea of how badly they want the deal. If they don't, and we really want to make the deal, we can always reopen the talks by saying, "Look, let's forget that one for now. Let's talk about other things." We can use the sticking point, what they're now focused on as the deal-breaker, to win concessions on other points—"We can't give you that unless you give us this." Notice that I didn't say, "We could give you what you're asking for if you give us this."

That's because there's a huge difference between the two. A lot has to do with the way you phrase what you mean. The first way of putting it gets them to make a concession, or at least show that they're willing to make one, without you giving up anything. If they say, "Well, yes, we could do that," that's only an opening bid. That's the point you can start working from. If they'll give that, will they give that plus something else? The second way does just the opposite. It shows that you're willing to give up. They get to work from there and try to get you to give in on whatever it is even without them giving you what you want.

Or, if the sticking point is important to us, we can give certain things to get them to soften up on it.

But the key to it is time, and playing poker.

Always use time to your advantage. Especially if you know that the other side has a deadline looming—they need money before the bank forecloses on them; their investors have given them until the end of the month to start construction or they're pulling out; whatever. Look for clues, listen for hints.

To give you an example, my partner and I have used New Year's Eve to our advantage. I've been in my tuxedo, with my wife waiting downstairs, while I've been in a conference call trying to hash out points of a deal—because I know the other side is in the same boat, and that their wives are waiting, that they have places to be, and that they have to be there before the ball drops in Times Square. It's a psychological deadline I use to my advantage. I don't tell them my wife is waiting. I let them think I've got all night to get this done. But the closer we get to midnight, the more they're under the gun to get this finished, and I know it. Their wives are tapping their high heels on the floor and starting to glare, they know they have to drive however far it is, and the pressure is mounting.

Have time. Don't be desperate. Desperate people will always end up badly in a negotiation. Don't put yourself against the wall. And if you are, don't show it.

As good as people are, if they smell blood and they can do a better deal for themselves, nine out of ten times they will make a better deal for themselves. So watch your back.

COMMANDMENT #7: WHATEVER CAN GO WRONG WILL GO WRONG

Whenever we reach agreements, we act on them very rapidly. We take our time getting there, but once we settle the details, we move fast.

Once we reach an agreement, we have a contract out the next day. Because whenever you let go of things and time goes by, my experience has been that they start to fall apart.

You've already settled everything, so there's nothing that can go in your favor. But there are a lot of things that can go against it: They win the lottery and don't need my money. They find a developer that's even bigger than we are, with greater expertise, who will pay them more money, and they won't do the deal with us.

Murphy's law applies in real estate just as much as it does anyplace else: whatever can go wrong from the moment you make that deal will go wrong if you don't tie it up. I tell my people the same thing: If we found a great site, we have to act on it. If I don't act on it somebody else is going to take it. Or else it's not a great site. So you must act before you lose it. You must act before you allow bad things to happen.

Often, the things that come up are totally unexpected. It's like stepping off the curb and getting hit by a bus. Or getting hit by lightning when there's not a cloud in the sky. Because if you've done your job correctly, you are prepared for the things you anticipated could happen. You still have to expect the unexpected. Always think that what can go wrong will.

> **Always think that what can go wrong will go wrong.**

I was once putting together a deal to build a condominium tower project in Miami. The site belonged to a well-established private hospital, Mercy Hospital, and sat right on the water, right next to ritzy Coconut Grove, overlooking Biscayne Bay. Beautiful location. Beautiful view.

On one side you've got the water. On another, the hospital, and, beyond that, separated by a thicket of mangrove trees, one-story homes. Opposite the water are more low homes in a neatly wooded neighborhood. And, finally, opposite the hospital side is a thick snarl of mangroves and lowland on the bay. That goes for the equivalent of a few city blocks before you hit the next patch of development, which includes waterfront mansions formerly owned by Madonna and Sylvester

Stallone, among others. They sit just past a historic manor on a sprawling property with gorgeous garden mazes called Vizcaya, which was built in Miami's early days as the winter home of a wealthy corporate baron and his wife. Now it's a museum, open to the public. Which means no one is ever going to build there. Ever.

So, in all, you've got mostly unobstructed views on all sides, and almost zero chance that anyone is going to build anything that will interfere with those vistas in the next lifetime or two at least.

The hospital owns the site outright, so I'm dealing with only one owner, and they're motivated to sell.

What can go wrong?

We hashed out a tentative agreement with Mercy. Then we went to the three neighborhoods around the site and sat with them, asked them what their concerns were—and totally understood what they wanted. They were concerned with traffic. They were concerned with more cars going inside their neighborhoods.

So we made individual compromises with those neighborhoods. We made the deals confidential because we gave them a lot of money for the improvements they were going to have, but we didn't want to go to every neighborhood in Coconut Grove and have to give them the same because then the project would not have worked. We knew from the beginning how much we could give out. And we worked out compromises with the adjacent neighborhood groups.

So far so good.

We took the plan to the city and we got initial approvals from the city planning and zoning department. Still smooth sailing.

Then, as we got to the first city commission meeting, after more than a year of meetings, Murphy's law struck. Vizcaya had never come up once. It had never even entered my imagination. The neighborhood people never said a word. We had presented to the Coconut Grove Council. The museum folks never said a peep to us.

And then, all of a sudden, someone presented a photograph that showed through some trees, which had fallen because of a hurricane that blew through, how if you went out to the garden and looked almost a mile away, you could see the buildings. There, at the last minute, the Vizcaya people suddenly decided the view was impaired.

So I said, "If you look the other way you see Brickell buildings, and if you look the other way you see Grove Isle. Why did you even sell the land to Mercy Hospital?"

I understand historic preservation. But this I couldn't understand. If I was tearing down the park, okay. But we're talking about a site a mile away that they can't normally see because of the trees anyway.

And that became a huge negotiation, out of nowhere. We sat with them and asked them what it was they wanted.

Their response was that they simply didn't want to see the building.

So we went over the tree canopy with them and offered to redo the plants and trees that were knocked out by the storm, which would cover the great majority of the building.

Then they wanted assurances that there wouldn't be more development on the rest of the hospital's land. So we agreed to get Mercy to put a restriction on the land so that for the next twenty years there would be nothing else built there.

Then they said the project's density was too high and the height was too high. So we went from three hundred units and offered them a 20 percent reduction, which later on became a 25 percent reduction because the commission asked us for more.

The lesson is: Expect the unexpected, because what can go wrong will. But you can limit the number of unexpected things you'll run into if you do your research, you prepare, and you meet with the people with properties around your site to hear their concerns so you can work out compromises, gain allies, and neutralize opposition.

CASE STUDY

St. Regis—Neutralize Opposition, Gain Allies

One day, I was at a real estate conference and I started talking to Barry Sternlicht, who was then the head of Starwood. Starwood is one of the largest hotel companies. They own the Sheraton, St. Regis, W Hotels, Westin.

He said, "You know, we're thinking of upgrading all of our brands. The Sheraton we have in Bal Harbour is older, and what do you think of that location?"

I said, "That's the best location in South Florida."

And, for what he was thinking of doing, it was. The Sheraton they had there sat right on the ocean, and across the street from the world-famous Bal Harbour Shops. People travel internationally to shop in the exclusive boutiques and stores there. The truth is, I felt the Sheraton was incompatible with the location. I mean, you've got these great, upscale stores that rich people come from all over the world to shop in, and a hotel aimed at business travelers.

A little time went by, and we met with Barry's people at Starwood, and we ended up partnering with them to replace the existing Sheraton with a St. Regis condo and hotel, which included extremely luxurious hotel rooms and condos that people could buy in the same building. They owned the land, and we would be development partners.

Now, Barry is very opinionated. *Very* opinionated. And he had already gone through an exhaustive selection process with some of the world's greatest designers and architects competing for the job, and he had already had plans drawn up. And what they came up with was a very nice design, but it wasn't Miami Beach. That's very hard to tell somebody who's really opinionated, who had already spent over $500,000 in design selections. He didn't care. He wanted to go forward with it, so we said, "Okay, we'll work with it."

And we did. We took it to the city architectural review committee and they said, "We hate this building. This building has nothing to do with Florida. It doesn't even have balconies. This is the premier site in South Florida and you're putting in a building that doesn't relate to the South Florida environment."

So I went back to Barry and said, "I told you so." Then I convinced him and his people that the right thing to do was to get a design that was much more tropical. And we not only changed the building design, we brought in a new landscape architect to give it that tropical feel.

Now we had to fight the second battle. The Sheraton had aggravated some of the neighbors on either side. They had never done any real extensive community relations. And the two condominiums on either side were what the Bal Harbour village council listened to the most. Both had very influential people in the community living in them. Councils everywhere are made up of politicians, and politicians are people who want to get elected, and reelected. So they listen to influential voters. In Bal Harbour, they listened to the people in those condos.

We knew that if we wanted the city's approval, we needed to have the condos on our side. Or, at least, we needed them to not oppose us.

So we took the time and individually met with all the community leaders who were also condominium leaders. I met with them. I gave them the assurances they wanted: That we would wash their cars during the construction phase, that we would put nets over here, that we would give some money to the condominium association so they could do certain things, that they were going to get some special entry into the new spa. It was a long, long process.

> You have to take the time to get the community on your side.

This is important for anybody starting out, too. You have to put in the time to get the community on your side. It's a long process. You have to listen to everybody. You have to listen to the city. Often, the city and its residents will be really split between pro-development and antidevelopment factions. No matter what you do, some of them will always be antidevelopment. But it's important to get enough people in that community on your side so the politicians see they are not taking a vote that will get them all thrown out the next time they run for office.

Bal Harbour is no different. And while we knew we couldn't win everyone over to our side, we won over the ones we could, and tried to neutralize as many of the rest as we could. That's important, too. You never convince everyone. Someone who is adamantly opposed to the development is probably going to continue to be adamantly opposed to the development. But if you can get a guy who's opposed to stay home instead of going to the commission to fight you, then, even if he doesn't come to your side, you neutralized him. So go talk to him, look him in the eye, listen to what he has to say and try to get him to think you're not such a bad guy, and that this development is not going to be the worst thing in the world. Then, maybe, he won't go to the commission to blast you.

It's very important, too, to find out who the opinion makers are. Whenever you're going to fight something, you have to know who the people are that people listen to. Look for the people who are important in the community and the people who are friendly with the commission and the mayor.

So we went to the opinion makers and we met with them individually. And after meeting with them individually, we met with their boards. And we showed them we were listening to their concerns and that we wanted to be good neighbors. They wanted the setback to be a little bit more this way or a little bit more that way, so we worked within the parameters to accommodate them. And we got the approval of both boards of the buildings on either side.

Additionally, we had to work with the people concerned with historic preservation, because the building was done by the noted Miami Beach architect Morris Lapidus, who also did the Fontainebleau and the Eden Roc, two landmark hotels from the beach's heyday. So we went to his son and daughter and the historic preservation people who were going to fight us and we showed them that the building had already been changed from the original, that there were very few things that remained. We told them we would at least save some things. So we took some of the original things that were in the lobby and donated them, so that we could preserve some of the history that way. Again, we didn't win them all over, but at least that defused them. Some of them actually wrote letters in our favor, but the majority of those who at the beginning were against us did not come and stand in front of the commission to make a fight.

Some you bring to your side. Some you neutralize.

Then we went to the owner of the Bal Harbour Shops and got him to come over and be our ally, too. We made him see the advantage of having this great resort right in front. Because, remember, while we're building it, it's going to be four years in which he's got all this construction traffic and dust and mess across the street. The construction becomes a royal pain. Can you imagine that site with three buildings going up at the same time? With trucks coming in and out? A thousand workers? It's a logistical nightmare.

Not only that, but for four years, the people who used to stay at the Sheraton and come over to shop wouldn't be there anymore.

But we went to him and we said, basically, "Listen, you have the most expensive mall in the southeastern United States, the one that everyone associates with quality. You can't have a Sheraton next to you. That is Middle America. It's a nice hotel, but it's Middle America. The people who stay at a Sheraton are not the people who go to your shops and spend $10,000 on a dress. The people who go to St. Regis and pay $1,000 a night for a hotel room are those people. And the condominium people who are going to be there, those are real heavy hitters. Because the units that we're going to sell start at $3 million."

So we made him visualize what he was gaining in the long run. We said, "Forget about the short term—you are going to have some dislocations. But in the long term, this will then cement Bal Harbour as the luxury spot in the world. Now it's not just going to be your shops, but it's going to be the hotel. The best hotel brand and the highest-price condominiums."

We also knew he had plans to make improvements to the mall at some future date. So we said, "We'll be your partners when you choose to do that and we'll help you as much as we can."

And that brought him over to our side. And he was a real strong ally.

You neutralize some. You gain allies.

Then we went to the city. We showed the architectural board that we had listened to their concerns and redesigned the building to give it a Miami Beach feel. They wanted to be able to see the ocean, so we lifted the entranceway so that in the grand lobby you would have this glass building and you would still be able to see the ocean from the building. They wanted larger balconies. They wanted more tropical pools. They wanted more light. So we did all those things to get the approval we needed.

And by the time we went before the commissioners, they knew we had worked real hard with everyone to make our project good for the city, not just good for us. They knew we had worked with the condo residents and the historic preservation people and the Bal Harbour Shops to show them we would be good neighbors. So the commissioners felt that if they voted for this it was not going to be a negative for their political careers.

Be prepared for a long process. Be ready to compromise. And be ready for when whatever can go wrong does.

We had anticipated what we could. We had done our homework, met and compromised with neighbors to get their support, won allies or neutralized opposition among the preservationists, and modified our plans to meet the city's concerns.

Then came the unexpected.

In the middle of all this, Barry Sternlicht got thrown out. The board decided it didn't want him, even though he founded Starwood. So we had to start with a whole new set of players, all of whom saw us as Barry Sternlicht people. Which meant we had to convince them all over again that the project was good, that we were good, and that we weren't necessarily Sternlicht's people, we were Starwood people.

So I developed a whole new relationship with Steve Heyer and finally got everything clicking with his people and got the project rolling again.

And then guess what happened. They got rid of Steve Heyer. So now it's again going through the process of getting the new Starwood people to see things our way, to partner up, to trust us. For the third time.

Murphy's law.

COMMANDMENT #8: BE NIMBLE, BE CREATIVE

Negotiations evolve. They aren't static. Circumstances change. You can't go in with a goal in mind and a plan for achieving it and stay locked in, plowing straight ahead with blinders on. That's like planning a road trip, marking your course on the map, and driving the way you had laid out even when you find part of the road is washed out, under construction, or closed. You just don't do that. You adjust to the conditions and you choose a new course. If a deer runs out ahead of you, you react.

Negotiations work the same way. You have to watch for changing conditions, stay alert, and be nimble. You need to stay open, so that as you're talking you can understand more and more. Don't be closed. You have to always be listening for the subtleties and nuances, so you can use them in your favor. You've got to be totally open-minded so that you can understand what it is they're telling you—not just what comes out of their mouths, but why and where the gaps are. Don't stay so focused on what you want that you don't listen to what they're *really* saying. Be open to achieve your goal by either changing or modifying something that serves their interests.

So, for example, let's say somebody I'm negotiating with says that because of the tax implications, they have to sell a piece of property before the end of the quarter. That immediately tells me two things: They have a deadline they have to meet; and I can help them with it, or use it to my advantage. I'm going to recast my whole proposal based on that issue they have.

After every meeting, I re-sit with my partner and I say, "This is what they told us that we didn't know before. And this is the way we're changing our strategy based on what we learned."

You're constantly changing based on the things you hear. For example, I might walk away from a negotiation to give a seller time to stew, to make him think he might lose the deal. I'll want to give it a little time to soften him up a bit. But if I hear from good sources that there's another buyer who's ready to make a deal that's a little better than ours, I'll take a totally different course. I'll call him. Instead of holding out for a better deal for me I might give a little bit more than I did before, because now I'm in a different set of circumstances. So you have to be nimble and react to that set of circumstances.

Like that deal in Colombia—one of them made the statement that one of their cousins was the main judge in Cartagena. What does that mean to me in terms of the negotiations? I figured that if I ended up fifty-fifty partners with these guys, I lost. Because if we disagreed over something and we had to go to court, they know the judges who would be deciding the case.

That revelation showed me an area where I needed to protect myself. I put in the agreement that any issues between the parties would have to be resolved in Miami. Because I didn't want to go in as the Johnny-come-lately developer from the United States, fighting a battle against Colombians who have a long history in Cartagena. I'd lose that. So I took it out of Colombia, and I put it in Miami. We fought a little bit over that, but we convinced them that it was the right thing.

You have to be nimble, and you have to be creative. In real estate, no is never the final answer—unless you want it to be. Sometimes there are big issues separating you. So you need to be creative to solve those things.

> In real estate, no is never the final answer—unless you want it to be.

I'll give you an example involving two projects that wound up going together, the Slade and the Villa Lofts.

It started when I got involved in a site that had a condo building and an unfinished condo building next to it. The developer went broke and just left it there. He left a slab and steel bars coming out of the ground for more than ten years. It was an eyesore.

I came along and got the property next door rezoned from like 32 units per acre to 151 units per acre. I wanted to build a condo sixteen stories tall, the tallest building there.

So the condominium next door went nuts. They sued. And I thought that this was going to be a two- or three-year delay as the lawsuit made it through court.

We launched a grassroots effort to counter the opposition, going door-to-door meeting with people and asking for their support. We met with local activists, church pastors, small-business owners, and neighborhood groups to explain how our project would help the over-all neighborhood.

And I made a really interesting deal with the people in the condo next door. Both buildings were on the same plane. They were on the water. The condo I was building blocked a lot of the existing condos. So I bought a lot behind me and moved my building back forty feet so the people in the existing condo could see the water.

I also agreed to complete their unfinished building, their eyesore called the Villa Lofts. But I had to slide that one back, too, and that meant buying the parcel behind it from a large, slow-moving institutional company. We didn't expect the company to move very fast, so it looked like whatever time we had gained by ending the lawsuit would be lost getting them to sell.

Another out-of-the-box solution—I should probably say out-of-the-chocolate-box—saved the day. We skipped all the middlemen and found a direct way into the director's office through his assistant. We sent her two wrapped boxes of Godiva chocolate and told her one was for her boss when he sold the property, and the other was for her to get us into a meeting within twenty-four hours. She had the meeting set up in two hours and we bought the parcel within weeks.

I built the Villa Lofts at a $1 million loss. But it was worth it. In exchange, I got them to allow me to build an extra floor on the Slade. That provided me with another seventeen apartments, on which I made $1.7 million.

So in the end, I got rid of what would have been an eyesore for me, too, and made an extra $700,000. I worked all that out and was able to turn a very bad situation for both into a very good situation for both. You make a win-win situation from adversity.

There are no formulas.

You've got to be open to changing your original plan if that's what it takes to get it done. Nos are not roadblocks that stop you. They're just temporary obstacles you have to find ways around.

So be 100 percent prepared. But be ready to change courses. Be ready to reskin the cat differently as long as it gets you the results you want.

COMMANDMENT #9: BUILD RELATIONSHIPS

Building a relationship is one of the most important goals of any negotiation. The long-term gain is worth more than any immediate profit you can make.

We were recently negotiating with a big firm, and when we finished, one of my people came up to me and said, "Jesus! I'm not even going to bring you to negotiations anymore. You gave them this and this and this."

And I said, "I know exactly what I was doing. I know that I have to deal with these people for three more years. I want this job to be a job with people who like us and feel they have a good relationship with us. Or else the next three years, as we're building and selling this job, will be a nightmare. Everything we do, they won't trust us. They're going to want to argue with us."

You know what I'm saying? It's very important that when you finish and you leave the table that everybody feels that it's okay, they made a good deal.

Negotiations are not just about the deal right now. Building a relationship is more important than making one deal. That's why I always say, "Leave things on the table." It could be money, it could be addressing their concerns about having my building blocking their view, about the landscaping, about how we're going to deal with the construction traffic while we're building—any number of things. But if you give them something you didn't have to give, you show them you care about them. That builds a positive relationship.

The worst thing that could happen is if I end up with these people and they're my partners, but they feel like they got taken advantage of. If they're bitter over the deal, they're going to always be trying to get back what they think they lost.

That's why you always leave things on the table. Make a concession. Give them something that's important to them. Throw in a bonus. Even if they don't ask for it.

Let's say you've convinced the owners of an office building to partner with you, but they think the property they're putting into the deal is worth $100,000 more than you do. According to your pro formas, that's too much. If you give that now, and fixing it up costs what you think it will cost, and you sell for what you think you'll get, that $100,000 would eat up all your profit.

So you negotiate. You get them to see things your way. And they agree to value it at the lower price. But you know they're not happy.

You could leave it at that. But I wouldn't. I would say, "You know, I know you're not happy. But I know we both want this deal to be the best for both of us. My pro formas are based on what I think is the least I think we can sell it for, and the most it will cost to fix up. But if we get lucky and we make another $100,000, it's yours. I'll give it to you."

That's when my people will scream, "Are you *crazy*?"

No, I'm not.

Think about it: Let's say I was hoping to make $100,000 after we got it all fixed up and sold it. I had done my numbers and I was happy making that. Well, if I make it, I should be happy. And if we make more and they get the extra $100,000 they thought the land was worth, I still make what I was hoping to make. Why shouldn't I be just as happy? We should all be happy.

But if I can offer them what they want, even when they didn't ask for it, they're going to work harder to make this project work. They're going to trust me. They're going to come to me with other deals in the future. And they're going to tell the whole world what kind of a guy I am.

And it didn't cost me anything. What, you say it cost me $100,000? No, it didn't. They only get that *if* we make it. If we don't, they'll still work harder, trust me, and all the rest.

It doesn't matter if you're going to partner with them or you're just buying from them or selling to them. Make a seller or a partner happy, and they'll be looking to bring you more good deals. Make a buyer happy, and they'll want to buy from you again.

What happens is, people get greedy. They lose sight of the big picture. They want to squeeze every dime out of the other guy and they end up hurting themselves. Building a relationship is more important than one deal. Building a relationship is always one of your ultimate goals when you go into a negotiation. Be strong but fair. Leave things on the table. And build relationships.

It pays off—over and over again. Over the years, I've built relationships. And I've built a reputation. When I go into negotiations with someone, I know they're going to check me out, just like I check them out. And I know what they're going to hear.

I want them to be of the frame of mind that "this guy is fair and this guy I can trust and, if I partner with him, this guy is going to do the best not just for himself, but for the group as a whole."

COMMANDMENT #10: NO MATTER WHAT, INTEGRITY

Always maintain your integrity. No matter what.

One time in Argentina, for example, I had the best site in Buenos Aires. We had agreed on a price of $10 million, everything was done. And all of a sudden this guy comes to me and says, "Because of the tax situation I was in when I bought it, you have to give me half in black money."

So I asked, "What in the world is black money?"

In Argentina that's what they call cash that hasn't been declared to the government. He wanted me to give him $5 million in the transaction. So they would have posted that he sold it for $5 million, and he'd only pay taxes on that, and the other $5 million would go in a secret bank account somewhere.

And I said no. I lost the best site in Buenos Aires because I believe you can never lose your integrity. Because I could never go to sleep if I felt what I was doing was wrong. For two reasons:

One, the moral reason—it's wrong. Any way you look at it, it's dishonest. And two, I think that sooner or later bad people get caught.

And I have no desire to go to jail. I have no desire to have my reputation destroyed after working so hard. So I won't do it for both selfish reasons and moral reasons.

By the way, the story has since spread around Buenos Aires. Now, the only people who come to us are people who will never even broach a topic like that.

People say, "But that's the way many people do things there." I don't care. It's not the way I do things. Your reputation and your integrity need to always remain intact. Just because something is almost commonplace doesn't make it right. When I do business in South America, I start my relationship with any partner and any owner with a lecture on who we are, so that we never get a questionable proposal. I don't even want to receive it. We tell them, "We do things by the book. We always pay taxes. We pay all prices clean." So right off the bat everybody is going to know about our integrity and our way of doing things. And if that isn't their way, then I'm sure they can find some other guy to deal with. I simply won't do it if it's wrong.

Once you tarnish your reputation, once people see you are willing to take the short, easy way, others will lose respect for you and that will greatly diminish your capacity to grow in the future.

KEY PRINCIPLES

- Buy and sell from people who know what they're doing.

- Negotiation is not just talking and salesmanship. It's much more about listening.

- Ask yourself: What do you bring to the table that they don't have?

- Always go into negotiations knowing what you want to end up with.

- When you negotiate, the exit strategy needs to be part of the ultimate goal.

- If at all possible, don't be the first to make an offer.

- Always think that what can go wrong will go wrong.

- You have to take the time to get the community on your side.

- In real estate, no is never the final answer—unless you want it to be.

5 · THE FIVE RULES FOR SECURING FINANCING

> "It's always good to work
> with other people's money."

By now, you've found the perfect piece of property for your plan. You tied it up with a returnable deposit. Now you're wondering, "Where do I get the rest of the money to make this project work?"

As I told you in the introduction, there's a lot of money that wants to go to real estate. There are a lot of investors ready to put their money into a good land or development deal, and a lot of lenders who are willing to offer loans.

Why shouldn't they? It's one of the most secure investments. Real estate almost always goes up in value over time, unless it's in a really bad location. And it involves a product that's tangible, touchable, real. It's not some nebulous get-rich-quick idea. So it attracts a lot of money.

And one of the beauties of real estate is that because it is indeed real, the property you're buying gives you instant collateral for your loan.

But just because there's money out there looking for opportunities to get into real estate doesn't mean you can just stick out your hand and get some. You have to know exactly what the lender or investor wants, and give it to them. It's a sales pitch, with documents to back up what you're selling. If they buy in, you get the money. So the better the pitch, and the better the documentation, the better the chance that you will walk out of your meeting with the money you need.

There are basically two sources of money: investors and lenders. The biggest difference between the two is that, generally, investors only expect to be repaid if the project makes a profit. Lenders want their money, plus interest, no matter what.

They're not mutually exclusive. It's very likely you'll get some of your money for a project from investors and some from lenders.

Within each of those major sources, there are, by and large, three types. They might be institutional types, such as banks or investment funds, individuals looking for better returns, or family and friends willing to back you with either a loan or as investors.

No matter what the source, the more prepared you are, the more likely you are to get the most favorable terms.

Rule #1: Be Prepared

You have to be prepared for every question, know every detail. If you're not, trust me, there are a hundred others lined up right behind you who the bank can talk to. Every one of them has a project they think they can make money with. And at least one of them has done his homework and is completely prepared with the financials and the renderings and a perfected sales pitch.

That's what it takes. Investors want to know what's involved, what the risks are, and what their returns are likely to be. So do lenders. You're going to have to know the numbers—anticipated revenues, as well as the expenses of everything from the land and construction costs to Realtor commissions and swimming pool maintenance (if it's a property you're going to be holding on to and managing). And you're going to have to be able to answer questions about your sales operation or your management team, your customer pool, and more. You have to anticipate their questions and know all the answers. And by the way, if you ever get hit with a question you don't know the answer to, don't lie. Tell them, "I will get right back to you with the answer."

But you can do it, if you do your homework. Your accountant will help you with the numbers. Your market research and advisers will help with the facts. In fact, you knew most of the answers before you went shopping for the property and saw what was out there. You prepare the same way you prepare for any negotiation—drill, practice, role-play. Know which member of your team is going to say what; run through the answers to the questions.

And just like you do in any negotiation, you have to know the other side. Study the different lenders and investors. You have to know what each of them does, what each of them wants, and which is best for you.

It's always good to work with other people's money. It's always good to leverage. But remember, there's always more risk when you leverage. The more you borrow, the riskier the transaction becomes.

I'll show you. Let's say I have $1 million and I want to build a condominium. I figure it out and it's going to cost $1 million to build it. If I take my $1 million and pay it all in cash, I have no risk.

You say, "You risked $1 million." No. Assuming that I can finish the whole condominium, I can't lose my money. The thing is built. I can wait forever. I can't rent it? Of course I can. So the risk is much, much less.

Now, what if instead of having the $1 million in cash, I borrow it at 8 percent? At that rate I've got $80,000 that I owe to the bank every year for the interest. If the market goes sour and I'm stuck holding my building, I've got to find a way to come up with interest payments. Plus, I've got them telling me to pay back the $1 million. Now that's risk.

The more you leverage, the greater your risk levels are, but the greater the return on your cash. You always have to balance how much you risk against how much your reward is.

There are various sources of financing, with varying degrees of risk.

For most of us, our experience with lenders and real estate involves our own home. We, or our parents, found a house, agreed on a price, and asked a bank for a loan to buy it. That's why it's only natural that when we think of getting a real estate loan, most people think of the bank first. But there are two other lender sources to consider as well.

One is called seller financing. That's the kind in which the seller says, "Yes, I'll sell you my building for one million dollars. You can get a seven-hundred-thousand-dollar loan, and instead of you coming up with the other three hundred thousand dollars, I'll give you a second mortgage for one hundred fifty thousand dollars." That means the seller is going to act like a bank and extend you part of the cash you need for the purchase, and you'll pay back the loan—usually with interest—just like you would to a bank.

Or I might convince a landowner that instead of selling the land for $500,000, if he would sit in with me, not only is he going to get the $500,000 for the land, but I'm going to give him 30 or 40 percent of my profit. And if my profits are $1 million, say, he's going to make another $400,000. And he never risks his land because the payment for the land comes out first, before anybody even takes a profit. So I would build a program to which I would hook the players I need to provide cash into the deal.

Or maybe the seller doesn't want to do that. He just wants to get his cash in a lump sum and say bye-bye.

Then I might have to hook an investment source into the deal. I might go to a private person who has money sitting in a bank making 5 percent, and tell him I have a way to make 30 percent with that money. And to make him feel more comfortable about the risk, I might assure him that I'm going to give him his investment back and his profit before I take a single penny for myself.

You can also go to friends and family, your rich uncle the doctor, or whatever, and lay out your plan. You can say, "Hey, I don't have the money. Can you put up most of it? Here's what I'm going to do, I'm going to do the sweat equity. I found the deal. And I'm going to be in charge of renting it and increasing the rents and then, later, selling it for a big profit." You can ask for a loan, and pay him interest just like you would to a bank. Or you might convince him to become an investor. If he likes your plan enough, he might see an opportunity he wants to take part in.

Even after getting funds from the seller and from family and friends, though, you might still need to go to an institutional lender, such as a bank or mortgage company. They're the primary source for the bulk of the money in most real estate transactions.

And as I said, you have to find ones that specialize in what you're looking to do. Some specialize in home loans for people buying primary residences or second homes. Some only do commercial loans, for retail space or office buildings. Some do construction loans and some only loan money for existing buildings.

Within any of those specialties, you'll find a dizzying array of options—balloon, recourse, variable, partition, participating, and mezzanine, just to name some. Explaining all the differences can easily fill an entire book. What you need to know is that there are all kinds of loans out there that you need to discuss with your financial advisers so you can decide which loan or combination of loans is best for your specific circumstance. Because you won't always want the same one. What works great in one case can be all wrong in another.

Let's say you go to your financial adviser and say you want to buy an apartment building and flip it in two years. Then your financial guy might tell you it's best to get a variable-rate mortgage and mezzanine financing.

If you tell him your plan is to hold the building for a long time, then he might say you're better off with an FHA thirty-year mortgage in which your loan-to-value will be much higher, you get the government financing, you get the lower interest rate, but you have prepayment penalties.

Based on your specific situation, there will be choices in financing you will pick. If you want to go long term, I wouldn't go variable. Why? Because any jumps in the rate will kill you. You want to match the loan with the duration.

If you're doing long term, you want to make sure you have fixed interest rates. Now, if you're looking to flip, if you're looking to have the cheapest money, then you might look at variable-rate mortgages. You might look at interest-only mortgages.

And, based on what your goals are, you set your plans for your presentation. So if the lender all of a sudden offers you a fifteen-year loan, you already know that's not what you want. Your plan is to hold it for only two to five years.

You might want to have a contingency plan in case you need to hold it for longer than two years. That way, if your two years are up and you haven't been able to flip it, you don't have to go back to all your lenders again. I've done loans in which I have a two-year variable, but I buy an extension up front for an extra point. If at the end of the two years I need to, I can buy three more years, and I'm not going begging for an extension when the market might be turning bad. Don't ever leave yourself open.

You might want to go to a lender and get more money and give them some participation in the job. Some lenders now are splitting up the loans, and they become primary and secondary lenders. So what they'll do to you is say, "Okay, your costs are a hundred. Instead of giving you the traditional eighty and you put in twenty, I'll give you ninety-five." But they'll break up the interest rates, relative to the risk. So on eighty you will pay the traditional interest rate, and on the additional fifteen you will pay a higher interest rate because it's a riskier loan.

So they become all in one, because by doing that they have total control. There's not another participant involved in the deal. The lender feels more secure that way, because if something goes wrong with the property, he's the only player.

That's why you have to study lenders—because a lot of them don't do those kinds of deals. So if you go to them asking for them, you're wasting your time. You've got to know who your lender is, and know the lending tools that are there in order for you to sell them on it.

A mortgage broker will help you. The truth is that the loan business is very national, so a mortgage broker will be able to access everybody. All you have to do is go in the computer and you'll see; this is very transparent. They'll say, "This guy is giving office loans at the following rate." You can see it.

> The best deals are obtained through relationships.

And the best deals are obtained through relationships. So if you're starting out and you don't have a relationship, what do you do next?

Get somebody who has a relationship. That's why you need the mortgage broker. It's not that he's just going to send you to all these lenders. He already has the relationship with them. It's much easier for him to say, "Hey, Mr. Smith is a real good guy and you should give him the loan," than it is for you to walk in as a total stranger and say, "Hi, I'm Mr. Smith. I'm a real good guy." What else are you going to tell a lender? That you're not?

So it's very good sometimes to have somebody else describe you and do the selling for you. And they'll give you access. Believe me, in the long term your consultants will more than pay for themselves. So don't worry about if it's going to cost you one point more because you're using a mortgage broker. It really is not. And it's going to allow you to have instant access to somebody.

Generally the bank or mortgage company is only going to lend you a percentage of the total value of the project. It may be 70, or 80, or 90 percent, depending on your credit history, your track record with the bank, and the project itself. For the rest, you can look for second or mezzanine loans, take it out of your own pocket, or look for investors.

Real estate is very trendy. The herd mentality is prevalent. There are "in" investments and "out." So as you're looking at investment deals, be certain to look at not only what you like, but consider whether what you like is the flavor of the month. I've sat on bank boards where if hotels were not the popular thing at the time and the loan officers were brought a hotel deal, they'd throw it out—even if it was the best hotel deal in the world. Their attitude was, "Don't bring us hotels!"

The same thing happens with offices and retail and residential. Right now residential—condominiums, for example—is not selling well. Now, I could have the greatest condominium, because I found a niche or something very special, but it's still much more difficult to finance today than offices, which people are much more inclined to do.

For that reason, you should try to look for the investments that people want to go into. It's much easier for you to convince an investor today to go into an office project with you, or an income-producing warehouse with office buildings, than it is to come to them and ask them for some money to do a condominium in Miami.

They're going to say, "What? Are you nuts?"

You've got to look at that. Remember those luxury apartments I wanted to build in downtown Miami, the Island Club? Bank after bank told me I was nuts. The "in" investment was garden apartments on the outskirts of the county, where land was cheap. I was bucking the trend. I finally had to go all the way to Brooklyn to find a lender who understood and would lend me the money.

Today, if I'm going to do a condominium project in a market that is overbuilt the way it is right now, I need to convince them somehow that my building is not going to suffer from that overbuilding.

That goes beyond being a good salesman, unless I find a special niche. We did that with the Lofts, with affordable housing aimed at middle-income people. And in a market where nobody was selling, I sold 450 units, in the worst market, in a month. Because I found a niche. I found something that defied the regular market.

That's what I had to convince the investors of. I had to find the people who would believe that even in this terrible market, a place aimed at this underserved sector would be a hit. I had to show them the numbers and persuade them this was a worthwhile investment. I had to make them see that this was a new niche that wasn't being exploited, and that this virgin territory would defy the challenges of an overbuilt market and succeed where others couldn't.

In the end, I was proven right. But if I put myself in those investors' shoes, I could see why they were skeptical. Everyone could see the condo market falling. Everyone could see there were way too many condos being completed for all of them to make it. It didn't take vision to see that. It took vision to see a way to go around that and create something that would sell out in a matter of weeks, despite what the rest of the market was doing. If I hadn't been prepared, I wouldn't have been able to answer their questions and deal with their concerns. You have to be just as prepared when you go ask for money.

Rule #2: Show Commitment

Always put some of your own money in to show that this is much more important to you than it is to them. If somebody gets hurt here, you're the guy who's going to get hurt the most because you're putting in all your time and all the resources you have.

Now, you're probably thinking, "Wait a minute, there! You said you started with no money down. Now you're saying always put in some of your own money. Which is it?"

It's both. Just don't think of "money" as meaning the same thing as "cash."

When I'm dealing with lenders, the money I'm talking about is equity. That can be the value of the land, the value of the completed building, and a whole lot of other things. From the lender's point of view I still have a lot of money in the deal. But it's not money that you call money.

If you were buying a piece of property valued at $100,000, and you're only paying $50,000 for it, from the lender's perspective you've got $50,000 in there as equity. That's real. Because you can go and sell that land for $100,000. That's money, and it shows your commitment to the deal.

If you get the property rezoned to allow more units, that increases the value of the land. You can use that added value as equity.

Remember, too, your advisers' time is worth money. When I started, I would get the owners of these old buildings to hold the property for me with a $5,000 returnable deposit. Then I got an architect to draw me these plans on the basis that if I got everything done, he would get paid. And I got the contractor to do all of the takeoffs, to tell me what it would cost to rehabilitate the place, the same way. If the deal went through, he got the job.

That work has value. So I get to use all of that for equity. The architectural services are worth something. It might be $10,000, or it might be $1 million, but someone would have had to pay to get the plans and renderings drawn up, and to have scale models built. If you didn't have them done before you went to the bank, you'd probably pay for them with money from the loan. Since you already have them, you show their worth on your budget as part of the assets you have in the project, the same as the land. The bank counts that as equity.

Also, when you get preconstruction deposits from your condo buyers, you can bond them. With that bond you can take the deposits out and give them to the lender as equity. If something happens with the deposits and you can't repay them, you'll have to pay for the bond. So your skin is in the game. The lender sees that. It's a commitment.

How you structure your total budget is a very critical item in attaining the lenders. Each lender looks at things differently. You present the same budget, but in different forms, in order to tailor it to the needs of the specific lender. How you show your deferred costs and use of deposits can substantially reduce equity.

You can use the buyers' deposits to create equity. You use your land to create equity. The final option to look for is mezzanine financing. Mezzanine financing is the financing that comes after your first mortgage. So first you go with a lender who gives you a loan at 6 percent and covers 80 percent of the job. Then you go to other types of lenders and you say, "I don't want to put the other twenty percent down. I want you to give me some money that has a second position to the primary loan."

You might know it as a second mortgage. In development we call it mezzanine financing.

Now, with the combination of phantom equity—the deposits, the increased land value that you got them to believe in, and any mezzanine financing—you are obtaining the highest level of leverage. You're taking the smallest amount of money out of your pocket to achieve the greatest return on your investment.

What's important is that you show the lenders your level of commitment. They need to see you're in it for real, and that you're going to make it all happen.

The same principles apply whether you're doing your very first job or you're doing a $1 billion job like my Icon Brickell project in downtown Miami.

CASE STUDY

Icon Brickell—Using Other People's Money

At Icon Brickell, we wanted to do a building that was going to be the largest endeavor in Florida history. Not just Related history, Florida history. This is a 2-billion-square-foot project that we really couldn't do in phases. We had to do it all at one time.

In a typical deal the lender will lend me anywhere between 75 and 80 percent. That means, with close to $1 billion in total cost, I'm going to have to come up with $200 million in cash. There are very few people who have that type of money and very few people who want to risk that type of money even if they do have it. I'm not going to take it out of my company and put it all in one job. If something happened, I'd be gone. I needed leverage not only to maximize my return, but to reduce the risk of my own money.

Again, these numbers are huge because Icon Brickell is huge, but it works the same way if you're buying a four-plex for $350,000 and spending another $150,000 fixing it up. If you maximize your leverage, you minimize how much of your own money you have to put up.

For the Icon Brickell job, we acquired a piece of land for $94 million, and the total predevelopment cost—everything that comes before you actually break ground and start construction— was $128 million. That consisted of the $94 million for the land and the money I needed to premarket the job—for the sales center, some architectural fees to develop a plan I can price from, and so forth.

So what did I do before I tried to get my construction loan? I went to the bank to get a big loan appraisal. Our appraisal came in higher than the $128 million. Based on the larger appraisal, I got the bank to lend me $95 million. Then I got a mezzanine lender to temporarily lend me $28 million, because it's covered by the appraisal. And that allowed me to do the predevelopment with $5 million in actual cash.

In a normal transaction I would have to put up 20 percent of the $128 million, about $26 million. Instead, I did it with $5 million.

And as I built Icon Brickell, I never put up another penny. As soon as I finished predevelopment, I built success in my sales. I started taking deposits from people. But now I had to finance not just predevelopment, I had to finance the first phase, which included buildings one and two. So we closed on a construction loan. We started construction. We had, with those two buildings, a $682 million construction and development budget.

What happens now? If I had to do that with the usual 20 percent equity, I would have to put in $140 million in equity. But what I did was, I got a huge land appraisal—more than $128 million—that gave me tremendous land equity. I had already begun selling condos and taking deposits from customers. That put money in the bank I could borrow against, by bonding the deposits. So I took $65 million of bonded first deposits, and I used part of my construction loan to pay off my original mezzanine loan. Then I got a new mezzanine loan for $11 million. That left me $10 million in cash as equity in the land. So now I'm doing a project that is close to $700 million with about 1.5 percent in actual cash equity.

And the sales for the third building were so strong that I actually reduced my cash equity to $5 million. How? The mezzanine stayed the same. A new lender came in and covered almost all the costs. And I had further deposits for the other tower that I was able to bond. So over a period of three years, I will make $350 million in profits with a $5 million cash investment.

I know it sounds big. It sounds big to me. But applying the same thinking to the four-plex job, you can do the same thing with no money down.

Let's say the owner agrees to sell it to you for $350,000 and you put down your returnable deposit. Fixing it up is going to take six months and cost $150,000. You figure you can convert it to office condos and sell each of the four for $175,000.

Then you go to the bank and say, "It's close to the medical school, and it's been underutilized as a rental property for university students for all these years while all these doctors' offices have sprouted up on the block. I'm getting it rezoned to allow another doctors' office, then I'm going to convert it. If I don't, someone else will. Looking at it that way, what's it worth?"

The bank almost surely is going to say $500,000. Maybe more. If they give you 80 percent of that, that's $400,000. You would still need to come up with $100,000 in equity. Now you can go to a mezzanine lender to give you a loan for 70 percent of the $100,000 equity. That would give you $70,000 more, leaving you with a total equity of $30,000.

Also, by this time you've got contracts signed and deposits in for all four units, at exactly what you predicted: $175,000 each.

Six months later you finish construction, hand over the keys, get the deposits out of escrow, and collect the balance from your customers. You made $700,000 in sales and, if you stayed on budget, made $200,000, minus the interest on the loans.

Not bad for a $30,000 investment.

Rule #3: Make a Killer Presentation

Back to the beginning again: I launched into affordable housing, planning on having the federal subsidies guaranteeing my rents. I figured that with that rent stream I would go to a lender and say, "Give me the money, because when I complete it the federal government will give me the rent I need to pay your mortgage."

Surprise! The first bank said, "Well, how do I know you're going to manage it? And how do I know you are going to complete it?"

That's when I realized, okay, I've got to prepare my package better.

So I went out and got myself a really respected general contractor who bonded the rehabilitation that was needed, because I didn't have two pennies to bond anything, and I convinced him to do the work with me. He gave the lender a bond stating that for $500,000, he would totally rehabilitate the building.

So now the bank has the credibility of the contractor, who is not a start-up guy like me, with a bond that says I'm going to finish. They've got the federal government saying they are going to give them this rent. And then I set up a management company to manage the property. I went out and hired somebody who knew how to do property management and they told the bank that they were going to participate.

In effect, I was really the manager, but since I was trying to grow, I had to have somebody who was a known person who would manage this little thing for me. Because we were so little, I couldn't have a superintendent, so these were the jack-of-all-trades guys. Were there times at the beginning when I actually went to the property myself to fix the toilet and to be with the electrician and to clean up? Oh, yes, believe me, many times.

Anyway, I put all these things together because it's what the bank needed so that it would know that, yes, we were going to be able to complete the job, and then run it after it was done. That gave them the confidence to give me the loan.

The building of relationships has made it so that now I give them one sheet of paper that says I'm doing a project, and I have four lenders lining up to say they want to do it. When you have built the relationships that we have, the presentations become less important—still important, but less important. They still have to have a piece of paper that says this is the income and these are the costs so they can go to their board and explain why they're approving this job. But they don't need much more because we already know each other. They know I have never, ever defaulted on a loan.

If I'm going to someone I haven't dealt with before, my presentations are much more refined. I start with a corporate video that tells them all about Related, about our track record, and my renderings are much more elaborate. I use computer graphics and graphs and charts. But the basic concepts haven't changed.

If you're going to family or friends, you can take them to the property and tell them about your vision and you can probably get away with showing them the costs and revenues on a sheet of paper or two. Your enthusiasm and determination, and the fact that they know you to be a person who always does what he says he's going to do, is going to serve as your credentials.

But if the deal is bigger and you have to go to outside investors, your presentation should become better because you don't have the credibility you have with your uncle, or your mom, or your doctor, or whatever. The presentation now has to include a beautiful picture of the building, some slides, a computer presentation. Do something so that your passion for the deal is going to be infectious. So that they're going to buy into it.

Always think of a presentation as what is going to enable you to sell.

Your presentation needs to include a business plan in which it says, basically, "You're going to put in two hundred thousand dollars. I'm going to put in one hundred thousand dollars. We're going to split the profits fifty-fifty and this is what I'm going to do for you for this investment."

The plan has to be much more detailed than that, of course. You need to show the breakdown of the construction costs that your contractor wrote up for you. It's got to include the plans and renderings your architect prepared for you. It's going to have an explanation of how you arrived at your revenue projections—if it's federal subsidies, how they're calculated and how you get them; if it's rents, how your market research told you exactly what to expect and what the competition is, and so on.

And it has to be very, very clear.

When you're putting your presentation together, remember the two key things are: They have to be able to understand it well, and it has to tell them what they need to know.

Every bank you deal with has certain requirements and certain ways of analyzing deals. All banks have two people who will look at a deal: the relationship manager—that's the lender—and the underwriter.

The relationship manager is the one who is always saying, "Approve it! Approve it!" because he makes money on volume.

The underwriter guy is the control. He says, "No, no. This doesn't make sense. Give me more information."

So as you do your presentation, the guy you really have to convince more than anybody is the underwriter. He's the negative guy who is going to go and try to punch holes in your presentation. So understand what parameters the underwriter needs. When you go to the underwriter, you should already know the parameters of approval—for example, they won't go over 80 percent of loan-to-value. Or they won't allow phantom equity from the land. But they will allow you equity in bonding deposits.

Know what it is they want to see. Some lenders won't allow for a second mortgage, so it will be much more difficult to put in mezzanine financing later on. You can still put it in, but you can't put it in as a mortgage. You have to put it in as a pledge of the partnership. Some construction lenders say, "I don't want anybody to be in a second position to me." If they do that, then how do you get the mezzanine guy? You give him a position in your partnership. If the property goes broke, he has no claims against that property. He can only claim against the partnership. But your best bet is still to go to lenders who allow you to do a second mortgage, so it's easier to get mezzanine financing.

Always cater your presentation to the recipient. What does he like? Does he like great wine and want me to take him out to dinner? I'm going to do that. What is going to make that loan get approved? That whole presentation has to be geared to the person you're making it to. Don't do your presentations the same for everybody, because everybody is not the same.

> Your presentation has to be geared to the person you're making it for. Everybody is not the same.

The mezzanine lender, for example, needs a totally different presentation than the primary lender. The investor needs a totally different presentation. The numbers are going to be pretty much the same, but the way you accentuate certain parts of the presentation is going to be different.

All the primary lender really wants to know is that the loan is covered. So your whole presentation needs to convey the message that you have enough sales contracts to cover their loan.

The investor not only wants to know that the loan is covered, he wants to know that there's plenty of money left after the loan is covered so that he can participate. In this case you're showing them how you're going to make profits, and how much. So the presentation here not only has to be geared so much for the repayment of the loan and convincing this lender that this is a safe loan, but to what profits there will be and how they are going to participate in it.

So for each individual we set up a presentation that highlights the most important information for them. Basically, the most important part of the presentation is still your pro forma. You have to have numbers that are very easy to follow. "This is what we're spending here. This is what we're spending there." So, as opposed to the people who do extensive internal rate of return calculations and say they take up to five years and they do this and they do that, we like to have what I call my single-page pro forma—the one-pager. It basically, in a very simple form, says: Here's the sales price—there will be two hundred units with an average size of one thousand square feet and a target sales price of $400 per square foot; here are the other revenues—parking revenues, commercial revenues if you have commercial space, total revenues; and, very simply, a cost breakdown—architect, construction, land, engineer, lawyer, sales, marketing, and so forth. We'll break down the costs and the person will be able to see that the bottom line is profits.

We follow the single-page pro forma with a detailed pro forma, but most people don't look at that. So our presentation includes one page, and then there are like thirty pages that follow explaining each little item on the one page.

But if that summary page isn't good, they'll never even look at the rest of the stuff. When they have questions we go into the rest. If they ask, "Why did you put down two million dollars for staffing?" we'll immediately turn to the staffing page. And there we'll take a look at every person in that job and the monthly salary that we have to cover until we sell.

Everything will be in great detail, but you've got to make sure—particularly when you're making your presentation to decision makers who have very little time—that you hit them with the one-page pro forma. The other really important thing is a picture of the project. A picture is worth a thousand words.

I can't get them really excited about the pro forma. But when I open up my renderings and I start going, "Look at the architecture! Look at the interior design! And look at this!" that's when I can get them to buy into my passion. Because the numbers are really, "We're going to sell it for six dollars. We bought it for four dollars. It's going to make us two dollars." Not too much to get excited about there.

But if you can show them why this project is going to be successful, in pictures, that's when you do your sale. We get the best renderers we can to try to show them why, again, our vision is going to be better than the other ones.

The final part of the presentation is the market analysis. There's two parts, and they consist of exactly what you did when you were finding the property. You include the macro ones that tell them that your area is growing like crazy and these are the many households that will be in our universe and the money that they make. And you include the microanalysis, which tells them why you're going to do well, what the competition is doing, what they look like, and the price they're selling for per square foot.

Then you show them how your project compares. You always want to do that, because without that it's meaningless. "I'm going to buy an office building and rent it for twenty dollars." What does that mean? As opposed to what? What if I found out that everybody else was renting at $10? Then it's a stupid presentation. That's why we do graphs, charts, and comparison tables. We're great at doing different comps. For example, we'll have our price structure in red and we'll have the price structure of all these different projects in another color. The red dots will show them very clearly where we stand with our product. This helps convince them how our project fares vis-à-vis the competition. Make your own graphs and charts to show lenders and investors why you are better than the others.

Now, again, people are busy. Have a summary page that is unbelievable. One page as a pro forma. One paragraph that describes the job— one paragraph. And then you open it up and you have one great rendering of the building you're going to build or a picture of the building you're going to buy and how it's going to look when you're finished. Remember that the decision makers are typically very busy. And it's a world of sound bites. They've got to be able to look at it and make up their minds in ten minutes. And you've got to capture their attention. If you don't do that with your summary, you will lose the majority of people.

That's your basic lender presentation.

The lender presentation

1. One-paragraph description of the project

2. Single-page pro forma

3. Rendering or photo

4. Detailed pro forma

5. Market analysis (macro and micro), with comparison

In the old days you had it all on paper and you thumbed through the presentation as you talked. Now, we go and we say, "Please give us five minutes so you can see our new corporate tape." And we open up a laptop computer and we play the corporate video for them. It shows me talking about us and how we build, and our customers. It shows all the projects that we have. So we get them pumped up on who we are.

Then we'll go from the corporate video into a project video. One of the first things we do when we're starting any job is make a project video. And we'll have images of renderings and those images will go beyond paper. Our people have the big Apples with the big screen, which they take to the lender, so they can always make the presentations on very clear formats.

This becomes particularly important when we go to foreign countries and they have no idea where the place is or who we are. We have to show them through images what the hell Zihuatanejo, Mexico, is. Why our project is going to be so amazing. The pictures now become very, very, very important in securing the equity. Because the pictures do not just tell them the facts—the facts are the market analysis and the pro formas—they're going to show them the excitement of the property.

In the beginning, you're not necessarily going to have the whole corporate video and computer-generated graphics thing, but the more you show them that you're up-to-date with the latest technology, believe me, the more you're going to impress them. It's going to make a difference if, instead of giving them a piece of paper, you can go and say, "Let me show you on my computer," and you have a nice little video and some renderings there. It helps you create credibility.

No matter how you present—on computer or on paper—get it right. You can't come across as someone who doesn't know how to do anything. Because if you can't do the presentation right, the assumption is you aren't going to be doing the project right.

The biggest part of the presentation, though, is you. You've got to sell them. You've got to believe. The person delivering the message has got to sell. So not only do you have a project, but this mouthpiece you have has got to get into people's heads and make them believe in the project as strongly as you do. Your personality and passion will make or break the deal.

In fact, when we have a loan, a big one, that has to go all the way to Charlotte, for example, for Bank of America or Wachovia, my loan officer will ask me to get on a plane and make that presentation. It isn't that he can't explain the numbers, because they're pretty simple. It's that they want someone to infuse the passion and the vision into them. So the personality you bring in, the salesmanship you bring in, the passion you bring in has to be contagious. You've got to make them believe in you and in your project.

> ### Make your passion for the project contagious.

And really remember this: If you don't believe, you're not going to be great in your presentations. People will see through it. People know a shallow salesman from a salesman with belief, integrity, and depth. This is a case in which you're putting yourself on the line—your whole expertise, your whole reputation. You're telling that guy, "I wouldn't be doing this job unless I really believed that it's the best job in the world and we're going to be very successful."

Bringing them into your vision is key to any presentation.

People tell me, and it's true, that all of a sudden it's like I'm possessed. For some moments I'm totally out of that place and I'm just so much into the project presentation. And that way I can transfer. I can make you believe. That is the power of salesmanship. In securing equity it is unbelievably important.

You know there are a million great ideas and a million great projects that never come to fruition because the guy can't sell.

The number-one thing in securing a loan is to have a good product. Number two is to have a great presentation. Number three is to have relationships. Even with all of those, you have to have the passion and the salesmanship.

People tell me today, "But it's so easy for you, people are throwing money at you. You get financing when nobody else can get financing." Maybe that's true. But that's because all of those people who are lending me money are the same guys who twenty years ago were there with us and knew of the integrity, of the loyalty, of the fact that when things went wrong we just stood up and made them better. We never left anybody hanging. If they lost money, we lost money. And that's all they want to know.

So these relationships have helped me tremendously to grow. And not only did they help me with themselves, they helped me with others. All the bankers talk to each other. So when the president of Wachovia Bank meets with these other lenders or loan officers and they start trading stories about deals they're involved in, he's going to say good things about you. Then these people all become eager to do deals with you. They all want to loan you money.

It wasn't always like that, believe me. There were some very, very tough times in which my credibility was not there yet, my ideas were not yet proven. I think of the time when I tried to do my first high-rise and finance it in Miami. With all the passion that I had, I just couldn't convince local lenders I would be able to charge almost twice as much for a high-rise in downtown as I could for a garden apartment in a nice suburban neighborhood, even though the high-rise was in an incredible waterfront location. They wouldn't do it.

As I said before, lending is very much a national endeavor. So, certainly in the beginning, your mortgage broker will be able to connect you with lenders. Nevertheless, if you're doing a deal and you have a relationship with a local bank, where you keep your checking accounts and your savings account and you know the branch manager, always go to those guys first. Because they already know you. They've seen your business. They've seen that you pay your bills on time. They see all those things and many times they are the ones that will give you your shot. You've built a relationship. In effect, whether you know it or not, they know your history. They know you've been paying your bills and your MasterCard on time for the past five years.

So the first time it's probably always good to start with the bank you've been doing business with, if that bank is also in the business of whatever it is you're going to do.

But no matter which bank you go to, you have to put together that killer presentation. They need to be able to see the project, and see the numbers, to give you the loan.

Rule #4: Follow Up

After you get your loan, don't just walk away. You don't go in there and see the lender and get your loan and never talk to them again. Never, never, never get a loan, cut communication with the guy, and go until the end and just pay the money back.

Always keep them with you at all points. Communicate with them regularly. Keep them informed about what's going on with your project. Get them involved. Take them on site visits so they can see how the progress is going.

And always tell your lender the truth. If you have bad news, call them up immediately. "We had a construction bust." Don't give them surprises. And don't just say, "I had a bust" or "I had a problem"; have solutions to the problem when you tell them about the problem.

You want to be sure they don't get left in the dark. No lender likes surprises, and they love being well-informed. They will appreciate it and, as a result, your project may encounter greater flexibility if you do run into trouble.

One of the things we take great pride in is in believing that our lenders are our partners. We make sure they're treated like partners, and we go out of our way to answer any and all questions they have on our deal or any other deal.

Be straight with them. Show them everything up front. Get them to buy in. By assisting them in every way possible, it strengthens your relationship and they in turn will assist you if you need something. When the lender becomes your partner in good times and bad you will sit down and generally work things out. That's the importance of the partnership, that long-term relationship.

It's nurturing, just like we do with our customers. My chief financial officer must go to dinner ten times a month with lenders. He has them over to his house for barbecues. We know their families. That's nurturing the relationship.

We keep them posted about what new jobs we are going to have. We let them know the successes. We bring them to our sales parties. When we do our grand opening we are sure to let everybody know who the lender is and how much we appreciate them. We do that in front of everybody.

RULE #5: BUILD A TRACK RECORD

I have never defaulted on a loan. I have never been late with a payment. I have never renegotiated. I have never let a bank down. Never.

And I'm not saying we haven't had jobs that were hairy. Or that I haven't paid loans when I didn't have the money from the job to pay the loan so I had to take it out of my own pocket. I have. I've taken it out of my own pocket to show them that I stand behind my jobs. I think that has probably been the single greatest factor, even more than the success and the profitability, that has helped me get where I am. It's been that integrity, that honesty, that conviction that I will always pay them back.

As I take a loan I tell them, "I will not make a penny unless you get paid back. I'm going to do everything under the sun. I'm going to take money from every source I have. But I'll tell you this, my children aren't going hungry before I pay you. If it comes down to feeding my kids or paying you, my kids win. Other than that you're getting paid."

I did that from the very beginning because I wanted to establish a track record. When they thought of Jorge Pérez, I always wanted lenders to say, "He will never fail you."

I still want them to believe that. I want them to know that we are here to stay with them. We have never given up. We will not build a job and, if something goes wrong, leave them hanging. We're there until the end.

You want that lender to always think, "Things can go wrong, but this guy is always going to do what is right. He's always going to stay with us in the trenches during the hard times."

During the good times everybody does well. It's during hard times that you want the guy who will not lose one inch of that passion and that drive he's got and know he's going to be with you till the end.

At this point, I have been able to show them sixty thousand units we have done profitably, without ever being late on a payment. In addition, by working on more than a dozen deals with Wall Street types—Lehman Brothers, Goldman Sachs, and so on—we have established major credibility in the financing world.

Your track record establishes your credibility. Have successes.

> Your track record establishes your credibility.
> Have successes.

When you're starting out, you establish credibility by having jobs turn out the way you said they would, by paying your lenders and investors what you promised.

Here's another important rule when you're starting out:

Sell something, even if you don't want to.

When you're starting out, it doesn't matter whether you're a keeper or a seller, you have to sell some of your properties. Why? Because you've got to show results. Especially at the beginning. Selling shows returns. It shows success and builds your track record. It lets you put some money in your pocket or in your company's pocket. But it also shows your investors that you're for real. And there's nothing an investor likes more than making the money you told him he was going to make. You've got a relationship, and you've got a friend who will be there for a long time.

If I find a deal in which I buy four houses and turn them around and rent them and I get a fairly good return, I'll think it's a pretty good income source.

But if a buyer comes along who is willing to buy them, my advice would be to sell—if you're getting the right price and you're making the right profit. Because you're going to make your lenders and your partners believe in you.

So even if your nature is to keep, it's important that you sell some things and get them off the table so you show some returns to the people who are with you. When you do that, they'll want to invest and lend you money again next time.

You build a reputation. You build a track record. You build expertise. And then you have some money so you can invest again.

The Prado—Leveraging Seller Financing

The Prado is a case in which I bought a project from a rental developer who allowed me to presell it as condominiums before we closed on his project. And by the time I closed I had it all sold.

So all I did was transfer the people that we sold to and paid him with the sales of the project.

The Prado is this beautiful building in Palm Beach that was originally being built as a rental project. Usually, when you build rentals, you have one of two goals in mind: You're building it to hold long term, rent out, and make a slow, steady return on your money; or you're going to fill it with renters, which increases the value, and sell it right away. If you sell it before you rent it, you don't normally get as much as you do if you fill it with tenants.

But I saw it going up, and while it was being built I went to the developer and said, "Listen, you're going to sell this product at the end of the project anyway. Why don't you save yourself the trouble and expense of having to rent it. I'll buy it from you right now. You don't have to do your marketing. You don't have to do your renting. You don't have to do any of that stuff. All I want you to do is allow me to spend some of my own money to make the finishes more luxurious."

For example, the counters were mica, and I made them marble. The carpet was cheaper carpet. I made it real nice, plush carpet. The bathrooms were surrounded by linoleum. I made them all imported tile surrounds.

So we never had to be responsible for construction; we just had to supervise it to make sure they were delivering the right product. We never had to borrow money from a lender because the seller was doing all that. And all he had from me was a commitment that when he finished, I would buy the property.

I put $2 million down. As always, I made sure it was returnable to me if the deal didn't go through. If he had delivered a building to me that had so much as a scratch on it, I could have called the deal off and taken my money and left. And there's no such thing as a perfect building. I had my people documenting little things along the way so I could always point out the things that had gone wrong. And I'd get my deposit back. So in reality, I'm not taking a chance. The seller is the one with all the risk. He just has a promise that I'm going to buy the building.

Now, the greatness of this deal was that, without having responsibility for the loans that he had, I was buying something that I didn't have to pay for until it was finished. Meanwhile, I was selling it and bringing in the money I was going to pay for it with. What happened if I went to sell and it didn't work? Nothing. Because then I would have squawked about the construction errors, taken my money back, and left.

The seller actually allowed me to spend $1.5 million of their deposit for the upgrades and to use for sales, so I didn't have to come up with any more cash. This represented less than 4 percent of the total cost for the entire transaction, while we owned 100 percent of the deal.

So I put up an off-site sales office and started marketing and sold the whole thing out before it was even finished. As far as leverage is concerned, I didn't even have to get a construction loan. I didn't have to get anything. All I had to do was get a lender to lend me the money to do the predevelopment sales.

So for very little money I got a promise of a building delivered to me in the future, sold the building before the building was delivered to me, and with the sales proceeds I paid the seller and made all this money.

The owner made a healthy profit on his building without having to go through the trouble of having to get it all leased out first. And from the time I got involved until the time construction was completed and I handed the building over to the buyers was a little over twelve months, and Related made $15 million, net.

KEY PRINCIPLES

- The best deals are obtained through relationships.

- Your presentation has to be geared to the person you're making it for. Everybody is not the same.

- Make your passion for the project contagious.

- Your track record establishes your credibility. Have successes.

THE VENTURE AT AVENTURA,
Aventura, Florida
© 2006 Dan Forer

6 • SELLING IT: FROM BUZZ TO FRENZY IN FIVE STEPS

"What we do is not traditional selling.

It takes selling to a new level."

Believe me, in real estate, selling is the heart of it all. If you don't sell, you fail. I don't care how great your building is. It doesn't matter. Sales is where you make your money.

I'm a developer, yes, but the reason I've been so successful is because I'm a good salesman. Early in my career I figured out how to get people to buy. As I got better, I figured out how to get them excited enough that they would line up just for a chance to buy. Over the years, we've perfected those methods and standardized our process so much that now, in some very successful openings, we don't just get people to line up—we get them to beg us to take their money, literally.

You can, too.

THE BASICS

Most people think that after you've made your plan, found the property, and secured the loan, the next step is building it. It's not. First you sell it, and then you build it.

Remember the Little Havana example? I had a plan for rehabbing federally subsidized housing and selling the tax credits to syndicators. I found a twenty-four-unit building, and then I went to the bank. Then I went to the syndicators and got them to give me the money I needed to build it, plus my profits, up front. In other words, I sold it. And nobody had so much as lifted a hammer yet.

Then, while the work was being done to rehab the building, we went out and signed up the tenants. So we knew we had the federal money and the rents coming long before the construction was finished. You got it: We finished selling out the building to insure the other part of the income needed to make the deal work—*before* it was built.

The advantage is: You put your money in the bank. You reduce your risk. You know it's sold! That's the goal, right? Why would you wait to find out if people really want what you're offering? Sell it first and you eliminate that fear. Then you just have to make sure you don't overspend your construction budget.

Presales cut the lender's risk, too. That makes it easier to get a loan. It is much less risky for the bank to give you the money to start a condominium job in which you have 70 or 80 percent of the units presold with a 20 percent deposit up front, than when you go to the lender and say, "I'm going to start construction and then I'm going to start selling and hopefully it will do well."

Remember the example of the Yacht Club at Portofino in chapter 3? When we thought it would be better to turn it into a condo project instead of a rental building we didn't wait for it to be finished, then put up a sign and wait to see if we were right. As soon as I convinced the bank and the contractor to go along with the idea, we put our sales team to work. That way, if it didn't sell, we could always quit upgrading the units and go back to rentals. It would cost us a little, but it wasn't as bad as spending all the money to put in better kitchens and bathrooms and then find out people wouldn't pay for them.

We call this a preconstruction investment. During the predevelopment stage, it is very easy to fall into the trap of throwing money into something without having certain fundamentals secured. We tie our spending to our achievements: If our ads and direct contacts draw interest from enough potential customers, then we build our sales center.

If enough people make reservations to buy, then we hold our invitation-only, pre–grand opening sales events—many times in a temporary tent. When we get deposits from enough people, then we build. We spend some, then we spend more as the risk is reduced.

> Spend some, but only spend more when the risk is reduced.

Preselling works particularly well in hot markets when you have investors and speculators. They like the notion of the presales because it gives them a crack at the earliest time to buy and the longest time before a flip can occur. In a hot market, they can put down a twenty-to-one deposit to buy before the construction even begins, and by the time the building is finished—which is when they'll have to come up with the rest of the money to pay for it—they can many times sell it at double or triple their deposit.

And presales are a marketing tool for creating buzz. Initially, they help spark interest. They help spread the word. Then, when people hear that units are selling out, it creates a sense of urgency. People know they have to act fast if they want one. It sparks, or furthers, that natural human tendency to think, "If everybody's buying it, it must be good. I have to have one, too."

Speculation, however, can be very dangerous for both the speculating investor and the developer. It creates false expectations on both sides and can cause markets to crash, as sales many times are not real. That's why we try to limit the number of speculators in all of our projects by selling only one unit per customer and increasing deposit sizes.

One of our goals with every job is to sell fast. Most people focus on maximizing their profits. They want to make as much as they possibly can from every job. We're willing to give up some money to get it sold quickly. Our objective: Get in and get out as soon as possible.

So the whole sales process became an art form in which we were able to sell jobs in record time, many times working out of temporary facilities. Our marketing and sales became all-important. And we became known as an incredible sales organization. Even in a bad market, with an overbuilt condo market collapsing and buyers trying to bail out of their contracts left and right, we were one of the few able to create a buzz. In a horrendous market, we put out the Lofts III and sold 450 units in thirty days.

One of the ways we do that is we sell at slightly below-market rates. Instead of trying to make the most money possible on each unit, we make the project attractive to investors and to people who are just looking for a good deal. We know what the market is.

If you were an individual with only one building, velocity might not be that important to you. You might try to totally maximize your profitability on that one building. You might.

But what's worked for us is not the maximizing of any one project, but moving product as rapidly as we can so that we can go on to the next project. To do that, I will leave money on the table. I will say, "I don't want to price myself like the guys at the very top who are selling two units a month. I want to price myself below them and still make my margins."

So, for example, if my competitor is at $10 and I can sell at $9, I try to find that $1 savings in my construction costs. I still make the same mark-ups as the guy who's charging a higher price because I can deliver the products cheaper without losing quality. Some might work it both ways—save the $1 and still charge the $10—to make the most money. My goal is not to totally maximize the profit. We leave money on the table, for two reasons: One, we're going to have a more satisfied customer; and two, it allows me to move forward and start concentrating on other jobs.

If I have slow sales, it slows everything down. If I sell out fast, it allows us to move that sales team to the next job, to do other things.

You need to find the balance between volume and profitability. You may not make $5 on every bike you sell. But if you make $4 and you sell ten more bikes, you made $40 more.

And that trickles down. Because you're doing more volume, you're able to cut better deals with your subs and general contractors because they know they're going to have a lot more to build with you. So you're still making the markup, the customers are satisfied because they're getting a good value, and the lenders will give you the best deals. Why? Because if it's 100 percent sold they have very little risk.

So it all works together. You get a reduction in lending rates and construction costs that you can just pass right on to the consumer.

But people don't buy just because the price is right. People know what they like, and what they're looking for. If you want to sell to them, you have to know your customer. I'm always telling my people, understand who it is you're selling to.

If a person only wants to go to Disney World and does not like foreign cultures and foreign arts, don't sell them Tokyo. Don't try to sell them something they don't want. Now, sometimes you may be able to change them and make them believe that that's what they want. But those are hard sales. Typically, people have a mind-set. They know what they like and they know what they want. To sell them, you have to find out what that mind-set is, then show them how what you're selling fits perfectly into their mind-set.

> Understand your buyer. Give him what he needs to commit.

Understand what it is that sells people. Understand what you're going to have to do to bring them in. Understand your buyer. And then give him what he needs to commit. Whether it's a sales presentation or renting an apartment, selling is a process in which you take a person from having an interest to having a commitment.

When it's all said and done, we really are all salesmen. That's what you're doing all the time in business. When you look at the guys in real estate, that's what they are. Donald Trump is a salesman. Donald Trump sells himself better than anybody else. If you're going to go into business, you better be ready to be a salesman. Because if you can't get other people to buy into whatever it is you're selling—your concept, your image, your program—you're not going to be successful.

People buy from people. Remember that. People buy from people. So the messenger has to be just as important as the message.

> People buy from people. The messenger is as important as the message.

When I am looking at a Philippe Starck–designed luxury condominium project in Mexico, I'm doing a sales pitch that turns a lot of people off. I think they would never buy. I tell them, "Listen, if what you want is a resort-style pool with your waterfall and your fake little things and everything looking pseudo-Mexican that caters to the stereotypical American tourist, then you've got ten other places you can go to right here in Vallarta. And they're actually cheaper than we are.

"But," I tell them, "if what you want is state-of-the-art, if what you want is cutting edge, by one of the greatest living designers of the twentieth century, that is going to be unlike anything you're going to see in Vallarta, then this is the place you want to be."

Then we explain why: how the greatness of Philippe Starck's mind translates to amazing designs for better living.

But I tell them right then, "If you don't appreciate Starck with that level of design, it's not like you're right or wrong, but this is not the place where you want to be. Because you know what? The rest of the people who are going to be buying here are going to be people in that frame of mind."

And that's what's going to sell to the ones you want. And the other ones aren't going to buy. But that's okay, because the ones who buy are going to tell their friends, the people who are like them who do appreciate all the design elements you worked so hard to include, and they're going to come see you, and they're going to want to buy. They're going to be easy sells.

But it won't do any good at all to try to sell an opera ticket to a rodeo lover. Or vice versa. At least not in most cases. Generally, they're not going to buy no matter how hard you try to sell them. And if they do buy for whatever reason, in ninety-nine out of one hundred cases they're not going to like it. So they won't be happy, and what good does it do you to sell them something they're not going to be happy with? They're only going to be trying to get out of the deal, complaining, and bad-mouthing you everywhere they go. It's bad for you now, and it's bad for your brand.

So I always tell my salespeople, understand the client. If the person comes here and says, "It's me and my child and I want a two-bedroom apartment," please, do me a favor, don't show them the three-bedroom units. If they say, "All we can afford is one hundred fifty thousand dollars," and I check their income and they're right, that's all they can afford, then do me a favor, don't try to sell them a $350,000 unit. You're wasting your time. And you're wasting theirs.

When you know your customer, you'll also know where to find your customer. Just like you don't go to the rodeo to find opera lovers. So if you think your product is going to do well with a certain clientele, that's the one you want to target. Go where they are, not where they aren't. If you're selling multimillion-dollar condos, you look for people who can afford them.

One of the selling points of the St. Regis, the luxury condo hotel project across the street from the exclusive Bal Harbour Shops that I told you about in chapter 4, is that it's right up the street from a nationally known synagogue. While all my customers may not be Jewish, I knew that that would be an important selling point for those who are. I already knew that from the initial sales on another project I had built right up the street from the St. Regis site. And in selling that one, we found there was a strong Russian-Jewish connection.

So we said, "Where are your Russian buddies?" And with the market slumping here in the United States, we did the same sales presentation in their New York enclave and St. Petersburg and Moscow and got many to buy. So in the worst market, we were able to get $400 million in sales. Which in any other project would've been a fully sold project. So almost 40 percent of the project sold by doing all this premarketing and going directly to our anticipated customers.

You need to think the same way, whether your customer is around the corner, up the street, or in the next state. Know your customer. Know where to find them. Know what they like. Give it to them.

Guiding the Sales Team

Generally speaking, our projects take on an unorthodox method of marketing. This comes from a realization that in a real estate market, particularly one that offers a lot of choices to the consumer, something must set you apart from the competition. And you can't stop there. You can't be like a tree falling in the forest. If no one hears you, you're dead. Not only must you be unique, but you must also know how to hammer that message home effectively.

It's even more important in a tough market, where sales are dropping and huge numbers of developers have product they're trying to move, so they're screaming, "Buy! Buy! Buy!"

When the market gets like that your voice has to be better, louder, and clearer. We've been almost forced by bad markets to think outside the box. To do bigger and better marketing campaigns. So instead of giving up in bad markets, we just had to become sharper.

We've really, really studied our sales techniques to see what works and what doesn't. We've come up with improved programs, improved brochures. We've gone to the source of buyers instead of waiting for them to come to us. We've taken the trips to where our customers are and shown them our brochures. It's all about building that image as the best company there is in the business.

A common mistake is to leave the responsibility of this task simply to the company or agency that has been retained to provide this service. This is fatal to the process. We have created a sales organization called RCRS, led by my partner Alicia Cervera, who is second to none. She is the best sales organizer and people motivator in the world. We control the process by having the best salespeople, training them well, and providing them with a road map to sales success.

> No one knows your product and your target market better than you.

No one should know your product and target market better than you, and you must never forget that. Sometimes you may go to outside sales and marketing companies to give you ideas on how to best communicate to and reach your audience, the creative aspect of the campaign, logo ideas, taglines, advertising vehicles, and so on, but not about who you need to be communicating to. That is your job as developer. You guide the salespeople.

Before we start selling a project, I take all the salespeople to lunch one or two times so I can instill in them not how to sell—they know how to do that—but the knowledge of the project and why I am so passionate about it. I'll talk to them about the location. I'll talk to them about why our product is so much better than the rest. I'll talk to them about all the specifics, not just the cold facts, but in a very emotional way, because you want them to start feeling that sense of excitement and passion to participate in your vision. I meet with all the salespeople and I make sure they understand who their target market is and what the important aspects of this specific project are—and why this particular one is better than the rest.

Every one of those people is trained and tested on the knowledge we give them about the project and the area. We won't take a person who is just a pretty face and turn them loose to sell. Because pretty faces may pique your imagination, but they won't take you to the bottom line. People want to buy from people who are extremely knowledgeable, who can answer their questions.

If I have a salesperson who's not knowledgeable, he won't be able to tell my story. When somebody asks, "What about the schools here? What about the hospitals?" I will lose them. So we prepare books about the area and everybody has to be knowledgeable. Where are the schools? How many people live here? Where are the airports? How many flights? To where? Where are the hospitals? How are they rated?

We have a precise way for greeting and handling customers. We teach our receptionists and salespeople how to answer the phone. We don't say, "Hey, there. Jimmy here." We say, "Welcome to Icon Brickell, my name is Susie, how can I help you?"

We do the same thing with our rental units. Everything is in a manual. Because then we are consistent. How to answer the phone. How to welcome the customer when he comes in. How you show the apartments. Everything is in the manual. Because we want to make sure that the process is there, consistently, and that the client is getting a crystal-clear image of who we are.

In addition to that, we do actual one-on-ones with them in which they sell us. I go there, or somebody does, and we go through all the salespeople and we say, "Okay, I'm Mr. Jones. I'm interested. Sell me."

From that moment forward everything follows the steps in the manual. We don't skip steps.

Don't leave your sales process up to your staff. Establish your procedures and make sure everyone follows them. That way you can test the process, and perfect it. When you see that certain things are giving you better results, you can use those and drop the ones that aren't working. Done right, your sales process accomplishes two things: it sells your product and gathers valuable research. Use the research to improve your product and your process.

THE SALES PROCESS—FROM BUZZ TO FRENZY IN FIVE STEPS

The path to a solid sale never varies. The product may. The target customer may. The ads, the brochures, and the sales pitch almost certainly will. But the five steps to the sale never do. In every case, you have to lead the customer along a road from getting their attention to getting them to sign.

It's up to you to create the spark, build them to having an interest, then having a desire, having a want, and, finally, having a pressing need.

Pay close attention to that last one. It doesn't just have to be a need, it has to be a pressing need. It's got to be the one that leads them to sign that check. We all have plenty of needs that we don't necessarily do anything about. We may need to lose a few pounds. We may need to put some money away for retirement. We may need to get that work project done for our boss before the end of the week. But, somehow, until it's Friday morning, there are a lot of other "needs" that keep us from getting around to getting that project done. Then it's suddenly a pressing need and we don't stop until we're done.

The psychology behind the sales process is the same. We start with the spark and we develop a pressing need.

That's when they sign.

Where's the spark come from? Your product. You create a one-of-a-kind opportunity that they can't miss and they've got to have. You have to show them it's unique, it's irreplaceable. You have to make them believe this is the best thing they can do. It doesn't matter if it's affordable housing, market-rate apartments, or $3 million luxury condos. They have to believe this is a unique opportunity for them to get something they must have, and if they don't grab it now they won't have another chance.

But you don't let them have it all at once. You aren't selling a candy bar at the supermarket checkout that they'll just grab and gobble down.

It's a process. You go from showing them something and sparking their imagination. You show them a little bit more and create that desire. The desire becomes a want to have, then a must-have. And that's why we prepare and we get big lists and we get them to make reservations to look for the type of units we have. It's all about creating that desire to be involved in something that, if they don't, they'll never have that opportunity to do again.

It's a progression. And every step counts. They build on one another.

In order for somebody to really feel good about getting something, they can't get it easily. If you say, yeah, here it is, come on over and we'll give you a price break, then, in their mind the buyer is already saying, "This guy's like a used-car salesman."

I want to create the feeling of immediacy. I want them to feel, "I better act."

Over the years, we've perfected that sales process to the point where we have sold out projects entirely during the worst markets imaginable. When people were canceling contracts in other buildings, we sold out. And as we expanded into Mexico, we hired an international sales company called Playground that had the exact same philosophy to handle our sales there. They have slightly different names for the five steps, but they have the same concept about the path to a sale:

1. Develop awareness.

2. Build interest.

3. Create desire.

4. Create want.

5. Create need.

But Playground also peeled it back another layer and looked at the emotions connected to each of those steps, something they describe as the "magic versus logic" of the sales process. They say you have to:

1. Create unique opportunity.

2. Create a sense of privilege.

3. Create credibility.

4. Create perception of value that exceeds price.

5. Create fear of loss.

I agree totally. It's something I knew and did intuitively—and pushed my sales team to do—but just hadn't thought about in those terms. They perfected the process.

CREATING THE SPARK

I sell dreams. I build condominiums and that's what people pay for, but what they're really buying is a dream. They want a place where they can escape, relax in the pool, enjoy beautiful sunsets, and live a life that's better than they ever imagined.

What a salesman does is, he gets that dream and transports it into your mind so you become a dreamer with him, too.

Remember those luxury apartments I built in downtown Miami, the Island Club at Brickell Key? I told you about them in chapter 2, about how I realized I wasn't selling apartments, I was selling a life-style. That's just another way of putting it. I was still selling a dream: a dream of not commuting, of having affordable luxury just minutes from work. The amenities we included were just part of that dream.

The billboards advertising the Island Club that I put up along the most congested roads were just a way of tapping into that dream. I was creating the spark. As you sat fuming in stop-and-go, bumper-to-bumper traffic for an hour or more every day, I wanted you to be thinking, "Why am I doing this?" We wanted to provide the alternative.

We also started a series of mail-outs with the same message on them, targeting people living in apartments far from downtown. That was our list of prospective customers. It wasn't anywhere near as sophisticated as the client lists we use now, but, as rudimentary as it was, it worked.

You can do the same thing. You can buy lists from direct-mail marketing firms that break down potential customers by geographic area, income, whether they rent or own, educational level, age range, marital status, and several other criteria.

You can also work with real estate brokers who have their own customer lists and know how to cull them for the most likely prospects.

As time goes by, you'll refine your techniques and develop your own lists.

It's one of the things we've done very smartly, because you look at real estate developers and they don't even do it, and I don't understand why. We have over thirty thousand names on the list of what we call VIPs—people who bought from us and brokers who have brought us people who have bought from us. So at all times, when I start a job I have a huge advantage over the rest of the market.

When we're creating the spark, we reach out to brokers we've worked with before and "leak" the word to them that we're starting another project. I want them to feel special—and they are; they get the word before anyone else. They're the ones in the know. So they can start reaching out to their clients and tell them that they're among the first to know. That way, their clients feel special, too. They feel—and here's one of the emotional hooks Playground talks about—a "sense of privilege." They are VIPs, important enough to be given this—here's another one—"unique opportunity" ahead of everyone else.

What you want to create is talk about the uniqueness of the property, the fact that you don't want to miss this opportunity because a lot of other people are very interested in this opportunity.

So while you're creating awareness, creating the buzz, you also start creating excitement. You're making these customers feel like they're being given a chance to get in on this deal before it gets away, and at the lowest price level. And they are. But also, by extension, if there's a chance it can get away, that automatically makes them feel a sense of urgency. They have to move fast because others are going to want this, too.

As opposed to opening up the sales office and putting in an ad and saying, "grand opening," I hit as many people as I can with this VIP concept: "You're a very important person. You are one of the chosen ones. Before the general public, first come the chosen ones."

Through a series of e-mails, mailers, broker contacts, people who we know are interested in buying for whatever reason, we let them know this is coming. "But," we tell them, "you can't buy yet. You can't buy it, but I'll let you sign in. We're establishing a priority list. You can be on it. Give us your name."

This is where we move from the spark to having an interest.

People will give us their names. They'll say, "We want to buy." But we'll tell them, "No, no, no, no. You can't buy now. But give us a deposit and we'll put you on the priority list."

If I started selling the units, and then I did my opening, who's going to show up at the opening? They're all bought. We're funneling all that to create the tremendous excitement at the opening where people are there, screaming, "I want that!" You want to create that excitement. You want to build the crescendo to the act.

Now, of course, if I have a person who says, "I can't attend the opening. I'm going to London next month, but I want units," I'm not going to lose him. I'll make exceptions. Nevertheless, we do try very, very hard to stay within the process.

So in the beginning, we start collecting names.

After that, we'll continue to send these people messages and postcards and things like that. We'll let them know that there is a VIP sales event coming for the people on the priority list. They'll be able to come in to compete with other buyers for units "as long as they're available" before we do our general-public grand opening. But in effect, this VIP notice is going to thousands of people who are VIPs. They actually do know it before the big ads come in.

Then we start our teaser ads in the general market. But they don't say, "Sales are now open." They only say: "Coming soon." So the general market also starts buzzing. People start thinking they want to get on the list.

At this point, we also make our Web page available so people can see the project in greater detail. An incredible Web site has become an integral part of our sales process.

So now everybody is trying to get onto this list, because we've created a once-in-a-lifetime opportunity and they don't want to be left out.

Now we start moving toward having a desire.

As you already know, I always plan for the worst. While we're creating our VIP list and putting out our teaser ads, we build a sales center that shows them what these beautiful units are going to look like. We always build a professional sales center so it's not all just talk, so they actually see the meat. We put up a scale model of the project, and a full-scale kitchen and bathroom for them to look at.

The sales center serves three purposes: It's a marketing tool, another test of whether the project will be successful, but it's also insurance.

It works as a tool because it helps move them from interest to desire. They came in because they were interested. But as they see the beautiful marble in the bathroom and run their hands over the granite countertops in the kitchen, it kindles their desire. And that's what the sales centers do. You can talk to them until you're blue in the face, but as these people start going by our sales center to make their reservations, they'll get more pumped up toward that VIP sales event.

But seeing how many of the people who visit sign up for reservations also gives us another way of gauging how successful the project is going to be. It is a sure sign of how things will go at the sales event. Let's face it, if everybody who comes in looks around and leaves without signing up, something's wrong. If nobody wants the food you're serving, you better get it off the table and head back to the kitchen.

And, finally, when I do the pre–grand opening tent events, I never go in there thinking they're going to sell out. If they don't, then I'm going to have to have a sales center where people can see their kitchens and their bathrooms. We always plan, not for a sellout at predevelopment but for having a showroom so people can see what they're buying. You've always got to go in expecting a long sale.

The sales center also does something that Playground identifies as one of the emotional hooks: It creates credibility.

Once we have enough reservations, we set up a tent for our by-invitation-only, pre–grand opening VIP sales event. We call the people who expressed an interest and we let them know this event is going to happen right before we open up sales to the general public in our permanent sales center. They can't buy yet. They have to come to the VIP sales event. It's the only way they can buy. If they're not there, they miss their chance.

Now they move from desire to want.

By the time the event rolls around, we might have one thousand people standing in line for 150 units. The first time we did it, for the Venture in Aventura, we were so successful in reaching out to people who wanted to participate in this real estate boom that we had people camp out the night before to get in and get their names in early.

We always put out a huge spread for breakfast and lunch. We have contracts already in place. We set up one section of the tent as a waiting area to keep people in. And there's like twenty of our best salespeople in cubicles inside.

Why the best? Because as any fisherman can tell you, just because you have them on the hook doesn't mean you've reeled them in. Even though the people on the list came in, signed up, and gave you a deposit doesn't mean they're sold. It's easy to say I'm interested and here's a $5,000 deposit that's returnable. Now we've got to make sure that we have the right salespeople when we get over there, the right approach, so everybody gets signed and closed. You still need to have the trained salespeople who are not going to let them go.

The people who are going to be serving to the people waiting in line outside, by the way, are also trained salespeople who go around pumping the customers up. And the people can see for themselves how many buyers are lined up. They know there aren't enough units for everybody. So they start getting worked up, thinking this is the hottest thing around. Everybody wants one. They must be great. They have to have one.

And when they get to that point, they've gone from having a want to having a pressing need.

The reason we do this is not only so we can obtain greater sales velocity; as you create the frenzy you can move sales prices up. We typically go into these sales events with eight sales steps. After a certain number of sales, it goes up to a higher price. And it does it almost automatically in the computer. I want no mess-ups there. So when 20 percent of the units go, it bumps. When a certain number more go, it bumps up again.

But even before that we can understand if we priced something wrong. If everybody starts coming in to make reservations and 90 percent of them want a certain type of unit, immediately we bump the price on that unit type. Even if we haven't gotten one sale. That's the way we control it.

We don't leave this to the salespeople. All they want to do is sell. Sometimes they don't follow the procedures. So we have somebody doing the accounting. We have contract administrators making sure that exactly when this unit type hits this number of sales, boom, it goes up. We have the senior vice presidents and the project manager inside the tent, in the war room, looking at the price lines, to make the price adjustments right there. We don't leave it to chance. We don't leave it only to the computer. We don't want to be caught as a result of the computer not spitting out the right price. It's all really well programmed to get the maximum price increases we can.

And the salespeople get to use it as a tool as well. Because the buyers can see us putting colored dots next to unit numbers on a big board. And they can see, for example, that the one-bedroom units are going very rapidly. So the salesperson can say, "It's now going to the next price level, and if you don't get this price level now, it's going to go to the next." And it will.

In Playground's emotional terms, seeing the prices climb and knowing that in a matter of minutes the condo will be selling for more than they pay gives people a "perception of value that exceeds price." They realize it's a great buy because they can get it at a certain price and it will be worth more immediately.

This is extremely important. You have to make sure they feel you delivered value. That has to do with quality, and with the sense that they got something that's worth more than they paid for it.

So if somebody comes in early and gets a unit for fifty bucks and they know that by the time the sales event finishes there's been eight price increases, I've got to tell you, they feel pretty good. And even if you're the eighth one, you still got value—because, remember, the demand continues even after the sales. Right after the building is sold out, we open up for resales. The buyer knows that when the resales begin there are still lots of people out there waiting to buy his unit. So we try very hard to deliver on the promise.

The buyers also know, as they see the dots on the board and the contracts being signed and the long line of frantic people trying to get their hands on a unit, that they have to act fast. And that creates that last emotion on Playground's list, the "fear of loss."

As we're selling, we only release certain numbers of the various configurations and locations in the building, so my best units don't go first. You never want to release all the waterfront units, for example. Because what happens? All your best units are gone, and all of a sudden all you have are the less desirable ones that don't sell as well. So we release by price and by sectors, to make sure my building is all getting sold evenly.

What we try to do is dispose of as much inventory through that process as we can. But since we had to put an ad in the paper announcing the weekend grand opening, and we typically put the lowest price to attract customers, we have to do two things: We can't sell it out, because it would be false advertising if we announced a grand opening and there is no opening; so I always leave a certain number of units available. And at least some of them have to be at the price I advertised.

But we have done grand openings when we have had only five units left out of a five-hundred-unit job. And after I do the first one, they'll give me whatever I want for the last ones.

Can you do the same thing with a ten-unit building, or even a duplex? Of course. It's all about creating that spark in the buyer's mind. Show them why these units are *unique opportunities*—buy now or you will *never* get another chance to get one, at least not at this price, *ever.* Is it the location—an exclusive water view? The last spot at the top of the mountain, or on the lakefront? Is it the design—a one-of-a-kind architectural plan? Does each unit have individual elevator entry? Private beachfront or boat slip? Or is it the amenities—such as home theater rooms in every unit? Rooftop tennis? Secure, reserved parking?

Highlight whatever it is about your product that's unique, and that your research told you people wanted more than anything. And let them know, if they don't act *right now*, it will be gone.

The Venture at Aventura—The First Tent

One of the best examples of sales with the temporary tent was called the Venture at Aventura, an upscale city at the north end of Miami-Dade County. It was five hundred units, a large job for the location. It was one of the first times we sort of perfected the system of creating the initial buzz and making people believe that we had a one-of-a-kind product that was an opportunity that was going to disappear very rapidly.

The first thing we did was get Alicia Cervera, my partner in our in-house sales company, RCRS, to assemble the very best sales team. We selected six salespeople, which for a job like this is a lot of salespeople, got them together in a room and said, "Okay, without selling, without advertising, without anybody knowing, you've got to get on the phone and on the e-mail lines and talk to all your best clients and the brokers you know best so they talk to their clients, and you tell them, 'There is this project coming up. You can't buy it yet. Nevertheless, I want to let you know beforehand, so you can get your name in.'" We then gave them all the information describing the advantages of the project and its location. You need to really sell your salespeople before they can be effective.

And all they were allowed to do was give the approximate sizes and approximate prices of the units.

So they started collecting names.

While they were doing that, in order for us to expand that initial list, we started with teaser ads. These ads didn't tell you where it was or how it was, these ads said, "Coming soon. Premiering, the greatest project in Aventura, at unbelievable prices." They sparked your imagination. And, in the real estate market, when people saw this, we started creating great anticipation.

We backed our salespeople's lists by also providing them with our own lists of previous buyers, prospects, and brokers, and also by buying lists of prospective customers once we had determined the most likely type of buyer for our product.

At that same time, we developed our Web page and our project video. That pretty much followed the teaser ad, but had a little bit more. The Web page also ended by providing the contact information with the salesperson's name.

So from the teaser ads and the Web page we continued to collect names. So now, remember, we've gone through everybody calling everybody under the sun. I mean, they spent two or three weeks just making phone calls.

That got the "visualize this" list getting bigger. That's all we wanted. Because the bigger your interested universe, the better chance you have of creating that stampede toward sales, which is basically what we wanted.

By that point the Web site was more developed. Now you could see sizes of units, more defined price ranges by unit size, and better, sexier project descriptions.

Then we sent beautiful invitations to all the names we accumulated through the teaser ads and the Web page, our salespeople, and the brokers calling. The invitation was like a minibrochure, like a postcard that opens up, that says: "Because you are a VIP we want to invite you to the preopening event of this amazing new job." Now, this list had five thousand people on it, but it still said, "Because you are a VIP, come by, sign your name, and give us a check so you can be on the priority list." We didn't ask for the whole 10 percent deposit they would have to give when they signed the contract, but a $5,000 check.

So we got as many checks as possible—all returnable. And the invitation said, "The VIP grand opening event will be Wednesday and Thursday, before we open our doors to the public for our grand opening on the weekend, Friday, Saturday, and Sunday."

And we put a huge ad in the paper that they could see that said: grand opening, Friday, Saturday, and Sunday. So they would be thinking, "My goodness, the grand opening is coming right after this event, they're making this event just for me."

But we told them, "You must be there because we're going to start calling names, and if you're not there we'll call the next name."

Then we set up this huge tent and broke it down into two sections—they had shades so you couldn't see from one into the other. One had couches and chairs and food. That was the first place people could come into.

In the Venture, there were people who camped out outside the doors of the tent overnight. When we opened our doors, we only let certain people come into the interior of the tent, otherwise there would have been too many to process correctly. The rest of the people had to wait outside. So all of them were trying to get inside to get food and something to drink, or just to know what was going on.

And inside, we had these loudspeakers and we'd be calling names.

By now, outside, I had all these very excited people. Some of them were screaming: "Hey, you haven't called my name!" Some of them got angry. "These units are sold! Give me the next one!" They were going nuts.

We were constantly sending people from our team outside to talk to them so they wouldn't get desperate and leave.

In Aventura, in the first thirty minutes of this frenzy, we sold 495 units out of the 500 in the building. I kept the last five because I had already run an ad in the paper that said we had one-bedroom units starting at a very low starting price. And so it wouldn't be false advertising, we kept five units there for the general public. But in reality, the moment that Friday hit, the brokers who were so upset at us because they couldn't buy were lining up for the public grand opening as soon as they could so they could try to buy the ones that were left.

The frenzy was unbelievable. You have to picture this. Picture the tent. Picture people outside. Picture screaming brokers saying, "Give me this unit! My client is going to be upset!"

But we didn't just turn away the people who didn't get to buy. What we did was build that excitement into the next job. All my salespeople and the project manager were happy because we sold out. For me, I'm always thinking of the next opportunity. I started my buzz for my next job. We told those customers the same thing was going to happen with our next project. People were already calling. If they didn't get on board this time, they'd miss another opportunity.

So I got the buzz going for the next job with all these frustrated people who wanted units so bad. And I started creating prospective buyer lists for my next job.

The process works no matter what you're selling. Our buzz groups may be different, but we always want to create the feeling of "never before and never again." And never before and never again can be done in price, in quality, or in location. Or all of the above.

When we created the first of the Lofts projects, we wanted to offer affordable housing for moderate-income people. So our marketing went directly to City of Miami workers, county workers, school board employees, and college workers. We had the city send a letter with us to those workers saying, "This is a great opportunity." And we had cocktail parties and sales events just for those people, again, before we opened it to the general public.

What did we do? We created a group of people who were supposed to be very special. We made those people feel special, that they got a deal before the rest of the world.

It's the same thing you see when they have a huge sale before they open a Macy's at nine o'clock. You see the people there because they want to make sure they're the first ones there. They go running to that store to get the Macy's Day special before the supplies disappear.

When we did Lofts I, we sold out, just like we did at the Venture.

The strong sales strategies were developed in our company's condominium phase. But with our apartments, we did have very, very good rental strategies with grand openings and promotions and radio ads as we opened. In rentals, the key was also to attract as many people as possible. So we always had a big grand opening with food, celebrities, and excitement in ways no rental developer had done before.

But overall, the process evolved into an ongoing sales campaign. Because a rental project is not a finite asset. I mean, someone can rent an apartment, but they can also rent one of the fifty apartments all around you. How can you tell them this is the only apartment there is? It's not a diminishing asset. You can't tell anyone, "Either you rent right now or you're never going to rent again." Whereas condominiums are diminishing assets. You *can* tell them, "You either buy it from me now or you're never going to buy it from me, not at this price and not in this location."

Also, the levels of expenditure the condominiums allowed me were much greater. In a three-hundred-unit rental project, for example, your marketing budget might be $100,000. In a three-hundred-unit condominium project, your marketing budget is probably $2 million. So condominiums are much more marketing-intensive.

When I was starting out we didn't have marketing people. I was the marketing department. If we were going to have a grand opening of a market-rate project, I looked at it and asked myself how I was going to bring people in. I would bounce ideas off our project manager, who had been trained as a jack-of-all-trades. And it couldn't cost much, because I didn't have much money.

With the rentals we found that the biggest thing that brought people in, other than the product and them wanting to rent, was food and drink. For free. It's just like all those car sales events; you've seen them—what do they do? They offer free hot dogs and beer and free kids' things. Everybody wants something for free. It doesn't matter how rich you are. Go to a super-rich wedding, go to a super-rich any-thing. When you put the food out, people who've never stood in line for anything stand in line to get the freebie food. It's true, isn't it?

So early on I announced that we were going to have a grand opening and that there would be food. But I wouldn't spend a lot of money. I would get my project manager to flip hamburgers and hot dogs by the pool. We would get these deals in which it cost me nothing. I once made a deal with Hooters in which—for nothing!—I got the Hooters girls to come and serve everybody and have a great time and all that stuff.

It really was great advertising for them. And for me. Who doesn't want to go and have free food served by skimpily dressed beautiful young women?

I always was looking for ways to get the customers in.

Eventually we made it a much more standardized process, and everything was in the manual: from the moment you got in there, how you were greeted, how the people dressed, how they offered you a drink, how they took you out to see the model. Everything was in the manual.

At one of our rentals there will always be a greeter who stands up and says, "Hello, what's your name? Thank you for coming to our project. What are you interested in?"

You say, "I'm interested in looking at a one-bedroom unit. Can I go over there and take a look?"

But again, this is a process. For people to really appreciate getting something, they can't get it too easily. So we say: "No, we'll have someone show you. Here's our waiting area. A salesperson will be with you in a second."

In that waiting room, there would be a video playing about the company. There would be renderings of the apartment complex. Then a salesperson comes in, and they take over the whole presentation. This one is totally, totally, totally programmed. The salespeople studied it and took tests before they could meet with customers. We wanted to make sure that when the customer signed they were *really* sold. Because many times they come in, and they'll say, "I want the unit," and they'll sign. But then there's a period when they can rescind, and if the whole presentation was not done correctly, you lose them. They'll leave and they'll look at another project and they'll come back and cancel their reservation and ask for their deposit back.

You want to make sure they are really sold. That's why we have this whole process. In rentals, when you're starting, don't ever sign them up without showing them your models and without showing them your amenities. They must go through a whole path building up to the moment when you finally let them sign a lease. We used to call it "the marketing path."

For example, all our walkways in the whole project were made of concrete. On our marketing path, our walkway was made of this incredible Spanish tile. The landscaping on the marketing path was three times as good as the landscaping in the rest of the project. So as you went to see the model apartment you went past the amenities, you went past the bougainvilleas and all the colors. For the hallway leading to the apartment, instead of just using concrete we used Gyp-Crete, which is just like concrete, but it's a surface that is totally smooth and perfect. We had big potted plants, beautiful entries, and everything was beautiful. And then we always had a beautifully designed model apartment. A professional designed it, but with furniture and accessories within the price range that would seem affordable to the people coming to rent. We never offered furnished apartments, but we didn't want people to look at something and feel they could never live there. It needs to feel like it can be their home.

We wanted to create that dream of how good it was to live here. And we were very, very, very good at it. We showed them all around. We showed them all our amenities—the pool and the clubhouse and the play areas for children—everything the project consisted of. And at the end of the marketing path, after they'd seen it all, then the salesperson would invite them to sign the lease.

What does that do? It prevents people from canceling. We sold them. They knew our project. They're not going to go to somebody else and ask to look at theirs. Or see a FOR RENT sign with one month's discount and go in and check it out. *No.* Their minds are made up. By the time they sign the lease, they know they're getting an incredible value on an incredible place to live, and if they don't act fast, someone else is going to move into their apartment and there's no telling how long they'll have to wait to start enjoying this lifestyle.

So whether it's condos or rentals, you really, really sell them. It's not enough to just hook them. You have to reel them in and land them.

SELLING FOR THE FUTURE

You're never selling just one project—you're selling your brand, and all the projects you'll have after this one. You don't want to make a sale, you want to make a customer for life.

So the sale doesn't end when they sign the contract. You have to follow up. You have to nurture that customer.

When you buy a unit from us, we send you a quarterly newsletter. At some point we're going to call you and say, "Mr. Smith, come into our sales center to pick the finishes and accessories for your unit." So you'll come into the sales center to pick the color of your carpet, to pick the color of your counter. We'll show you the options. Not only do we have kitchen vignettes and the bathrooms in the sales center, we have samples of the different styles you can pick and the different color cabinets and all the other options.

Then we give you a link to a webcam so you can see the progress of the job going up. We send you a gift before it's done. We invite you to parties that we have, and to other marketing parties that we have for other projects. We continue building that relationship.

Right now, as I'm writing this book, we're doing a big condo hotel project in Celebration, the Disney development in Orlando. What we want to do is, instead of selling my project—do you know how many condo hotels there are in Orlando? how many hotels?—we want to sell Celebration. This is not going to be on International Drive with all the T-shirt shops. So I hired Daniel Azoulay, a world-renowned photographer, and we put together a beautiful hardbound limited-edition book with unbelievable photographs of Celebration. Nothing to do with our job. Just of the town—the golf course, the kids, the farmers market they have on the weekend. We want to give the image of small-town America. After you buy, we give you this book as a present. You'll keep this forever. And while your unit is being built, you can leaf through this book and you can dream about the life you're going to have there. You can picture yourself walking through this great small American town with your wife and the kids, at the hot air balloon rides they have on the weekends, at the old-style movie house.

> Nurture your customer's dream.

We are nurturing your dream, and nurturing you as a customer. Because not only will you be more satisfied with what you bought now, you'll show this to friends and relatives and tell everyone how great our project and company are. And at least some of them are bound to call and possibly buy, in this one or in the next one.

So remember, nurture. That's part of the whole sales process.

KEY PRINCIPLES

- Spend some, but only spend more when the risk is reduced.

- Understand your buyer. Give him what he needs to commit.

- People buy from people. The messenger is as important as the message.

- No one knows your product and your target market better than you.

- Nurture your customer's dream.

ONE MIAMI,
Miami, Florida
© Paúl Rivera/archphoto

7 · BUILDING IT: THE EIGHT RULES FOR BUILDING FOR PROFITS NOW AND IN THE FUTURE

"Every building we have
is our best marketing tool."

You really have to believe you are going to be the best, because only if you believe you're the best will people think you're the best. When you build the best, people will come to your product and pay more for your product.

That's a reality. It's also marketing and perception.

It doesn't do you any good to think you're the best if the whole world is not out there thinking you are, too. You have to project that. And in order to project it, you have to feel it.

RULE #1: QUALITY COUNTS

I can't sell you something that I don't really believe in. I can't tell you, "Go buy one of my condominiums," if I don't believe in it. I can't. If I don't believe it when I'm telling you that it really is the best and that you are making the right investment, I can't. I need to believe it to be able to make you believe it.

And the only way for me to believe it is to know in my heart that it's true. I have to build the best I possibly can. I always have. It doesn't matter if it's affordable housing that people pay $80 out of their welfare check for, or a $10 million penthouse condominium. I am going to make every one of them the best.

Some people think we should expect affordable housing to decay, that once you turn it over to the tenants, it's going to deteriorate rapidly, so you shouldn't put so much effort into it. I never expect anything to decay.

I do it for two reasons: One, I do it on principle. I cannot be associated with something that's a failure. That is run-down. That is mediocre. I just won't. I will not be associated with it. You talk about building self-esteem and pride when you're starting out—unless it's a fake self-esteem and pride you need to make sure that everything you have and you own is top quality. That's number one.

The other reason is long-term profitability. When you show people that you care enough to always build the best, people will stick with you. The lenders will stick with you. The investors will stick with you. Your staff will understand the value. I mean, I can go and tell my people this until I'm blue in the face. Unless they live my experience through my eyes and see my intensity and see my passion and live it, they'll never really understand it and incorporate it in themselves.

They need to see me perform and live by the ideals that I preach. If not, they become empty words.

Because everyone is going to tell you that they pay attention to detail and they want the greatest job. Because no one is ever going to come and tell you they don't care if your job is good or not.

No. They'll tell you they care about building the best, but words are cheap.

You have to deliver the best every time. It's good customer relations. It's that nurturing we just talked about in the last chapter. People appreciate it. They'll buy from you again. And they'll tell their friends.

No building is ever completely finished when you turn it over to the buyers. There are always some outstanding issues—it could be loose tiles in a unit, a leak in the pool, any of a zillion little and not-so-little things.

When we finish a condominium project and hand things over to the condo association, we separate the remaining issues into three areas.

The first of those are the issues that are clearly our responsibility or the contractor's responsibility—because we didn't meet code, because we didn't do it according to the plan or the specs we had, because of whatever.

Second are those issues that we call the gray areas, when the buyers claim one thing and we claim another, and, ultimately, who knows. Two real good experts would give you two real good opinions, and both could be right.

And then there are what I call the "wish list" issues. Those are things like, "I didn't like the pool furniture even though it was picked by the greatest designer in the world. You need to change it just because I didn't like it." Or, "I didn't like the painting you put in my lobby." Well, you know, those are what my designer picked. We didn't do it because of cost or anything. So we don't feel that we're in any way obligated to do something about them. But we'll try.

We try very hard to go out of our way to do everything we think we or the contractor are responsible for, and to do almost everything that is in the gray area. And then we take some of the wish list items and offer to do some of the things even though we're not responsible for them.

Why do we do that? It creates a brand; people will talk about you as an honorable person. And it will give you future clients. You do it hoping that those people who bought from you will buy again and that they'll go to their friends and tell them to buy from you because you do things right.

I always tell the developers who are working for me, "When you think of the customer, put yourself in their shoes. What would you want out of this apartment? Would you live in this lobby? Would you think that this lobby is the best?" You don't need to be a rocket scientist. What would you want for yourself? If you were the buyer and now this guy delivers to you, what would you expect?

> Don't give your customer any less than what you would expect for yourself.

Don't give them any less than your expectations. Now, unfortunately, I've had some guys who have some very low expectations and I've had to get rid of them.

Rule #2: Details Count—All of Them

If in your own life you don't have that sense of detail, that sense of perfection, you can't practice it. If you have a guy who's a mess in everything he does, don't assign him to be the head of a project. Maybe he can be the shell construction guy who only deals with the structure going up and not with the details. But that sense of the best, that sense of perfection needs to have somebody who pays great attention to details. That's what differentiates good from great.

> The difference between good and great lies in the details.

There isn't one job, using the best designers in the world and the best architects in the world, that I come and look at and I don't say, "We're spending more on this job. I want more pots here. I want more artwork there. I don't like the way they finished this wall. This pool needs more of this, more of that."

Everybody may be going, "Wow!" But they're all looking at what's going great about it. I may be going, "Wow!" too, but I'm looking for what's not right. What does it still need to be perfect?

If I find things from designers that are not to my satisfaction, where I think they did an inferior product, I will be upset. Right then and there I will call the designer and I will call the manager and I will say, "I want to spend more money in this lobby. It's not up to Related standards and I'm upset about that, particularly since this designer has done three or four previous jobs for us, and you, Mr. Manager, have been with us for several years, and you both should have known better without me having to come tell you that."

Many times, when things are finished, they're not complete. Or the execution is so bad that what looked good on paper does not look good in reality. That happens a lot. And it drives me crazy to see things that are not up to standards.

For most people, even some people in my own company, the fact that a place is 100 percent sold is good enough. And they let it go.

But it's not. People are going to go visit. People are going to go see it. It's your own pride that's involved. It's your building. Everybody who goes by and sees that is going to know that you did this. And they're going to either think that you cared enough to make sure everything was perfect, or that you didn't and the building looks imperfect.

So be relentless about quality. It's something you can never get enough of.

Rule #3: You're Building a Brand, Not Just a Building

You can't settle for less. You need to insist that things are done right. Because even on a job that was totally 100 percent sold, oversold, I still would not accept an inferior product. I mean, I could say, "You know, it is what it is. People like it." I don't. Settling is something that we won't do. It has to be the best in every detail.

It's more than pride. Every building we have is our best marketing tool. Yours will be, too. Every building says something about you, about your brand.

Brand is more important than profit. If you're looking to succeed in the long term, being known for quality will take you a lot further than making a quick profit. Excellence is what matters.

So if I was to do a job and all of a sudden in the middle of the job we found out we blew the profit and there was no profit to be made, I would still deliver the best job, with the same intensity, as if we were making hundreds of millions of dollars.

The main thing driving us is making that job great. The pride of making that job great. So I would never leave anything in the middle just because it's all of a sudden not profitable. I'm going to finish it and I'm going to finish it right. On principle. On pride.

One time I was with a *USA Today* reporter, and we went in to see my latest project. We had just finished building it and people were starting to move in. And there was this one guy who saw me and came up to me and said, "I've been waiting half an hour here for the elevator."

I'm thinking, "Well, you know what? We've got one hundred people moving in here at the same time. Even though we plan for that, there are times that delays are going to happen."

But that's not what I said to him. You can't—you know, the customer's king. Without aggravating the customer you have to, in a very nice way, say, "I'm really sorry and we're going to do everything possible for this not to happen to you again."

Which is more or less what I said. And then I went to the building manager and said, "Do we have two guys doing move-ins? Then let's have four guys doing move-ins. Let's prevent the delays that are causing customer dissatisfaction. This is the Related brand that you are representing."

You know what? I'm not saying this company is perfect. We're not. But I'll tell you what we are: we are honest. And where we are not perfect, we're going to try to make it perfect. So the message has to be, "Yes, we make mistakes. But we fix them." Because you want to be known for the quality of your product and the quality of your service. You're building a reputation with every project. You're building your brand.

RULE #4: DON'T BE PENNY WISE AND POUND FOOLISH

"Penny wise and pound foolish" is an old saying that basically means you're so busy saving on the little things that you end up costing yourself more in the long run. Example: You save a little bit by not changing the oil in your car, and you end up burning out your whole engine.

The rule holds true in real estate as well: Don't cut so much that you diminish the long-term value of your asset.

One thing that's important here, as a businessperson, is building a legacy. You want to do things that withstand time and will build your reputation. So anything you do to build that legacy will have long-term effects. If you do a building and people afterward say, "That's amazing!" even if it cost a little bit more to do it, you'll have long-term fruits from that. That is very hard to measure. You do it based on your interpretation of what value is on a long-term basis.

We put together a very expensive hardbound volume filled with exquisitely vivid photographs and depictions of sixty-four of our current and future projects, on more than 280 heavy-stock glossy pages. We hired the best photographers and artists. We called it *Related: Building by Design*.

What's the value of that? It's not like someone's going to come by and buy an apartment because of it. But you're building value by showing people what you do. I'm expecting you to look at those things and say, "Wow! Those guys really care for the things they do when they do something that's a little better." I'm sure that when you do that you will tell your wife and she will tell a friend. And so on. So that's how you create value. But it's very hard to measure.

More directly, on a building the extra touches are the ones that make or break your reputation. I focus on landscaping, color schemes, and decor. I call many of those things the sizzle. Those are the ending touches to a great job. And they're superimportant. Because you build your brand not just on kitchens and bathrooms.

What do you do above and beyond the kitchens and bathrooms to make the project more livable, to make the project great? And that is when we use things like great design and great architecture: Yabu Pushelberg, Philippe Starck, Arquitectonica, Robert Stern. And we advertise it heavily.

That's also why we put such an emphasis on art. Every job, when we finish it, we do an art book and give it to every one of the buyers. All the pieces are there so they know not only what the art piece is, but also who the artist is. Because I want them to become knowledgeable about the art. As they do, their lives become better. I really do believe that. They grow as people. They start having a greater level of understanding of something that should be very important in our lives.

Choosing the art is always important, in every job we do. But not everyone appreciates that. For one building, the Murano in South Beach, we spent all this money on an Edouard Duval-Carrié sculpture. It was a little unusual. It's a Haitian god in Plexiglas at the entrance of the building that lit up at night. It must have been ten feet tall, or something like that, and it lit up red and orange. We also did these floors by an artist that were all done with inlaid seashells and forms. Unbelievable.

And after we handed the building over to the condo association, the people came over and said, "We want marble on the floors." And they wanted to get rid of Duval-Carrié's sculpture. So we went over, brought the artist, and explained to them the process of the art. What it meant.

And what it did. And then we went to them and gave them the track record of the artist. We explained that he was in the Museum of Modern Art and other famous museums. And so on. We even had the auction prices of some of his pieces.

So I said, "Why don't you guys do this? Look at it for a month, and if you don't like it, I'll buy it from you at the price I paid for it. So you can put in whatever you want." Somebody wanted a fountain. Somebody wanted three palm trees.

And they came back in about two months, and they said, "No, we decided to keep it." And now it's become their pride.

So when we do the art and we do these little catalogs we do it with the mission of improving life. Art grows on you, and people need to learn about it to better understand it.

What do you do when you're starting out? You can apply the same concepts without having the same budget. I always paid very close attention to the landscaping and the paint, the color schemes, and the cleanliness. You can put potted plants around the lobby to add color and life, and use the pots themselves as part of the décor. Line the entrance and grounds with carefully selected landscaping. It doesn't have to be expensive to be beautiful, and it doesn't have to require a lot of maintenance. Landscape with drought-resistant native plants that don't require a lot of upkeep. Paint the walls in bold burnt reds and golds, add some hardy bougainvilleas, and you've got a Southwestern theme going. Paint the lobby in pure white, add just a few thin, tall topiaries, and you have a modern minimalist thing happening.

And art doesn't have to be by Picasso to be good or nice to look at. Use your imagination, and if you don't have an eye or the knowledge yourself, get a good local decorator and art adviser. You want your project to stand out. That's always true, but even more so when you're starting out. The touch of distinction that the extra touches add to your project will more than pay you back. Don't save your money here. Don't be penny wise and pound foolish.

You can't skimp when you're thinking of the long term. Saving a few pennies now can cost you lots of dollars in the long run. Spending a little more is an investment in your future that will pay you back many times over.

Rule #5: The Contractor Is Crucial

The best plans in the world won't be worth the paper they're printed on if you have a bad contractor. Plans are just ideas until the building is finished. If you don't build it right, no one is going to want to live in it. It could cost you twice as much as you anticipated, or more, to fix the mistakes a shoddy contractor made. You could end up getting sued by your customers, and spending Lord only knows how much to sue the contractor.

So before you start construction, you have to check out your contractor to make sure they are licensed and are bonded and haven't been sued a bunch of times or have a bunch of liens on their former clients' properties. You have to check their track record, visit their job sites, and ask their past clients.

I would check all that. Typically, an attorney does all that. So that's again hiring the consultants. They will check that. You should check it, too. But much more than that, you should do what I did at the beginning: I would go to the job sites they were doing and take a look at their work firsthand. I wanted to see how clean their job sites were, and if they were delivering on time. I would talk to the owner who hired them to see if they had any complaints, if they were honest, if they were change-order artists—the kind that give you a price and then change-order you to death, adding on charges here and there for things that "need" to be changed on the job.

That was all part of my due diligence. I would actually go to the site. I also would check with people who had used them previously to see what complaints they had. I would check with the subcontractors they used to check on their payment record.

When I was considering a contractor for a job, the first thing I would ask for is a list of projects they were doing or had done. Once I had that list it was very easy to track the owners. I used to do this all myself. I would drive to the construction site and go to the superintendent and say, "This is a great job, who owns this?"

"Oh," he'd tell me, for instance, "Juan Pérez owns this."

Or the contractor might be doing a small office building and I would go and ask the owner, "So what was your relationship with this guy?"

And he might say, "Forget it. The guy is the worst. I'm ready to fire him."

Or he'd tell me good things.

Before you leave you ask every one of them, "Do you know anybody else who has used him?"

And you go talk to them, too.

You do all that in addition to asking the contractor for his references. Because the thing you have to remember about references is, unless someone's an idiot, they won't give references that are going to talk badly about them. So when people tell me, "He gave me five references. I called them all up and they say the guy is great," I go, "What did you expect?"

When I'm hiring contractors, I don't ask them for their references. I talk to them and ask questions, like, "Who did you work for? And who did you report to on that particular job? And who owns that company?"

And then I will do my own reference checking, apart from the ones he has given me.

You learn from doing. And if you don't check out your contractor, you could wind up getting a very expensive lesson.

If you're careful, you won't make expensive mistakes, and you're bound to find contractors you can trust and who you want to work with over the long term. It's that relationship-building thing again. We've done that over the years, and it has translated into money in our pockets.

Why does everybody say that Related builds for 20 percent less and faster than anybody else? Because we have built up those relationships, along with a reputation for doing a lot of work and for paying promptly. When you're a subcontractor, your interest is not just in making money. You want to make sure you're going to get paid and not get messed around with. You want the developer to release your retainage—the percentage he was holding to guarantee completion of the job—as soon as possible. You don't want a developer who delays your payment or who, at the end of things, starts renegotiating with you.

So we have this whole group of people who follow us and know how we are. The plumber will give me a price that's much cheaper than the price he'll give somebody else. But it's worth it to him because the levels of risk with somebody else are much greater than they are with me. We have the same subs today that we had fifteen years ago.

We also give the general contractor incentives to finish faster. Sometimes those are passed on to the subs. But we give the general contractor incentives, so if they finish the job ahead of time, they will share in the savings they produce for us by finishing ahead of time.

Nonetheless, you have to keep very close tabs on the contractor. Construction cost overruns, or mistakes that have to be fixed, can kill you.

Our follow-up meetings in construction are well known. We get everybody involved—the architect, the contractor, my construction guy, my project manager, everyone—on a weekly basis and we go to the job site. And we're not just talking about problems we're having now, but also visualizing what problems we could have.

When we do our biweekly staff meetings and we do the budget, particularly when it comes to building construction, there's a whole section we devote most of the time to, in which we examine potential cost increases. And we separate those into the ones that we bring in because we want to make it a better project and those we have no control over, like the fire department comes in and says we forgot to put new and unexpected fire alarms in. You should always be looking ahead so you don't get into big trouble, you only get into little trouble. You want to be able to cure your problems by taking aspirin, as opposed to getting cancer and having to have major surgery.

A good contractor—who watches the details the way you do, who wants to build the best, who wants to finish fast without compromising any quality—will make the process smoother, and the project better. A bad contractor is another source of problems; a good one is a source of solutions. That's why picking the right contractor is crucial.

One Miami—Follow-up,
and the Value of Relationships

Over the years, John Moriarty & Associates had become my preferred condominium high-rise contractor. But they were doing so much for us that we had to look for a new contractor. We had grown so much that Moriarty just got totally full. So we were looking for other people and there was this very large construction company that had always wanted to do a project with me, Turner Construction Company.

So I said I'd give them a chance. But the way we work with construction is I set the preliminary budget with the contractor and we negotiate what the contractor's fees are going to be to make sure that they're standard—3 percent, 4 percent, whatever it is at the time—and the general conditions. The general conditions are all the things he needs to produce the job: his trailer, his staff, his equipment, and so forth.

So once we negotiate those two, we say, "You're going to show me the subcontractor bids. We are going to get to our budgeted price and you're going to guarantee that price."

I have a budget. The budget says I'm going to sell this building for $100,000. It's going to cost me $80,000. That way I make $20,000. Based on that, it's very important to me that the $80,000 is real.

My risk is that I'm going to sell it at $100,000. The risk on the construction price, they need to take.

So we prepared the budget based on history, what it cost me to build projects similar to One Miami in the past. Based on the experience of both of our companies and the One Miami plans, we set a preliminary budget of $120 a square foot. And they said they could do it at that price. This was a thousand units we sold for a total of $250 million.

I kept on meeting with Turner's Florida president as we went along. I told him when we started sales. I told him when we finished.

And all along, he kept telling me things were looking good. Not an iota of a concern.

Then, out of the blue, he said he needed to talk to me. And he goes, "It's not one hundred twenty a square foot. It's one hundred sixty a square foot." This wasn't that he missed by 1 percent or 2 percent or 5 percent. He was off by $40, more than 30 percent.

I said, *"What?* Are you crazy?"

We were already done selling the condominiums. That meant my revenues were fixed. I couldn't suddenly go back to the buyers and say they needed to give me more money. I couldn't just give them back their deposits and start over. So my construction cost needed to come in on budget, or less.

So I told him: "Either you knew all along that this was happening and you didn't want to tell me, thinking that maybe I had such huge profitability that I would just say, 'Fine.' Or you are the dumbest guy in the world, because you're in the construction business and you had no idea of the costs! Because last week you told me we were okay."

So not only did I fire him, but I fired the two people in my company who were the project managers. Because if they had been meeting with these people for six months, they should have damn well known of the coming disaster.

That took a huge amount of courage because I didn't have anybody in the background to take over the construction. But I knew enough about building towers and I have enough experience that I knew I might not get it down to 120, but that 160 was absolutely ridiculous.

So what did I do? I got Tom Daly, a partner in many of my past projects and one of the best construction guys around, and I said, "Let's go see John Moriarty." Tom and I both have an excellent relationship with John Moriarty.

Tom said, "They're too busy. They don't want to do it."

I said, "Let's go see John Moriarty."

And we did and I said, "John, here's the thing, I think it can be done at one hundred twenty."

He said, "Jorge, I don't have the people. I don't have the staff. And one hundred twenty is really tight."

I said, "Listen to me. I need you. On the other ones I didn't need you. Now I need you. This is a relationship. I've already sold it. I've got a problem."

So they spent three months working on the cost, while I'm thinking, "Oh, my God! The guy still doesn't have the staff." They bring it down to 120 but with almost no contingency. If they had the staff, maybe, but hiring outside management was going to cost more.

I said, "This is what I'll do. I'll take ten million dollars, in addition to the contingency that I had, and I'll put it in an escrow account. So if you muck it up, you blow your contingency and you blow my contingency, then there's still an additional ten million dollars in there. Please, I need you."

Construction prices were starting to zoom up. All my other developer friends were saying to me, "There is no way you can build the thing for even close to one hundred twenty a square foot."

But Moriarty brought people from their Boston office in order to build One Miami. As a favor for me and Tom. And we built it. In record time. And we didn't touch one penny of the $10 million additional contingency.

The moral of the story: Perseverance pays off. Relationships matter. And keep a really close eye on your contractor.

RULE #6: KNOW WHAT PEOPLE WANT, KNOW YOUR CUSTOMER

The market research we do before we embark on any job is immense. And this was from day one. From the very beginning, I believed in the value of research. Not just market analysis and macroanalysis, but also examining the competition and questioning our customers.

It became an extremely important part of what we do.

All of our salespeople questioned the people who came in to look. "What would you like to see, Mrs. Smith? What would you like in your apartment? What don't you like?"

We would do focus groups and interview our tenants about what they liked and didn't like about our rental apartments. We were always learning, for the next ones, what we were doing wrong, what we should add, what was wrong with our kitchens, what was wrong with our bathrooms, what was wrong with our amenities.

We were always evolving by asking. We were always looking to the consumer to tell us what it was they wanted.

It helped us learn to make a better product, and it made our tenants feel important. They felt somebody was listening to them.

We emphasized in the management company that the customer was always king. If your air conditioner goes out in Florida and it takes three days to get maintenance to go to your apartment to fix it, you've got problems. We really wanted to have a very rapid response system. And every time we would go to an apartment to fix something we would bring questionnaires and ask them to fill them out. But we weren't only asking them if they felt their apartment was fixed rapidly. We asked people what they liked and what they didn't like.

So all the time we would learn how to become better operators and developers of properties.

You might be asking yourself, "But I don't have a building. How would I know what tenants want?" Well, we found out from other apartments.

We went and visited all the competition, and even though we weren't asking directly, they would give us information in the responses they gave us. We would ask them, "Wow! You have three choices of kitchen, which is the most popular? Which is the one that people are picking?"

And they would say, "Oh, by far they are picking the blue one. Because this is the new color and this is like the latest thing you see in the magazines from Italy. And they love this rain shower. We can't believe everyone is paying the extra money."

So don't say that just because you haven't done it and you haven't been talking to a million prospective buyers you can't find out what they want. You go out in the market, and you find the answer in the market. We did that with our Section 8 affordable housing at the beginning.

We are immense believers in market research. Immense believers. And in being great imitators. We have no qualms about imitating what we think is great.

When I started, the areas that were doing apartments more than Miami were California and Texas. They were having all the apartment innovations. They were applying a lot of the new marketing techniques. Not only what they put into the apartments but what they put into the common areas and how they did the advertising.

I would take trips to California and Texas almost every quarter to look at new product. I would go to the sales offices to get all the brochures and I would come back with all these brochures. Then I would sit with my marketing people and pick the best sections of the best marketing brochures.

We'd get all the newspapers and magazines in the different cities to see how they did the ads. And then we'd start picking what I thought was the best. I would make my people do the same. We had this board in our office, and anybody who saw something really outstanding would put it on the board. We would have discussions and we would be looking at all this. We would talk about it. We studied even the smallest details. The way they did the utility closet. The new washer and dryer. The windowsills.

It was all about figuring out what people want so you can give it to them.

But sometimes people don't know what they want. They think they do, but they can't see that what they really want is something completely different.

For example, our project in Acapulco. What have people heard about Acapulco lately? That there have been a bunch of drug-related murders. Acapulco is the center. And, sure enough, what can go wrong will, so right after we got this incredible site, there was a murder.

The impulse, of course, is to think that it's all over and that no one is going to want to go there anymore.

And that's right. But the problem isn't that people don't want to go down there. The problem is they don't want to go down there *until* they feel safe.

Now that's a problem I can do something about.

I saw it as a two-part problem, needing a single solution. I had to create a place that would be a magnet—that they would want to go to—and that would be safe.

I came up with two great ideas. One, Acapulco is still an hour-and-a-half drive from Mexico City, yet all of the rich people, particularly the young rich people, go there for the weekend, because it's got the best discotheques and restaurants on the cliffs. So I asked myself, "Where do hip Mexicans and Americans who go to Mexico City on business go when they stay in Mexico City?" Easy answer: W Hotel. The W Hotel is not a hotel in Mexico, it's a hangout place. They've got the coolest restaurant, the coolest bar. You go there any evening, particularly on the weekend, and it's a hip hangout. All the beautiful people in Mexico go there.

Now, if that's going to be my market, I'm sure as hell not going to do advertising that shows a sixty-five-year-old couple holding hands on a deserted beach with a tagline about "a beautiful retirement village."

My market is the kind of person who wants activity, action, modern design. So based on that, we got ourselves the greatest modernist in Mexican architecture, a guy named Enrique Norten of a group called TEN—The Enrique Norten Group. And he was just put in *Forbes* as one of the top ten trendsetters in architecture in the world. This guy is amazing. He designed unbelievable buildings: 350 condominiums with a W Hotel, all stuck in a mountain. They look like concrete and glass sculptures popping out of the mountain. It will be in every architectural magazine in the world. We've had him do those plans twenty times over—I'm not exaggerating—because I really needed to create a great concept for them to want to come. So, W provided the hottest five-star international brand, and Norten matched it with extraordinary architecture. And we did not stop there. For the interiors, we got David Rockwell Art of New York, another icon in creating spectacular places recognized all over the world.

So the first problem was creating the coolest place for people to come. And the other was security. So I didn't want to go to a private beach. People would be afraid on a beach. So we created a private, secluded beach club on the mountain, with pools that drop down to about thirty feet from the water. And do you know how they get to the ocean? I have a private elevator coming down from the pool to a series of swimming platforms on the ocean. And only our customers can use the elevator. So you have total privacy for bathing, total privacy for anything you want. If you want to go topless there, you can. There's going to be a separate adults-only location. And we are making this a really cool and exciting place for the young and wealthy.

That's what we created in Acapulco. We saw a market that had problems. And we immediately asked ourselves how we could solve the problems and make it so that people wanted to go there and would feel safe. And that was done through incredibly creative architecture that combined great freedom with total security.

Can you do the same thing when you're starting out? Of course. It doesn't take a multimillion-dollar budget. All it takes is finding out what people want and giving it to them. Just remember, often enough they don't really know what they want until they see it. And sometimes they think they want one thing, but they really want something else. It's up to you to use a little creativity to give them the thing they need, even if they didn't know it. You can do that on a shoestring.

Let's say you have affordable market-rate apartments and you're targeting young professionals. That's the market you believe has the most potential. Because of their age group, it's a safe bet many will be single, but many are going to be young parents with small children. Most of the time, single people don't want little kids living next door, and parents with little children worry about noise and parties from the single people.

What do you do?

You could pick one market or the other and fight harder to fill your apartments from a much smaller pool of prospects. Or you could get creative. Maybe you could split your complex into two parts—one for adults with kids and one for those without. You could do that with simple landscaping, or by how you place your parking lots. If you have a slightly larger budget, you could give them each their own pools, at opposite ends of the complex. Spend a little more and they could each have separate rec rooms, with pool tables and big-screen TVs and a wet bar for the singles, and a carpeted children's playroom for those with children.

See where I'm going? Every creative solution makes your apartments more attractive than the competition, expands your universe of potential customers, and diminishes your risk.

Take it a step further. Say that one of the problems you keep hearing about when you're doing your research is that the parents want to stay closer to their jobs because they have to drop the kids off at day care, and the extra stop makes their commutes even more horrendous. Could you take one of your rec rooms and make a deal with a company to offer low-cost day care on-site? You give them free or low rent in exchange for them giving your tenants priority, and they pass their savings on to the customer.

Think you could fill your apartments now?

I'm telling you, be creative and make sure you always work to give your customers what they want.

Rule #7: Put Your Money Where It Can Be Seen

You have to give people what they want. As a businessperson, though, you have to make decisions about which things bring more revenue than your expenditures. That's a real hard process that comes through experience and, also, through talking to people.

Let me take you back to the very beginning. When I started out renting buildings, we would ask our customers to fill out questionnaires that would ask: What did you like? What didn't you like? Please rate them on a scale of one to five. What is important and what is not important?

We did constant market research. When you do that, you find what the consumers' preferences are and where you should be putting your marginal money to produce the most effect. You need to spend the money on work that can be seen, that will produce additional revenues.

> Spend your money on work that can be seen.

Obviously the building has to meet standards and codes and everything else, but what sells it is bathrooms, kitchens, flooring, landscaping, and amenities, those things that are highly visible and that people consistently note as higher priorities. People know. Even when you had a good market here and people were selling well, nobody sold with the speed that we did. Nobody. And it was almost invariably because of our ability to understand our customer's desires.

There are some things you could do in an apartment that people won't pay you any more for, like balconies. They said they wanted this type of balcony over that other kind of balcony, but in their surveys they didn't see it as something they were willing to pay more for.

We found that changes on the outside were always much more important than changes on the inside. In reality, nobody cared whether your plumbing was cast iron or PVC pipe. If one lasted thirty years and the other one lasted twenty-five years, that's all nice and dandy, but it didn't make one bit of difference to the customer.

But we have found, particularly in the for-sale product, that changes you made to bathrooms and kitchens were of extreme importance. People will pay you an additional amount of money for those expenditures. If I spent $2 and I did it correctly, they would pay me $4 for the more beautiful kitchen.

My standard kitchen, when we were doing condominiums, might cost me $3,000 a unit. But if, all of a sudden, I brought in cabinets from Italy as a marketing tool, this Italian kitchen would cost me $2,000 more per unit but people would then be willing to give me $6,000, $7,000, or $8,000 more per unit. The additional expense added to my bottom line profitability.

As a matter of fact, when you have sales offices, the vignettes you do are of the kitchens and bathrooms. Because everything else is just spacing. Apartments are, by definition, small. The wife—who is very, very, very important in the purchase or rental decision, believe me—is most interested in kitchens and bathrooms.

What I found, though, when we did the market analysis and customer surveys, was that while bathrooms and kitchens were important in all these rental jobs, the fact was that the bathrooms and kitchens we did were within a standard we really couldn't deviate from too much. Because if we deviated the costs would be prohibitive.

So it wasn't like I could put Italian cabinets in a rental. What I did was put in—and we coined this phrase—"European-style cabinets."

What was that? Instead of having gaps between the two doors when they close, which was the standard American style, we did it so they were flush, like the European style. And we still got the same guy in a factory here to build it for us, at the same price. But now it was European style.

So you use words. For example: "Garden tubs." Those were the same tubs, we just made them a little bigger. "Decorator carpeting." We asked our decorator to pick three colors of the same carpet. So the words you use become extremely important to the marketing of your product.

The other thing was I watched people and I always looked at things that people did. And then I wondered why I didn't have this or that.

Let me give you an example. Apartments are very small. So the kitchens were never the built-in, very expensive appliances. When I went into market-rate rentals—this is a long time ago now—I saw that nobody was providing microwave ovens even though many of our tenants, after moving in, would buy these larger ones that barely fit into the small apartments. At the time microwaves were much more expensive than now. But I made this incredible deal with a manufacturer in which he would provide me with large quantities of microwaves for around $70 each, a great price then. I got these small ones, because we had small kitchens. And they were under-mounted under the cabinet. I didn't have any space where I could put this little microwave except for right underneath the cabinet. So that's what I did, and it was a big hit!

The other thing I saw was that a lot of people, whenever they were cooking, were looking at little TVs they had in their kitchens. And I decided to give them as an inducement to rent. No one was doing this. At the time, the only thing I could afford was a little black-and-white TV that I under-mounted on the other side of the cabinet. Can you imagine? Again, it was a huge success.

You have to keep looking at trends and patterns, and figuring out how to put them to work for you. They need to be highly visible and of importance to the customer.

In rentals, we were among the first to do open kitchens. We had been doing kitchens that were either totally closed or maybe had a little pass-through. I totally opened them. In a small place that's what people wanted. They wanted to have their friends come over and be talking to them while they cooked.

They were another hit. Everybody started copying us. In a while everybody had open kitchens, under-mounted TVs, and microwaves.

When I started the garden apartments nobody had a washer and dryer in the units. All of them had laundry rooms with those coin machines. And we were making a fortune with those coin machines. But I started thinking, "Who wants to go in their pajamas and put change in the machines and do their laundry with everybody else?" Their things got lost and it was a pain to leave your apartment to go start and then retrieve your laundry. So first we came up with the idea of adding washer and dryer hookups, and they could buy their own washer and dryer if they wanted. And that developed into us providing washers and dryers with the unit and just charging a little more rent.

So we were changing all the time. And if you want to be successful, you have to be changing, too. You have to always be looking to see what people want. You read it in magazines. You see it on television. You see it by constantly checking the competition, not only in your market but in what the hot markets are across the country.

As I mentioned before, when I was doing apartments, California and Texas were the hot spots. Atlanta became one with Post Properties, a competitor of ours, which started doing great innovations when it came to landscaping. So you know what I did? I called up John Williams, the owner of Post. I said, "This is going to sound like a strange thing, but can I have somebody show me how you do things?"

It was a great honor for him and he agreed to show me. This guy was, I don't know, ten years older than me, he had more experience. And I was the guy who was growing and becoming a force in Florida real estate. And he took me all through Atlanta, and he showed me the landscaping, how they had gotten the nursery, and how he made the landscaping an integral part of his sales process. And I was like a sponge.

Never be afraid to ask. Learn from others. If somebody calls you up and says, "I think you're the best and I'd really like to know how you do certain things," it's flattering. If people see that you're well intentioned and you're going to get somewhere they will share with you.

People like helping people. People like to tell you why they are good. People like building relationships.

John is still a friend. And today we're doing some deals together. He understood that you have to put your money where it can be seen, where it has an impact on the customer's decision-making process. You have to do the same.

RULE #8: ONE BIG CHANGE CAN BE WORTH MORE THAN TWO HUNDRED LITTLE ONES

One of the problems with putting the microwaves and the TVs in was the cost. Individually, $70 for a TV or a microwave is not that much. Put one in every apartment, though, and it adds up. In a one-hundred-unit apartment complex, you're talking another $14,000 just for TVs and microwaves. Change the counters and appliances and you could be talking $3,000 per apartment. Again, not that much—until you add it up. Then you're talking $300,000 in extra costs.

With that kind of math, the expenses for little touches can quickly grow astronomically. So I had to figure out, always, where I had to spend my money in order to get the most bang for my buck.

We realized that amenities were very, very important. In condos, for example, I've found that people are really, really concerned about the first impression not only that they have but that their friends have when they come see the lobby. So I might have a $1 million budget for a lobby in a three-hundred-unit project that is costing me $100 million to build. If I make a change to the lobby—to put more art in the lobby, or to get the best designer—that might cost me 10 percent more. So I spend $100,000 more.

It might sound expensive, but, remember, that is one change. There's only one lobby.

If I make changes in the apartments, then it's three hundred times whatever that cost was. So changes you can make that create an impact by doing one thing that emanates to the whole building are typically more economical. They produce better leverage in the expenditure of your money than changes you have to multiply by the number of apartments.

It's true now and it was true when we were considering upgrading the cabinets or the tubs in the apartments when I was first starting. It was much cheaper for me to change one thing in the common area than to change three hundred things.

We had to do it in all the apartments. But with the amenities, there was only one: the clubhouse and the pool. That was one thing. It was much cheaper, and much easier, for me to make the change in the amenity package than to make a change in the apartments. And the change was highly visible and reached all the renters or buyers in the complex.

The other thing I started understanding when I was looking at the market was that apartments, by definition, are very small. Your one-bedroom is typically seven hundred or eight hundred square feet. Your two-bedroom is between nine hundred and eleven hundred square feet. So people know they're going to a small place.

If you invited ten friends over you couldn't fit them in your apartment. You had to take them to a restaurant. In our projects, you could take them to the clubhouse. The clubhouse had a kitchen, a bar and billiard table. So you could be with your ten friends and it was like having a five-thousand-square-foot home. Because the clubhouse was made for them to entertain. You could invite twenty friends to Monday Night Football. You couldn't do that in an apartment anywhere. But our clubhouse not only had the space, we had Monday Night Football every Monday night. With large screen TVs, popcorn, etc. The money, again, was spent on one clubhouse which was highly visible.

We gave them these incredible pools, these clubhouses with billiard tables, kids' rooms where we had Nintendo games, movies, and so forth. Your apartment was small, but we made the living space outside your immediate apartment great. We made you visualize this great living experience in which you got out of your apartment and you would go to your clubhouse.

We created programs that made the lifestyle very cool.

Over time our rentals became known for the life style our amenities and landscaping delivered. We always had the highest occupancy rates.

The other thing we did was from the very beginning we always thought that a tree was the most beautiful piece of architecture. I don't care what kind of apartments you build, for me landscaping was always more beautiful. So we covered our properties with landscaping. Even today, when you go to many of our places you don't even see the buildings. And we became known for giving that extreme natural beauty.

All that came from our market analysis and from investing in the things that really matter.

KEY PRINCIPLES

- Don't give your customer any less than what you would expect for yourself.

- The difference between good and great lies in the details.

- Spend your money on work that can be seen.

CITYPLACE,
West Palm Beach, Florida
C. J. Walker Photography Inc.

8 · THE FOUR KEYS FOR MANAGING AND GROWING

"Hire tough and

manage easy."

T he fundamentals of development never change. Whether you're doing your very first job or juggling twenty at a time, the principles remain the same. You have to know the numbers. You have to know your people. And you have to take a long view.

As your company grows you'll have more numbers and people to keep track of, and more things to keep an eye on and think about. That's just the way it goes. As you gain experience, you'll be able to handle more things at the same time. You'll be able to assimilate information about a job more quickly, and zero in on what's important faster.

In some ways it's like going from being a musician concentrating on playing a single instrument to being an orchestra conductor. In the beginning, it takes all your concentration to read the notes and place your fingers in the right spots. It's slow and laborious.

As you gain experience, you stop thinking consciously about where your fingers are. You play more smoothly. You can handle more complicated compositions.

When you become a conductor, you're not thinking about one instrument and whether it sounds right or not. You're thinking about the whole orchestra. You're reading the whole score and guiding each and every musician to create the symphony you envision. And if a single note on a single violin is off, you know it immediately and you can call for it to be corrected just as fast.

It's the same in development. It doesn't get easier as you grow. It requires constant, unwavering attention to every single detail. But as you gain experience, you'll learn to spot that sour note immediately, long before it ruins the project—or your company.

Key #1: Know the Numbers and the Details

If you don't know exactly what you're making, and how much you're spending, you will fail. That's all there is to it. You will fail.

Your main goal at any for-profit company is to maximize returns, and there are only two ways to do that: increase revenues or decrease costs. You're always looking for ways to do both—but don't let short-term profits undermine your long-term plan of providing quality, value, and customer satisfaction. That's the way you build the brand and ensure long-term profitability.

So you have to know all the components of the revenue side well—marketing, sales, comparable studies, economic trends, collections, customer satisfaction, and so on.

And you have to watch your expenses—*closely!* That means every single dollar. You have to watch your personnel costs, your material costs, and your overhead. Right down to the cost of copies and long-distance calls. If something kicks up suddenly, you have to spot it and figure out why. Then you have to figure out how you can bring it back down again.

You do that by putting detailed controls in place and remaining perpetually vigilant.

In the beginning, in managing my management company, the ones handling my rental buildings, I used to be brutal. I had meetings once a month and I would make them go over every dollar at their project—their revenues and their expenses on a monthly basis broken down by utilities, real estate taxes, staffing . . . hundreds of line items. I would make them compare them against the budget they said they were going to achieve. And against last year's results.

But not only would I make them do that, I made them compare them with all the other similar jobs we had. And we had ratios that we kept. One person inside the office per one hundred apartments, so many for maintenance, and so on. So I had all these charts and ratios for all these different jobs. And I could tell you what I was doing to the penny. I could tell you when something was wrong with utilities—for example, if there was a leak—because I had all the per-unit comparisons in all these apartments. And I would say, "If we've been spending forty dollars a month here, why is this other one spending eighty dollars this month?" So either we got a double bill, or there was a leak. And I was exhaustive with the review of the numbers.

We ran a management company that was so efficient it was unbelievable, because nothing escaped us. And they were so ready when they came to the staff meetings because they knew I was on top of things.

For many years, I trained others to do that for me, to keep an eye on the numbers at meetings so I wouldn't have to. Matt Allen, my COO, is now the person who does that. I am fortunate that he has thoroughly learned the exhaustive review process. And what I do is, once a quarter, I will look at the results, which are now done for me in a summarized form, but also still showing relevant comparables. That way I can very rapidly look at the results, compare them with budget expectations, and concentrate on looking for exceptions, such as when costs in an area seem out of line with other, similar projects.

So now I am managing by exceptions. And annually they prepare the budgets for the whole year. Then we have a big planning session in which we do everything we used to do once a month. We ask, "Why is the budget like this? Why is this so much for utilities? Why are you spending this a month? Why are you projecting these rent increases and this occupancy?" We go through that extensively, and now others do what I used to do on a monthly basis. They check all the expenditures and the revenues.

Those are called property management meetings. In them, you discuss whether the products are being managed correctly, if rents are being maximized and expenses are being reduced, and if the properties are being kept up the way they should so they maintain their value and their attractiveness.

We also continue to do extensive market studies in the rentals. We determine whether our competitors are increasing their rents, giving rent concessions, or putting out new advertising. We examine their occupancy rate compared to ours. We are constantly going through the market so we can be on top of rent increases. Because expense control is important, but you always need to be increasing the revenue. That's the way you really impact the bottom line.

That has been a very important part of our company. And we've made a lot of money. And always by keeping the highest level of rents, and by keeping the highest level of professionalism in the company. That's why I have a management company—because I wanted to control that as a way of making sure the value in the future is there. That's one part of management.

The other part of management is managing the financial condition of the company. We have meetings in our company that we call the cash needs meetings. It's still called cash needs, because in the beginning they were really cash needs: How do I make payroll?

So it's the same philosophy whether you have a lot or a little—I want to know once a month what money is coming in and what money is going out.

We do this religiously once a month. I sit with all my financial people. It takes a few hours. We look at what happened last month: This was coming in, this was going out, this is our position. And these are lines of credit available to us if we need to support that cash position. These are taken out into six-month time periods in great detail and then, in lesser detail, in one-, two- and three-year segments. At all times we want to make sure we are adequately protected in the short and long term.

That way I know how much our revenues are, how much we're spending, and what possible problems are out there. We play different scenarios, the what-ifs, to see if there are scenarios under which we could be financially squeezed. Fortunately, our review of corporate cash and our conservative project funding has allowed us to maintain very strong cash reserves, should that rainy day ever appear.

We also have development meetings, every two weeks. One is focused more on marketing and the other more on budgetary matters. The project managers are expected to be the lead in every one of those meetings. We have the senior VP there to correct or to add, but the project manager leads the way. So our young guys who have grown to be project managers take charge in the development meetings. They are in charge of preparing the agenda and leading us through it. I tell them I don't want the senior guy to do it. I want these kids to handle it. I want to see what's going on. I want to see what they know and how they have grown.

These meetings really have two main purposes. One is to bring me up-to-date with what is going on so I know if problems are developing. I no longer have the time to go visit everything every week like I used to. So I need to see this project through their eyes. The second important reason is that I am seeing the way the project managers think and grow. Are they really thinking about this? Are they really getting everything down? Are they really seeing the issues with the jobs? Are they connecting the dots? Do they understand all the development functions: development, marketing, construction, budget?

My role is to ask questions critically so things don't get lost. They'll give me something that says, "We've had five sales over the past two weeks, and our new marketing is this and this, and these are some of the new things we're trying."

So I'll look over what they've done and ask them what's bringing in the sales. I want to know what's successful and what isn't. I want them to determine if the ads are bringing people in, if the brokers are bringing them, or if they are attracted to us by our Web site.

Or, for example, if a project has been selling for a while, the market conditions might have changed. Then I'll tell my people to go into the marketplace again and update all the comps. They need to find out who's selling, who's not, and why. Just because we're selling slowly doesn't mean the whole market is selling slowly. If we're slow and the whole market is slow, it's even more important. Then we need to figure out who's getting the few sales that are going through, and how.

In that meeting, we'll go over construction issues and look at the work schedule to see if the job is proceeding without delays and within budget. I expect them to tell me everything that's going on—are slow deliveries or missing materials slowing down the construction? Do all the subcontractors have enough people working the job?

I've got to see things fairly rapidly as I go through these meetings, to spot problems early. It's the project manager's job to be on top of these things, to see—and foresee—problems, and find solutions before little issues turn into major ones. So I need to be inquisitive, because many times they don't tell me everything. Many times they don't want to tell me about the problems because they don't want to get in trouble, but that's the most important information. So I've got to get that information out of them.

That's how I manage the whole development process. I make sure they make those agendas comprehensive and meaningful—that they include all the relevant and significant information we need to spot issues and make decisions.

Each project agenda might be three or four pages long and cover development, construction, and marketing and sales. They break it down by categories. Development issues are anything from building permits to political issues, those types of things. Construction issues, of course, deal with the contractors and subcontractors. Are they keeping pace? Where do we stand on deliveries? Are material cost escalations affecting us? Marketing issues have to do with: Are we selling this thing the best way we can? How many contracts do we have signed, and for how much? Which sales are in the works, but haven't closed yet? What are we *not* doing that we could do to sell better? Tell me what we're doing and, even more important, be ready to tell me why. There's always a tendency to become complacent. So one of my roles is to be the gadfly—the one who says, "Hey! This is not enough."

While they're talking and answering my questions, I'm making notes. Because the next time we meet I'll take out the previous agenda with all my notes to make sure that they're following up. Because when you've got sixty jobs, there is no way you can keep it all in your head. I still keep a frightening amount of it fresh in my mind, but those are the big things, or the little things that I'm afraid are becoming big things. But even then, all of that is backed up on paper. I always say, "Make notes; make to-do lists." That's how you really keep track of everything and make sure none of the details slip through the cracks. Otherwise, you'll be amazed at how quickly small problems grow, and things that you forget about become major, expensive, time-consuming issues. And all the while, you'll be kicking yourself for letting them get that way.

Take notes. Catch problems early. Save yourself time, money, and headaches.

> Take notes. Catch problems early.
> Save yourself money and headaches.

When they finish going through the agenda, they will have their own to-do lists, but I will have my own list of things I need to take care of myself: a partner is not reacting to this, and this kid is too young to really call the partner and make him do certain things; I will have on my to-do list: Call the partner. Tell him we need to do whatever it is. If I see somebody is slacking off in construction, I may need to talk to the head of the construction company to tell him, "Hey, you better get your project manager to handle this." I will make some of those calls. If we are having trouble with the city and I need to call the mayor or call the head of a department, I will write that down.

So I will have a list of my to-do things, things that it is better for me to do, or more effective for me to do, than it is for some of the younger people. I'll have my list; they'll have theirs. Each of us takes full responsibility for ours.

And then, before the meeting ends, we will have a set of instructions as to what the expectations are for the next couple of weeks, when we're going to come back and talk about these things. So, for example, many times we don't bring the construction people to the development meetings. But if we're having construction problems or delays, I will then make the decision that for the time being, for the next couple of meetings at least, I want the head of construction for the job to be there and to be reporting directly. And then he will tell me directly about the window delays, the construction, who is late, who's not. That will give me a much better feel for what is happening.

So the development meeting is a detailed meeting about the status and the possible problems the job will have. Don't tell me about the problems now, as they're happening. Think about future problems you may be having. Don't tell me it's a problem when the plumber went broke. Tell me it's a problem when you see a guy who should be having eight people at the job site only having four people, and he started to fall behind. Tell me then, don't tell me when it's too late.

We have early-warning signals in all of these jobs. In marketing. In sales. And in construction. That's the way you manage the process. And those are the basic things you have. You have development issues. You have construction issues. You have marketing and sales issues.

We cover all of that in what we call the informal meeting. Two weeks later, we do what we call the formal meeting—where we do extremely extensive budgets. Once a month we will go in there, and we will not only talk about change orders that the contractors might want or increases in insurance that the insurance company told us about, we will be asking, "Are there any *potential* change orders?"

Potential change orders can be of two types: the ones you make because you want the project to be better. For example, I don't like the balconies and right now we could have this other balcony type that would make the building look much better, but it will cost us another $100,000. So then we collectively ask, "Is it better to put in that type of balcony? Why? Will we be able to get our money back for them in the sales price? Even if we can't, is it still important to us to do it?" We discuss it and we make a decision. The other ones are not of our choosing: The engineer messed up and the fire safety system they designed does not meet code. The fire inspector came over and said we've got to change it. So I ask my construction guy whose fault it is.

"Clearly it's the contractor's fault. He should have done this." If that's my construction guy's answer, then we tell the contractor, "We're not going to pay for this change order. This is your baby."

Contractors will always try to get you with the change orders. Because usually we are in the middle of the job and we can't change contractor or subcontractors and they will try to inflate prices. For example, if we have to do new sprinkler heads and they each cost $50, they'll put $100. It's a way for them to make extra money. So we have all of our technicians price it all out ourselves. Then we will fight the change order with credible information.

And I have all the young project managers in my company there while I'm doing this with all the construction people so that they're learning. You might have been with me two or three years and you're learning everything that has to do with marketing because you're there making all the marketing changes and all the decisions with me and the marketing group. You're learning everything about construction. So a guy with an MBA who knows nothing about construction and nothing about marketing and sales will become pretty well versed in those things after he finishes a couple of deals with me.

So the staff meetings allow us to manage the jobs and to train our young developers at the same time.

So those types of decisions come with discussions that happen as you manage. Management is an interchange, but I expect that all the people who are in those meetings talking to me are prepared. If they aren't, that's when I get really annoyed. If you're not ready to discuss this with me, and if you're not ready to come with ideas, then don't come to the management meeting. Don't just give me facts, tell me what they mean and if we need to do something about them.

I want them to come prepared to discuss issues. What can we do better? What are some problems we can have in the future? And how do we prepare for those problems we can have in the future?

Visualizing problems. Expecting things to go wrong. It is highly important.

Informal Development Meeting—Know the Numbers and Details

Agenda—Informal Staff Meeting   June 6, 2007

❖ *SALES*

➤ **HUD contracts—115 contracts** totaling **$221.8MM**. All contracts are hard with full 10% deposits. *(See enclosed Sales Report.)*

➤ **Potential sales** *(See enclosed Hot Prospects List.)*

- An offer has been received for 3902, a sky residence, for $3.4MM ($439K below first price level). Details will be presented at the meeting.

- We have mailed out a contract for unit 2604 to the broker in Turkey.

- There has been no further activity from the broker with the 10-unit bulk-purchase deal since the contracts were prepared two weeks ago.

➤ **2nd Deposits**—We have received **60 ($12.1MM)** in second deposits out of 111 contracts that are due at groundbreaking. This includes $580M in partial deposits on 7 additional contracts. We are at **59%** in collected second deposits of the **$20.5MM** required by our lender by the end of August. *(See enclosed Second Deposits Schedule.)*

We have announced the incentive program to the outside brokers to increase their second advance on commissions to 40% on contracts completing their 2nd deposits by the end of June. We are also providing a bonus to the in-house staff subject to their collections this month.

❖ *BUILDING PERMIT*

➤ Tower/East Parcel—Approvals have been received for all disciplines, only pending final approval by the Building Department. Issuance of the full building permit is anticipated by June 15, 2007, well within the 120-day conditions precedent established by our lender.

➤ West Garage—Foundation permit documents have been received and will be walked through the county BCEPD this week. The foundation permit documents will then be submitted to the city on Monday, June 11. We are working to obtain the foundation permit by no later than July 12, per the loan requirement.

❖ *GENERAL CONTRACTOR* (24-month schedule)

➤ Coastal Construction has submitted their 1st requisition for payment, which is currently being reviewed by the lender.

➤ 251 of the 805 tower piles have been installed to date, which accounts for 31% of the work scope. We are 3 weeks into the anticipated 12-week duration schedule.

➤ The contractor is excavating for pile cap installation along the eastern building line.

➤ The GC is obtaining the building permit for the construction trailers on the west parcel. We anticipate relocating our project administration to the field the week of June 15.

❖ *MARKETING*

➤ **IMI—Contract Termination**

As discussed at the last staff meeting, the IMI contract has been terminated as of the end of May 2007. They have turned over the marketing material and have agreed to a 60-day transition period to download the data from their system to SMW.

➤ **New Ad Agency**

We have presentations scheduled for next week from 3 agencies (Bridger Conway, T.J. Sabo, and Seraph Miami). They will be presenting a mock-up of the newsletter and a new ad concept for the next season.

➤ **Events**

In the month of **May**, we had several events at the sales center:

• **May 5**—Happy Hour for the CKG Mastery Convention for 150 top producing brokers from all over the USA and Canada.

• **May 6**—Lunch for 4 brokers from Catag Commercial—Top Brokerage firm in Rome, Italy.

• **May 16**—"Pick up your check party," a broker cocktail for about 80 brokers to distribute their commission checks, over $3.3MM.

• **May 18**—Brunch for Citi Group Realty in Sunny Isles.

• **May 30**—Broker lunch.

• **May 30**—Broker cocktail for 70 brokers and investors from Australia and New Zealand.

(continued)

- **May 31**—Broker lunch with French broker interested in promoting our project in Europe, especially France and Italy.

In the month of **June**, the following events are planned:

- **June 9–10**—Expo, 7,000 investors and prospects to attend.
- **June 28**—(Pending approval) Chamber of Commerce cocktail for 40 chamber members.
- **June—TBD:** Breakfasts, lunches, and cocktails with area brokers.
- **June–July**—The Hamptons. Looking for venues where we can participate as sponsors of events and tap into this important market.

➤ **Sales Promotion Trips**

A number of trips are planned during this summer to continue the outreach to the brokers and prospects abroad. Special attention will be devoted to New York City and the Hamptons. Our new sales associate is developing a schedule of trips to NY. (See enclosed list.) Some of the trips taken in the last months that will be followed up with repeat visits this month were as follows:

- **March 27–28**—Buenos Aires, Argentina: Meeting Points RE conference.
- **April 11**—Wall Street Showcase: event at Cipriani's with top Wall Street brokers.
- **April 15–18**—Caracas, Venezuela: *Gerénte* magazine Expo, 500 top brokers.
- **May 10–16**—Sales trip to Istanbul, Turkey. Top broker from Turkey presented project during a cocktail party for over 300 affluent prospects. Had great media coverage. A contract has been mailed out for unit 2604.
- **May 28–June 2**—Madrid, Spain: SIMA.

Trip schedules are pending confirmation to the following cities:

- **Moscow, Russia**—being planned with the local Russian broker who has sold 3 units to her Russian clients.
- **Paris, France**—planning to support French broker who sold a number of units at Villa Magna and is looking to move the contracts to other properties.
- **Brazil**—working with local Brazilian broker to set up a trip to São Paulo.

- **Mexico, Venezuela, Colombia, and Argentina**—to reinforce our product awareness prior to the So American mini-season traveling to So Florida in late summer.

➤ **PR**

- Press releases have gone out on the ground-breaking event, construction loan closing, broker event, and payment of commissions and the BASF Platinum Award.
- *El Nuevo Herald*'s special article on the BASF Platinum Award for architecture will be published sometime in June.
- Extensive coverage of the groundbreaking event has appeared in the *Miami Herald*, the *So Fla Business Journal*, *Selecta* magazine, *Las Olas*, *Biz Bash*, etc. Other coverage will include such magazines as *Edge*, *City & Shore*, *Home Ft. Lauderdale*, *House King*, *Social Affairs* (Hamptons issue), *Harper's Bazaar* in Spanish, etc.
- The May issue of *Miami Update* features project's interiors designed by Yabu Pushelberg and great photos of the sales center's interiors.
- We met with Phyllis Apple and are reviewing her proposal for international PR coverage thru a program sponsored thru the U.S. Commerce Department.

➤ **Video**

- We have retained Palm Beach Broadcast to produce a video. In addition to our sales center model interiors, they will shoot ground video of area attractions, such as the Diplomat Country Club Golf Course, the Diplomat Spa, Nikki Marina, the Bal Harbour Shops, the Ft. Lauderdale Airport, the Hard Rock Resort & Casino, the Gulfstream Park Race Track, area restaurants, etc. It will also include aerial video showing the site's oceanfront location and intracoastal frontage and the surrounding areas as far south as Sunny Isles and Bal Harbour and as far north as Las Olas Boulevard.
- We will be installing a camera on the sales center trained on the construction site to document live the construction progress. It will be wired to the Web site to provide current updates to our buyers and prospects.

(continued)

> **Signage**

- Additional signage will be placed on the intracoastal side of the property to capture the marine traffic.
- The construction fence on the beach side will be covered with signage screening as well.

MILESTONES	Original _Date_	Actual _Date_
• Start nonspecific Reservations	Feb 03, 2006	COMPLETE
• Finalize OLI's P&S Conditions	Feb 21, 2006	COMPLETE
• Opening of Temporary Sales Center	Mar 10, 2006	COMPLETE
• Site Plan and Zoning Approval	Apr 05, 2006	COMPLETE
• HUD Approval	Apr 15, 2006	COMPLETE
• Opening of Permanent Sales Center	Jun 01, 2006	COMPLETE
• Installation of Test Piles	Sept 2006	Mar 30, 2007
• Ground breaking	Oct 2006	Mar 30, 2007
• Sign GC Contract	May 2006	Apr 19, 2007
• Close Construction Loan	Oct 2006	Apr 30, 2007
• East Tower Foundation Permit	Sept 2006	May 03, 2007
• Construction Commencement	May 14, 2007	May 14, 2007
• East Tower Full Building Permit	Oct 2006	June 15, 2007
• West Garage Foundation Permit	July 2006	July 12, 2007
• Complete Tower Auger Cast Piles	Aug 2007	
• Complete Tower Pile Caps	Sept 2007	
• Commencement 1st Elevated Floor	Dec 2007	
• Commencement Condo Floors (Level 5)	Mar 2008	
• Complete Tower Superstructure (Top Out)	Oct 2008	
• Lobby, Arrival Court & Pool Deck	Apr 2009	
• Service Elevator Machine Rooms	Apr 2009	
• Temporary Certificate of Occupancy	May 2009	
• Certificate of Occupancy	Sept 2009	

Key #2: People Are All-Important

I'll say it again: People are all-important. You have to train and empower them so your company can grow and expand beyond you. At some point, as an entrepreneur, you need to get back to what it is you started doing. You are best at finding the deals, structuring the deals, making sure things are not going wrong, preparing the contingency plans.

But then, as you grow, the day-to-day, the execution, starts taking more and more of your time. If you let it, it will consume you and you won't have time to focus on the real core of your business. Yes, you have to keep an eye on the business details. But if you're not spotting deals and applying your vision to turn a site into something great that no one else has the imagination to do, you won't have any business to worry about. As you grow, the day-to-day operation has to be left to other people, those who you have hopefully taught well and empowered.

Even from very early on, as you assume the role of the guy who is going to go out there and get all the work and grow a company, you need to have somebody that minds the store, manages the product, deals with a lot of the stuff that is going to let you be the business getter. You need to be the guy who negotiates and does the deals.

So from the very beginning, I had to surround myself with people I could trust and hand things off to. I needed them to take care of a lot of the chores that need to be done so I could focus on finding and negotiating deals, on applying my vision to create great projects, to do many of the things we've already talked about. Without those people, I would have been so consumed by details that I would've never been able to grow.

That's why people are all-important. And surrounding yourself with a good team of talent begins with hiring the right people. I was reading a book that said hire tough and manage easy. And that is so true. It is so important to get people with talent who have energy, who have fire in their bellies. It makes the management process so much easier.

> Hire tough and manage easy.

I'm a strong believer that when you hire, hire talent. You can look for experience, but talent is more important. I can give you experience. I can teach you skills. I can't teach you talent. You either have it or you don't. Not everyone who picks up a paintbrush is Picasso. You can learn to hold one like him, how to mix the paints, how to draw. But you either see and execute like him, or you don't. That's talent. And I believe it's more important to fill my company with budding Picassos than with capable clerks.

Gut is extremely important. But then you have to test your gut. That first feeling you have when you meet somebody, when you talk to somebody and you get to know him and his family, speaks volumes. But it can deceive you. I wish I could say my gut is always right. It isn't. I have been really wrong. You have no idea how many times I've interviewed guys who I thought were great, and then I check them out and I go, "Oh, my God!" Some people are great salesmen, but they don't have the backbone. They look really good, but there is no depth to them at all. I call them the postage stamps: they look good, but they're paper thin. Then there are those people you meet and, in the beginning, you go, "Ewww!" Later, though, they turn out to be great individuals and employees. They're just different, you know? So yes, gut and first impressions are extremely important both for people and for deals. But then you have to dig in.

No matter what your gut and your experience tell you, and no matter how well they answer the questions, you have to check them out. That means not just references, but outside the references they give you, too. I wish I could say I haven't found the idiot yet who would give a reference who is going to say, "Don't hire him. This guy is terrible!" But you know what? I have.

Most people, though, won't put references that have anything but nice things to say about them. So check, yes, but don't stop at the people they worked *for*, talk to the customers they worked *with*, talk to the other companies they dealt with in their job. A project manager works with contractors and vendors. A general contractor deals with subs. An attorney deals with judges and other law firms. There are always sources who can help you round out your picture of someone.

And then, when you do bring them on board, keep them under fire. Keep them doing more things. Don't let them become placid. Don't let them become satisfied with themselves. Always give them more.

Keep their expectations growing. When you're dissatisfied with them, tell them! And tell them why they could've done better.

The hiring of people and driving them to be the best they can be is extremely important.

For example, the other day, somebody hired this guy who happened to be from a country where they are much more meek by tradition than perhaps we are here in the United States. This person has a great college background in economics, but he never spoke. So one day, I went to my senior guy and I asked, "What's he doing?"

"Well, you know, I've got him checking this and that."

I said, "Wait a minute. This guy is forty years old. He's got a master's degree from an Ivy League university and you're telling me he's not doing pro formas and not getting involved in some of the financials. That's stupid."

So I took them both into my office and I turned to the new guy and I said, "Look, in order to grow in this company you've got to speak up. And it may not come easy to you, but you know what? I have not learned how to read minds yet. So in order for me to know if you're good, better, or medium, I need you to open your mouth. What the hell are you doing? I don't know. I need you to start doing pro formas right now. You can do those budget updates that we do every month. When the senior guy has to do it you're taking away from his time, when I could be using him for other things. If you can't do market studies and go out and get an update, then you're never going to be a developer."

Then I turned to the senior guy and I said, "It's not only his fault. It's your fault. You're supposed to throw him in the pool and give him the tools and tell him to swim. If he can't do it the first time, tell him why he didn't do it well. Second or third time, he shouldn't be here with us."

My God, what a change. The guy talks now. And he had it in him all along. It could have turned out that he didn't, but then at least we'd know. But he did have it in him. He was just from a different cultural background, was very respectful, and you had to bring it out of him.

So my role is to bring it out. To be the guy who is always questioning them. The guy who won't let them be lazy and who will bring out the best in them.

I really believe that managers need to do that to earn the respect of people, so they know that whatever I'm asking them to do, I have done myself—and I am still willing to do it. I am not beyond the everyday involvement it takes to get us there.

I think that makes them sharper. It makes them respect you and obey you when you ask them to do something. Because they know it's based on experience, not just on some idea you came up with in your head.

They know that. I hear stories through lenders and others. They say that imitation is the best form of flattery, and I'm proud when somebody says, "You've got a bunch of little Jorge Pérezes running around." That's good. I hope I do. It's what I try to do.

That's why we give them so much responsibility from the very beginning. We're growing developers by putting them to work developing. That's why we have the junior guys, the project managers, handle the development meetings. We want them to be able to handle all the aspects of a project—development, construction, marketing *and* sales.

Other companies tend to specialize. They've got a guy in construction. They've got a guy in marketing. I have always liked to work with people who are generalists. So I build managers who can do everything.

The reason I've always liked this is twofold. First, because that's the way I am. That's the way I tend to think. And I think that if you don't have people who know something about all the different aspects it takes to develop, they don't tend to connect the dots as well. There are decisions you make in construction, for example, that are good as a construction manager. And you might have a guy who's a real expert in construction, who would take care of you that way. But those decisions are not necessarily good for the overall development. So I like to have the guy who thinks about the overall project.

How do you train the guy to be all-around? You do it by mentoring; instead of having him take courses, you do it by mentoring. And if they make money for you, let them participate in the earnings. They'll work harder and make you even more money.

So what we do is we take a young guy with an MBA, for example, and we say, "You're going to work with this guy who's a project manager already." And just like I said I needed people who could do things so I could grow, so do the project managers. So they get these assistant project managers to help them in everything. And while they do, they're becoming knowledgeable in all the details so they can become project managers themselves.

It's on-the-job training and there's somebody who can guide them. We have never had training programs. We're not a company with how-to programs. We define responsibilities in the job description and tell them that these are the things they're going to be responsible for. Then they learn them as they go along. It's a lot of throwing them in the water and pushing them to swim. When they're not swimming we give them a hand and help them a little bit. But it's really up to them. They start doing this and then they do pro formas and then they deal with the construction guy and then they deal with the building department, then they deal with the marketing people and the PR people and the salespeople. But all the time they are being corrected and receiving feedback.

So by the time two years go by, they can do everything they need to to handle a project from the day we break ground to the day we hand it over to the condo association. I always say, "I'll put my young guys against anybody in the whole country." Because they know about the whole development process very well.

People become very, very important for the whole success of the organization.

I want my people to go out and really use their creativity. I want them to bring me deals—to look at a piece of property and say, "This one is perfect for . . ."

I want them to do that, even if it's the dumbest deal in the world. I will always sit with them and say, "Thank you. This is the dumbest deal in the world. Nevertheless, keep at it because I really like what you just did. You brought me a deal. You used your imagination. What I don't want you to do is just sit and do what you're doing and never bring me a deal. I don't want you to just take my orders. Use your imagination, and let's see how we can improve what you've got." Then I will take time to explain to them why the deal they brought to me didn't make sense.

I love it when they come over and say, "Hey, I think the way we designed the pool—and you approved it—is wrong. But if we did this thing I saw on another one . . ."

I might totally disagree with them and say, "No, stick with that." But I would say, "I love the fact that you were thinking, that you brought that to me."

And by the way, I never get so enamored with my own thinking that I would not change it right away if I thought they were right and say, "Awesome thinking!"

You empower people, and you let them make decisions. You let them know you're still going to get mad if the decisions are the wrong decisions, but that you are going to be madder if they don't make decisions. They're only going to grow by taking chances and getting burned. They know that my wrath is part of growing up, and part of becoming a great developer.

That prepares them to take on other responsibilities and allows you to promote them. If you're developing talent correctly in your company, then you should find the best talent for higher levels within your own company.

Whenever possible, I like to grow internally. It gives people the opportunity to go up and then opens up a space and somebody else can go up. Also, he will be better than an outsider because I already know he is really brilliant and full of energy, and he knows the company's ways.

Being right for a position isn't about just having the technical expertise of how to run a project or a company. It's about dealing with the personalities and adapting to the corporate culture. Every company does things differently. Our pro formas are different. And our reporting is different. The way we do the meetings is different. The way we do our projects and budget updates is different. The way we do sales and marketing is different. When you bring somebody from outside they have to learn all of that.

If you look to somebody from within, this is a guy who has been sitting through all these meetings. And I'm always watching to see how they handle things. You want to see how they interact with other people, how they resolve conflicts, how they make decisions. And you want to see if you can trust them.

Trust becomes immensely important, particularly as you get larger and bigger in whatever you do. Because the less you see things and the less you're personally involved, the more you have to trust others to come through for you. You have to let people make decisions. You are entrusting them with your livelihood. You've got to remember that when I do a project in Acapulco it's a $200 million job. Almost any one of these jobs could cause serious damage to the company.

So you rely on a lot of people making decisions. You question and so forth, but you rely on them following certain procedures—both partners and employees. That's why one of the greatest frustrations for me when something goes wrong is not that the person wasn't intelligent, and didn't achieve this, but that I really put my hopes in this person and they let me down. They let me down because they just did not want to achieve what they could have—either because of dishonesty or not trying. So I misplaced my trust. You meet a lot of very bright guys, but what I have tried to do is meet, above all, good people. I want to hire and partner with people who have a very high moral standard above other considerations, people who practice my guiding principles: honesty, integrity, and morality.

> More important than hiring smart people is hiring good people.

That's why a lot of my partners become my friends, because they are people I would want to be friends with. I start out with that notion. I would never want to be friends with a person who doesn't have integrity and loyalty, so why would I want to be a partner with that person?

I assume, at the outset, that everyone might be trying to take advantage of me. My mind is always capable of understanding what can go wrong and what bad things people can do. So while I am not thinking someone's going to do certain things to me, I'm prepared for the possibility that bad things can happen.

That's why I dot the i's and cross the t's, at least until I get to know them well enough and deal with them in enough deals that experience tells me I don't have to do it anymore. Through many years of doing deals with my partner, Steve Ross, I know that I can trust him implicitly. We have flowed tens of millions of dollars into deals that he comes up with or I come up with without the other one having an iota of an idea of what the deal is about. Forget about having a paper signed or anything else like that. I have total, absolute 100 percent trust in his capacity and loyalty and integrity and moral fiber.

Pick the right people to work for you, and with you as your partners. Surrounding yourself with trustworthy, creative, and capable people will increase the ease with which you manage and grow your company.

Key #3: Consolidate to Control the Variables

Another thing we've done from the very beginning is to try to integrate as many facets of the development process as possible under one roof. From the start we felt that controlling all the variables gave us an edge and did not leave us vulnerable.

> Integrate as many facets of development
> as you can under one roof.
> Controlling the variables gives you an edge.

For example, when I have a buyer who wants one of our condominiums, it's important for that person to know he can get a mortgage for his unit. So instead of making that process a horrible one of, "Oh, God! Let me go see twenty people," I said, why don't we establish a relationship with a major financial institution—it happens to be Wells Fargo—and have our own crews of people that will solve a very important part of the buy?

"Mr. Smith, if you need a mortgage, here we are and we are the best. It's not Related, it's Wells Fargo–Related, and we have all these mortgage programs."

That way, Mr. Smith doesn't have to shop around for a loan to buy one of our condominiums. It's good for him and it's good for us. The sale going through depends on them having the money. I don't collect until they get the backing. So why would I leave such a crucial element of my profitability to someone else?

And we'll use an outside contractor, a general contractor, negotiate with them and so forth. But we have in-house senior construction people who are the best. We also hire people who are owner representatives, so that should there be a hiccup, and this has happened a number of times, we would have enough expertise in-house to take over that job and finish it. That's an important thing for us to know. And for them to know. Because if they think they've got you, they've got you.

You've got to keep them honest. If you don't have major construction expertise, how do you know that the change orders are real? That they're charging you the right price? That they're going to finish on time and there are no problems? So we were very sure from day one that we should have that construction expertise in-house.

Same thing with the management company. How do we take the rentals we produce and give them to someone else to manage? These are great assets. We wanted to add value to our inventory by being responsible for the management.

Marketing, too. Why depend on somebody to tell us what we should do? We did hire outside companies, but we had tremendous expertise to guide them. We wanted to create books about our projects and our company, but we're not printers. We don't do that. We don't have the designers, the guy who does the drawings, or any of the other technical expertise it takes to make a book. But we do have the people who are capable of guiding them, who know enough to know when it's bad and can say, "Go at it again."

We have marketing and communications departments. One handles public relations and the other handles marketing. And they are in charge of working with the developers and making sure that all the agencies we are using are the best and that they're not slacking off. That they charge us the best prices. They do all the media buys. They are the most creative and the most responsive.

The same with sales. I could hire a sales company. And then what happens if somebody was a bigger client? They would take all their best people and put them elsewhere. So what did I have to do? I had to go in-house so I knew every one of my jobs was getting the attention it deserved.

How do I control financing so that I get the best deal there is? I can go to brokers, and they represent me and they represent a hundred other people. So I wanted us to have those relationships with the lenders ourselves. I didn't want to go through an intermediary. I wanted to look them in the eye and know they knew who we were and that they knew they had to give me the best deal. So we became the best friends of all the lenders and we took the financing function totally within the company.

So we felt all those things had to be controlled by us in order for us to be able to deliver and manage the type of end product we wanted to see.

It works. It works well. It will work for you.

And you don't have to wait until your company is handling billions of dollars' worth of deals to do it.

From the very beginning, when I was just starting out and I couldn't have that staff, what I tried to do was make allegiances with people that I became very important to. I wanted to work with a construction company where I would be his most important client. That way, he became almost like in-house. I went to a marketing agency that was small, but that could see that with us they could grow. So they weren't going to pay more attention to other people.

Back then, I didn't have a marketing person or a communications person or a construction person. I was it. I was the construction guy. I was the marketing guy. I was the sales guy. But I picked my allegiances carefully and built the relationships so that they would almost be like in-house personnel. They would almost feel like they were part of the company and would have a vested interest in the growth of the company.

And as I became stronger and larger and financially more capable, I hired them. They became my head of marketing. They became the head of my management company. I had Alicia Cervera as an outside sales contractor, and when I saw what an asset she was I brought her in. She became my partner in our sales company, RCRS. I did the same thing in marketing and PR. I got the best people and brought them in. When we needed in-house counsel because we were having so many legal issues, we brought them in from the law firms we had used before.

When you're starting out and you can't afford staff, outsource the functions you need. But look at those arrangements as trial periods that allow you to see how people work for you and with you. They allow you to develop a pool of potential partners and staff to draw on the day you do want to consolidate a particular function within the company.

Key #4: Take the Long View

If you're staring at the tip of your nose, you're going to run into walls. You have to look ahead to see where you're going. In the same way, if you can't see past the immediate issue on your project, you'll lose sight of the big picture. With your company, if you're only thinking about today, you won't be prepared for tomorrow.

You're going to be making decisions every day. Even when it seems like what you're dealing with only matters right now, it doesn't. Short-term decisions affect the long term. So never lose sight of your long-term goals when you're making them.

> Never lose sight of your long-term goals when you're making short-term decisions.

You could be dealing with something as simple as picking paint for a building exterior. Does the color matter for the long term? You bet it does. Do you want people associating your name with some ugly building? No. If you use some gaudy gold instead of a delicate amber, everyone is going to associate your company with eyesores. Does the quality matter? Even more. If it's peeling in a year, they're going to associate your name with shoddy work.

What happens? You make a short-term decision to save a few pennies and you strip untold value from your reputation.

I told you in the chapter on securing financing, sell something, even if you don't want to, so you can establish success and a track record. That's taking the long view. You may be a holder instead of a flipper, but in the long term you need people to see that you produce profits and pay back your loans. Your track record cements your credibility.

We already talked about building the best. You want to be known for quality work. If you make a short-term decision to skimp, or to deliver a lesser product, you're being penny wise and pound foolish.

You always have to remember that you're building a brand, not just a building. Your brand is what will decide how much your company can grow, and what kinds of projects you'll be able to take on. It allows you to leverage what you've done so you can take on the next bigger thing. If you're known for turning out junk just so you can make a quick buck, Donald Trump is never going to partner with you. I'm never going to partner with you.

I've told you again and again about the importance of building relationships. If you're nearsighted about your company, you'll take advantage of others in negotiations. You'll try to take advantage of people and "win." In the end, you'll lose. Take the long view: Leave some money on the table. Treat people fairly. Do that and they'll come back to offer you profitable deals in the future. They'll spread the word so that others will want to deal with you. That's how you really win negotiations and grow your company.

It's also true that people buy from people. Remember that? They do. So give them a face to associate with your company if you want your company to grow. Steve Jobs and Apple are one and the same in people's minds. Bill Gates is Microsoft. Richard Branson is Virgin Airways. Your name and your company's name are inseparable.

In the beginning, I said, "I don't want to talk to magazines." Then I realized that giving interviews is a great way to build brand and name recognition. It's free publicity. Here I was, spending thousands of dollars on advertising, and telling people who wanted to put me in their magazine, "No." Talk about stupid.

Then I realized I was doing it wrong. I needed to talk to magazines to build the Related brand. So we made a conscious effort to accommodate as many magazines as possible, always trying to pick quality publications to enhance our company brand. If you go to my office today you'll see there are dozens of covers: *Time, USA Today, Poder, Forbes, Lifestyles*, and many others.

And now, if they really want me to do the interview, we'll try to be on the cover. Not because of ego but because many people don't read what's inside. They look at the cover and the pictures. What's important is the first pitch. So pictures are very important.

It's also important to do magazines that are important with my customers, even if most of the world will most certainly never see them.

For example, a guy called me up from this magazine called *Lifestyles*. You might never have heard of it, but it's a big, glossy, beautiful magazine. Why would you have never heard of it? Because 95 percent of the covers and the articles are about very wealthy, charitable Jewish people. So Eliot Spitzer, Ronald Lauder, Steve Ross, Ron Perlman are all there. But this man calls me up and says, "I want you to be on the cover."

I said, "I'm not even Jewish."

Then he explained to me that the magazine only goes to people who give more than $1 million to charitable organizations, and Jews are typically very charitable to social and philanthropic organizations. I have no idea why. But they are incredible givers. So they don't charge for the magazine, but they make a bundle off the ads because the advertisers know it only goes to the very rich. So I thought, "Jewish, rich. Bal Harbour, St. Regis. Perfect."

You may never have heard of it, but it's right on the bull's-eye for the target market for the condo and hotel project I wanted to promote.

You also have to take a long view with the company's funds. I'm always reinvesting. I am putting a lot of our revenues into our corporate kitty so that our cash continues to grow and our strength continues to grow. I don't want to be the guy in the negotiations that the other guy knows as the guy who's got a deadline and has no money to close.

It helps us grow, and it helps us insulate ourselves against downturns in the market. You're never totally insulated because you don't control many of the things around you. But you protect yourself by making sure your company is financially strong, that there are corporate reserves to get you through lean times. You insulate by having the staff meetings and asking your staff to alert you to potential exposures—like, for example, that the market is slowing and it may be getting overbuilt.

So the best way to insulate is by being a worrier. What can go wrong will go wrong. Don't fall so much in love with your job that you think you're the only one who's going to survive. You don't know how many smart developers I know who will come to me and tell me with a straight face that the whole economy is down, then say, "But I've got the best site and I've got the best product and this one is not going to suffer."

They all suffer. Even if you do everything right and everyone else does everything wrong, if they go down and a lender takes the property back and all of a sudden they start discounting it, what do you think happens to your property, even if you did everything right? The lender puts it at $300 a foot and all of a sudden your $500-per-square-foot building—which was a real good price, because everybody else was at $700 a foot—isn't such a hot deal anymore.

So what do you do to protect yourself? Watch the details. Do constant market research. And worry. Worry. Worry. Worry.

We have a planning meeting once a month in which we project six months out in immense detail. And the six-month projection is done with the finance and accounting people sitting with the senior project managers and going project by project, and they ask, "What are you going to need in cash for these new jobs we're doing?" But even more important, they ask, "Are there any worst-case scenarios that should be played out so we don't get in an unexpected bind?"

In addition to that, we look out over a three-year period and beyond, because that's the time it takes for a building to be built. And we look at all the money we've advanced on projects, which will come back into the company as the projects are finished and sold.

And I will always, always, always be thinking of the downside. I'm always playing the negative. The good news will take care of itself. If I close them all that's awesome. If I don't, what happens?

> Always think of the downside. The good news will take care of itself.

You also insulate yourself by being really nimble. You look at trends. You see the problems. And you start planning for them.

There are three steps I always follow to shield myself from downturns:

1. I plan for the downside market by shoring up the project. What does that mean? I make sure that I'm taking care of all those people who bought, keeping them informed, giving them newsletters, telling them how great the project is.

2. I become very cash conscious, and I build up reserves in the company, thinking if there's a downturn I better have my cash ready. I never want to be left in a situation in which I have no money left

to put into a job. I am making sure I overspend, if necessary, to make the project perfect.

3. I'm looking at everything in the market. I'm looking at all the competition and seeing what is happening, not only with my closings but also with other people's closings. I'm looking to see if there is a trend of people not going through with their closings. I'm looking at people writing us letters trying to get out of their closings. You start seeing the craziest things happening. People write and say, "My mother is sick. I can't close. . . ."

So we shore up, we visualize, and we play what-if . . . ? games: What if 20 percent of the people don't close and half of them sue? What if 30 percent don't? What if? What if? And we do it with everybody involved—our attorneys, our marketing people, our salespeople, our accounting people.

And we say, "If that happens, given the lousy market, what can we resell them at?" We will play all the different scenarios and how we will react to them. That way I've got everybody thinking about the possibility and we won't get caught with our pants down.

> Play out scenarios of what could happen and figure out how you'll react to them.

And when we see a downturn, we start finding new areas where there are still niches—affordable housing again; rentals; investments; buying some product or some land that now has been corrected in value; or locational changes.

I might say, "Hey, the Atlanta market or the New York market is still a good market. Or South America, with certain types of product, has become a very good market." So I'm looking to move out of the market that is stagnant into areas that are growing. But I've got to do that early because I don't want to be the guy who goes into those areas when they're already full-grown and they're starting to come down.

But I've been around long enough that I see the light at the end of tunnel. When downturns happen, I know that upturns will follow.

Now, I can't tell you if it's a year. I can't tell you if it's two. I can't tell you if it's three. But I know that long-term trends always push real estate prices up, unless your specific property is in a really bad location in a declining city.

Taking a long view also means looking beyond buildings, brands, and real estate trends. It means thinking about your legacy. When all is said and done, what do you want to be known for?

As our projects became more and more important, the idea of establishing a legacy, the idea of participating in things that are of greater importance, of doing great buildings that inspire others and change cities, has become by far the most important consideration that drives me every day to go into the office and do what I do. Much more so than the profits.

There comes a time when you ask yourself, What's important? What's important in what I'm leaving behind? How are my children going to remember me? Are they going to say, "Oh, wow, we had a rich dad." Or are they going to go around and look at the buildings and say, "Whoa! This guy really did a lot of cool things for his time." I think that's what's important. The idea of leaving behind something you will be remembered for becomes very important.

You can do that a lot of different ways. You can build an iconic building, like the Empire State Building, that people will admire. Or you can consciously choose to change the way people live, by creating projects that redefine lifestyles and remake cities.

I have tried to do both, by building great, architecturally unique buildings filled with world-class art and by developing visionary projects that changed downtowns and the very way people live.

If you take the long view, you can, too.

CASE STUDY

CityPlace—Changing Cities, Redefining Lifestyles

CityPlace, in West Palm Beach, proved that vision and determination can totally change an urban center.

In the mid-1990s, the West Palm Beach mayor Nancy Graham came up with an idea for revitalizing the city's downtown by partnering with a developer on a seventy-six-acre site in the heart of the city.

When we got involved, there were three bidders. Related was one. The two biggest office and mall developers in the country were another one. And an extremely powerful local Palm Beach group, extremely politically connected, was the third. We were the outsiders. If I was a betting man, I would've picked one of the other two. Because one involved the largest developers at the time and the other was a powerful local company. And then there was us.

The others had a much, much smaller vision for the site. They felt it would be pretty much a strip mall and an office building and that was it. But we had a vision for a cluster of offices and condominiums and retail space that could grow into a twenty-four-hour city where people would actually live and work and shop. We created a minicity with linkages to the main street downtown so that the existing downtown would not suffer.

In the presentation the other people actually said that our idea was way, way too grandiose for West Palm Beach. That we didn't have the kind of land to do it like that. That it had to be done incrementally.

We convinced the mayor that if it was done incrementally she was going to be dead before she saw any real growth down there. I convinced the city that with things like this you either step in or you don't. You don't change a neighborhood by building one building at a time. You must build a mass and create a whole new mind-set in order to create a new city.

We had to convince them that West Palm Beach could be a great town in the future. We had to make them see not what it was then, but what it could be. And let me tell you something, as I was doing this I was absolutely petrified. Because I was going in and thinking that this was an area nobody had touched for years. It had a bunch of crack houses in it and not much else. And the downtown had nothing in it either. All they had was this little Clematis Street with two nightclubs in it, which they thought was a hot thing. Creating a mixed residential and commercial center in what was little more than an urban wasteland was a daunting challenge.

The other guys were talking about a strip mall and low-scale offices and garden apartments; we were talking about changing that city and changing the way people lived in it. We created a design for a mixed-use development that included national retailers, specialty shops, restaurants, office space, along with town homes, lofts, and rentals and condominium apartments for over one thousand people.

We had the whole thing planned out, and we made them share in our vision.

We spent more money than the rest in making these amazing presentations with the whole city built-in to show our exciting master plan. And we walked them through the plan. So we put them, already, in CityPlace. We took them, through photographs, to the great, comparably sized urban centers in Europe. We made them believe that they, too, could become one.

We gave it our best shot, but we still thought, "No way." The mayor was close to the other people. But you know what? The mayor had the vision and the honesty to go with what she felt, and not with what was politically expedient. She went not with the groups that had the track record and the connections, but with the developer who had the vision and the passion to make it a better city.

And by the way, not only did they give us land, but they raised millions upon millions of dollars that we used for infrastructure improvements, to make it into a truly beautiful place. So they really had to believe in us. But it gave West Palm Beach the jump-start they needed to revitalize that area and sent their tax base soaring, making it one of the great investments for the City of West Palm Beach. The project changed urban West Palm Beach forever. It won almost every architecture and urban planning award, including ULI's prestigious best large mixed-use development in the country.

Today we have already completed close to one thousand residential units, 600,000 square feet of retail space, a 250,000-square-foot Class A office building, a historic rehabilitation of the oldest church as a town center, and we're continuing to expand into Phase II of this catalytic project.

This isn't meant to be just a "gee, maybe someday" story for you. For the person just starting out this is a great example of not just managing and growing, because we had never done a project of this type and magnitude, but of how sheer determination and salesmanship and passion can carry the day. We took the long view. We thought big. We looked beyond today and the immediate future. And we convinced them to share our vision, to think in terms of legacy and changing their city forever—and to trust us with that vision.

KEY PRINCIPLES

- Take notes. Catch problems early. Save yourself money and headaches.

- Hire tough and manage easy.

- More important than hiring smart people is hiring good people.

- Integrate as many facets of development as you can under one roof. Controlling the variables gives you an edge.

- Never lose sight of your long-term goals when you're making short-term decisions.

- Always think of the downside. The good news will take care of itself.

- Play out scenarios of what could happen and figure out how you'll react to them.

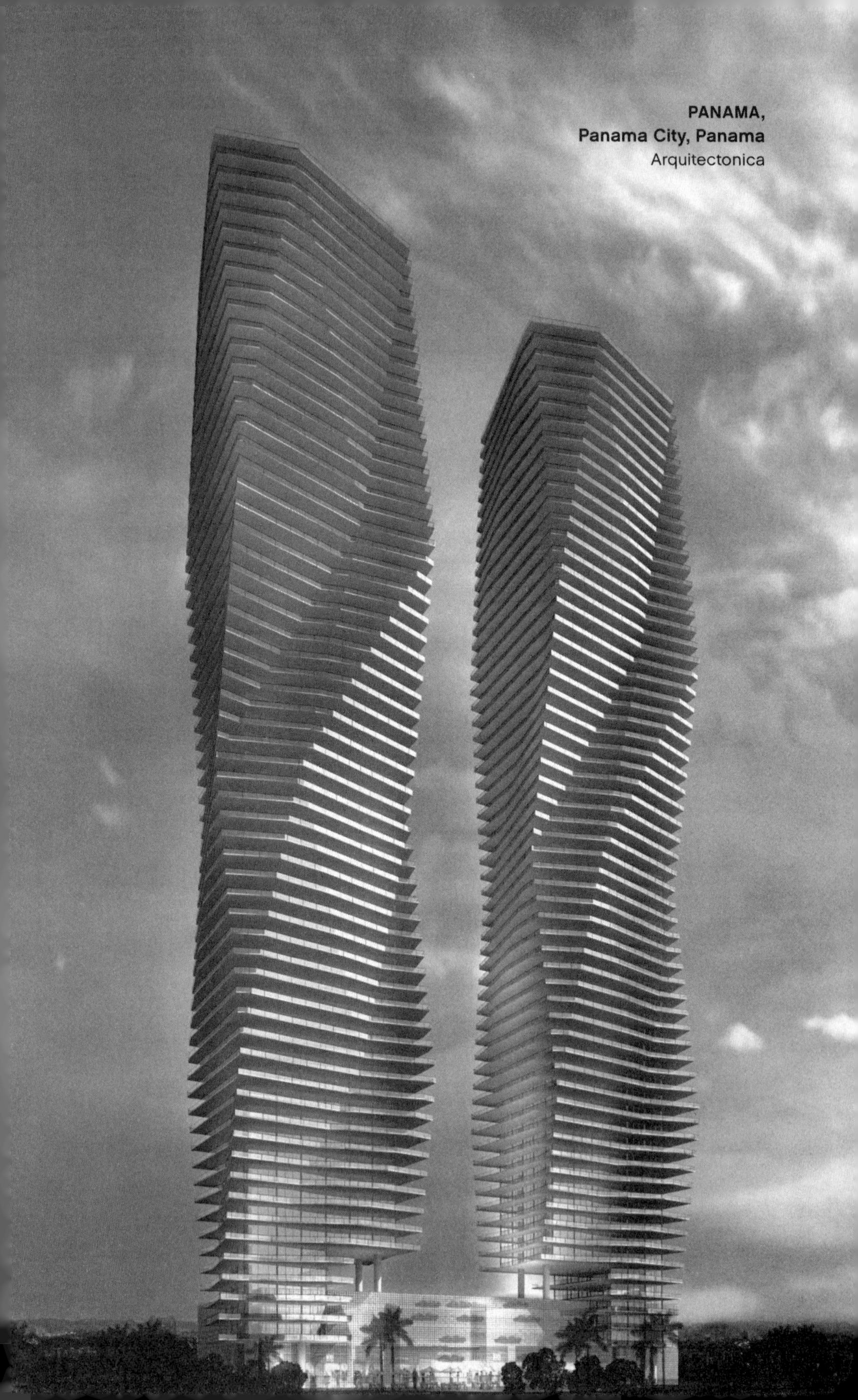

PANAMA,
Panama City, Panama
Arquitectonica

9 ■ THE THREE PRINCIPLES OF CHANGE

"The minute we stop changing as a company, we die."

or "Change alone is unchanging."—Heraclitus

At Related, we have embraced change. That means we don't sit still.

What my role is, particularly mine, in the company, is to be the one to ask, "What are the new opportunities that the market is giving us?"

Not, "What are the ones that it's taking away?" But, "What are the new ones?" And "How do we take the plunge? How do we again take a leap of faith? How do we learn something new?"

And that's always scary.

That's the first thing about change; it's always scary. Anybody who tells you that change and doing something new are not scary is either a liar or a fool. Because if you go to something new and you're not afraid, you're going to get massacred. That means you haven't studied it and you haven't seen the pitfalls. But if you're going to survive, you're going to have to change. That's the one thing that never changes.

Principle #1: Change Is a Given

The world is about change. Constant change. And change is happening much faster than ever before. With all the ways people are finding out about everything through the Internet and all the new means of communication, everything is changing exponentially.

When I started, compared to the way it is now, it's night and day. You'll say the same thing when you look back twenty or thirty years from now.

If you plan for your company to be around that long, you're going to have to be extremely alert and extremely agile. Because, as the economist John Maynard Keynes said, "In the long run, we're all dead." But because change is happening so quickly, the long run arrives a lot sooner—especially if you don't keep pace. So if you want to delay Keynes's ultimate outcome for your company as long as possible, you must change constantly, and rapidly. Those who don't adapt, die.

I tell my people all the time, "The minute we stop changing as a company, we die."

I want that to be an ingrained philosophy. Because, as I said, this is a rapidly changing world—particularly in real estate. That change affects the way we do business, the way we build, the way we live. Kitchens change. Bathrooms change. Technology changes. Tastes change. And you must not only change with it but stay ahead of it.

If you're going to be successful over the long term, you have to keep your eyes open so you can spot the trends, and keep your mind open so you can get there ahead of everyone else.

Nothing stays the same. Not fashions. Not markets. If Miami is the hottest spot for condominiums right now, I can assure you that Miami at some point will not be the hottest spot for condominiums. So as a real estate developer, you have a choice. As the market in your area of expertise becomes less available, you can either take a breather—because you think, "I worked really hard making all these condos while the market was going up. Now let me take a breather until the market comes back." You can do that. You see a lot of companies that ride out downturns and let their incomes go up and down over time.

Or you can do what we do and embrace change. You can see the market slowing down in a specific location, like Miami, or in a specific area of real estate—like offices or apartments—and you can move into something new. Rather than sitting there and watching your pond dry up, you can find another ocean to swim in.

If you do nothing, you die.

If you want to survive you've got to study, you've got to be prepared, you've got to be willing to continue to reinvent yourself and be willing to go into other areas and other locations where there is greener grass, where there are better pastures.

That's the difficult part: you're taking the plunge again, you're going into the abyss, the results remain to be seen. There are a lot more questions than answers as you delve into the market. So it becomes much, much more important to have a well-thought-out plan that has contingencies set all over it.

PRINCIPLE #2: DON'T GET COMFORTABLE

You know that old saying, "If it's not broke don't fix it"? That's nonsense. We are always fixing and fixing and fixing. I need to reinvent that wheel every time. I fear complacency. I fear that when we attack a new job, we just plop the old job in a new site.

There is a tendency to do that because: (a) it was successful, and people tell you if it's not broken don't fix it; and (b) it's comfortable. It's comfortable to do the same project—it was successful; it looked good, so let's do it again.

> Fear complacency.

The question is: Once you have achieved success, gained experience, mastered certain areas, do you settle or do you go to the next level? Those who settle and don't change in this fast-moving world get run over and die.

To my people, I call it re-creating ourselves.

And that's something you've got to push your people to do, because many times they fight you. Many times they say, "But this has been very successful, why don't we just do it that way?" And you've got to say, "No, I think there's a better way. I think we can do something here that's highly creative and different."

You really have to work hard to do that. Change is not easy. It's easier to think inside the box than outside the box. In every project we have done and every place we have moved into, we have thought outside the box.

We don't have formulas; I think people with formulas in real estate who just apply them religiously will end up in trouble. You need to always continue to improve your product. And that means every aspect of it—management, systems, people, design.

That process is hard. Change is hard. Because every time you have to go through that fear again, of doing something new. There's a lot of pain attached to that. There's a lot of satisfaction, but a lot of hard work and pain attached to it. It's like again taking that leap of faith. You're going into areas you don't know.

When I made that decision to go first from subsidized housing into market-rate rentals and then from market-rate rentals into condominiums and then from condominiums to mixed-use projects in which there were office components and retail components, they were all painful, because they meant a new set of criteria, a new area of expertise I had to familiarize myself with and learn.

When you are comfortable in the areas you are in, I think the natural reaction is to stay within your comfort zone, to follow the path of least resistance and do things as you always have. But that way only leads to failure. You won't always be able to sell adding machines in a world of calculators. If you're going to succeed, you have to refocus your vision, and look for new venues and new products that will lead to new opportunities.

Principle #3: Take What the Market Gives You

If you want to survive in real estate, you have to watch for change and adapt. If you want to thrive, you have to anticipate trends, see where markets and people's choices are going, and let market forces and your expertise guide you into new areas.

You must constantly monitor market trends. You need to conduct ongoing macro- and microanalysis to know what's going on in your area, examining the competition and surveying customers. Research never ends. Read data like tracks in the snow, constantly. When you see the herd thinning out, or moving in a different direction, it's time to change the way you trap them.

But just like those tracks in the snow, market trends will show you where things are headed. If you use your intuition and your experience, you can spot the new opportunity and position yourself to profit. New areas mean new challenges, and new opportunities.

The real estate market always changes. It takes away opportunities. And it brings you new ones.

When I see one area drying up, I start finding new areas where there are still niches—affordable housing again—and find an overlooked market, just like I did with the Lofts; rentals; investments, such as buying some product that now has come down in value; or locational changes, like the Atlanta market or South America, which has become a very good market for certain types of product.

So I look to move out of the market that is stagnant into areas that are growing. But I've got to do that early because I don't want to be the last guy who goes into those areas. I don't want to get there when they're already mature and they're starting to come down. You need to be anticipating. And then, be nimble. Don't stay with one product line. Change. Change. Change.

What you do now is just like what you did when you started. You switch gears and go into a new area. You go and examine all the areas that are available to you and decide which area you want to go into. Because when you look at all the possibilities, there's a million things you can do. You might go into another part of real estate that you haven't been in before, like offices or apartments. You look at the opportunities that the market has and ask yourself what you feel most comfortable doing with the knowledge you have accumulated. Ask yourself what you like doing best. Then pick. Just like you picked your first investment, you pick your new investment.

When we saw the signs of the condominium market in Florida coming down rapidly because of an oversupply vis-à-vis the demand, we knew we had to do something. It isn't just that we built a lot of them. We built a lot of them when the demand wasn't there. It's very different to build thirty thousand condominium units in Shanghai, where there's a million Chinese coming into the market every year, than it is to build them in Miami, when the demand is not there for that level of supply. So I looked at it and I said, "There are two things I can do. One, I can look at certain markets in the United States, where I see the long-term growth and I don't see the oversupply in the condominium market that we have in South Florida. Two, we can expand overseas."

We decided to concentrate on two areas. One was Orlando, because we felt our condo hotels, a product we had been very successful in developing, would be very good for Orlando. Orlando has one of the highest growth rates, with the Europeans and Latin Americans wanting to be next to Disney World still coming in droves. The other was Atlanta, which had the highest projected growth rate of any U.S. city and did not have the condominium expertise we had. So in my mind, I saw that we had an opportunity in Atlanta, because the market had not produced as many condominiums, the area was growing tremendously, and we had a type of product that had not been perfected the way we had perfected it in Miami. Atlanta was like Miami ten years ago when it came to luxury condominiums.

So what did we do? Here are the lessons from the past for both. I felt that if I was going to attack a new market, I wanted an exit strategy. I wanted sites I could buy at a price that, even if we guessed wrong and the market was not right, would still be incredibly good buys.

I looked around and found incredible sites in both places that were premier sites at great prices. One was in a beautiful little town called Celebration, which I've already told you about—the last site available there for that type of product. As a result, we had no competition in Celebration. And I bought it—because Disney needed to sell that particular last site—at an incredibly low price.

Same thing in Atlanta. We discovered a central site next to the two largest malls in the city, both high-end. And I got these twenty acres that, due to very unusual family circumstances, had been left behind from the growth around it, and I was able to rezone it to allow me to do forty-three hundred units there, thus creating great value. I bought the land for $40 million, and after getting it rezoned was offered over twice what we paid for it.

Always be thinking not only of the upside, but of the downside. You need to buy well to stay out of trouble. If something happened today and I wanted to sell those pieces of land, it would still be a very successful venture. Without even building.

I also was able to shift some people within the company whose projects no longer existed because we were no longer investing heavily in South Florida, and put them in those new locations. That way, we didn't have to hire new people and lose all the expertise we had internally. We have a team in Atlanta and a team in Orlando that know everything about Related: They know how to report. They know all the idiosyncrasies of Related. They know all the systems of Related. And that allowed us to enter those markets well prepared.

The rules of the game were very much the same. Atlanta and Orlando are somewhat different, but still in the United States. A market study was a market study. The law was the law. Development is development. Getting a permit is getting a permit. Was there a different cast of characters? Yes. But the system was very much the same.

The huge plunge we took was in South America. Mexico. Argentina. Uruguay. Panama. And Colombia. But particularly in Mexico. Why Mexico? Because in Mexico, we saw huge amounts of international demand, particularly U.S. demand. We had already been very, very good about attracting that international and U.S. market to Miami. We knew what it was they wanted. We knew what it was they were willing to pay extra dollars for. So we were able to use some of that expertise in transitioning into the Mexican market.

We also felt that our brand was already known to a degree there because of the large number of South Americans who were familiar with our product in Miami. And we saw a large customer base that we felt was ready for a product like ours.

As we looked at Mexico, and particularly at the resorts in Mexico, we saw this horde of Americans and Europeans coming to visit. Why Mexico? Because they felt at ease with Mexico. Mexico was their natural neighbor.

We saw that the prices in Mexico were much, much lower than they were in the United States. Where it might cost me $200 a square foot to build a condominium here, it cost me $100 a square foot to build the same condominium in Mexico. So I looked at that and said, I think there is a huge opportunity to change the product that is being offered there, to change their lifestyle and create a niche in the market for high-end, highly branded product, where people will pay us much more than they're paying the typical Mexican developer.

So, what are the lessons for you as you're starting out? First, realize that the things you're learning now will serve you well in the future. It's like learning to ride a bicycle. The pedaling you learn on a tricycle stays the same when you get on your first two-wheeler. The balance you learn when the training wheels come off stays the same whether you ride a mountain bike or a road racer. Things change, but the basics remain the same. And the more expertise you gain, the easier each transition becomes. Riding around the block is a tremendously big deal the first time you do it. But even Lance Armstrong started that way.

> Things change, but the basics remain the same.

If you're going to grow, you have to seize on opportunities to do things you haven't done before. You have to welcome change. You have to see change as an opportunity. And you have to use what you know to grow.

Always use areas of expertise you are comfortable in to move into a new area. Don't go from real estate to building submarines, and don't go into areas in real estate where you don't bring anything to the table. Find common ground. I'm comfortable moving into Latin America, where I lived until college and I speak the language, but not Dubai or China.

We still had a lot to learn in Mexico. The way land is treated is something that we're just absolutely not used to at all. Land ownership isn't as clear-cut as it is here. So it's almost like being in kindergarten. You're learning all these things for the first time. Now, if we had gone in without studying these pitfalls, I'm telling you, we would've made these land investments, and we would have put down a lot of money for land that we don't own. We'd be fighting title problems right now. We would've had people coming in front of our property and putting up businesses that would've ruined the value of our land. And then we would've closed and we would've been invaded by squatters if we had not fenced our sites.

That makes it, as you can see, much, much harder.

In addition to that, Mexico has a totally different legal system. Laws change rapidly. There is a lot of local interpretation of the law. So you have to be very careful how you write the contracts. It is a totally, totally different legal system. In the legal system here, if you have a complaint, you go to a judge and you get it resolved by fairly well-defined standards, which don't exist there. There is no transparency there the way there is here.

And I couldn't just go there and hope that the tax system is the same as in the United States. It's not. Now you go to Mexico, you're not only going to have to deal with the Mexican tax system but with the American tax system. And if I'm not careful with the way I set up the corporation, I pay twice. Once I make it there and once when I take whatever I've got left and bring it back to the United States.

So I realize it's like Development 101. I have to learn all over again. What takes you one permit here takes you six permits in six different agencies there. I knew, though, that if we were going to go there, we had to learn how to play the game. When you're in Rome, do as the Romans do.

The one thing that always must remain the same—and I tell my people this—is you must remain aboveboard. Because morality can change in different countries, but yours can't. Like the time in Argentina when I was asked to pay half the money under the table, and I simply refused. You must always take the high ground. Let there be no doubt about it.

And that's the bottom line: You must change, or die. But you never change your principles. Your principles will help guide you as you chart a course in new territory. As the world changes and business changes—and as you have to change to continue to succeed—your principles will serve as a compass. Never lose sight of them as you forge ahead.

KEY PRINCIPLES

- Fear complacency.

- Things change, but the basics remain the same.

ICON VALLARTA,
Puerta Vallarta, Mexico
Methanoia Studio
www.methanoia.com

RELATED GROUP PROPERTIES

The Related group and its affiliates were founded by Jorge M. Pérez in 1979. They have developed more than fifty thousand units across the United States, the Caribbean, and Latin America. Following is a sample of their developments.

50 BISCAYNE, MIAMI, FLORIDA • 500 BRICKELL, MIAMI, FLORIDA • 2080 SOUTH OCEAN DRIVE, HALLANDALE BEACH, FLORIDA • APOGEE, MIAMI BEACH, FLORIDA • AQUAZUL, LAUDERDALE-BY-THE-SEA, FLORIDA • AVENTURA MARINA, AVENTURA, FLORIDA • BLACKSTONE, MIAMI BEACH, FLORIDA • BOCA GRAND, BOCA RATON, FLORIDA • CITYHOMES, WEST PALM BEACH, FLORIDA • CITYPLACE BUCKHEAD, ATLANTA, GEORGIA • CITYPLACE SOUTH TOWER, WEST PALM BEACH, FLORIDA • COLONY LAKES, HOMESTEAD, FLORIDA • CIVIC TOWERS,  MIAMI, FLORIDA • CONGRESS BUILDING, MIAMI, FLORIDA • ENCLAVE AT DORAL, MIAMI, FLORIDA • ENCLAVE AT WINSTON PARK, COCONUT CREEK, FLORIDA • FALLS AT BONAVENTURE, WESTON, FLORIDA • GABLES GRAND PLAZA, CORAL GABLES, FLORIDA • HARBOUR HOUSE, BAL HARBOUR, FLORIDA • HALLANDALE BEACH CLUB, HALLANDALE BEACH, FLORIDA •

ICON BRICKELL, MIAMI, FLORIDA • ICON CELEBRATION, ORLANDO, FLORIDA • ICON LAS OLAS, FORT LAUDERDALE, FLORIDA • ICON SOUTH BEACH, MIAMI BEACH, FLORIDA • **ICON VALLARTA, PUERTO VALLARTA, MEXICO** • ISLAND CLUB APARTMENTS, MIAMI, FLORIDA • LAKES AT PEMBROKE, PEMBROKE PINES, FLORIDA • LAKES AT WELLEBY, SUNRISE, FLORIDA • LA COSTA, MIRAMAR, FLORIDA • LAKES AT DEERFIELD, DEERFIELD, FLORIDA • LAKES AT JACARANDA, PLANTATION, FLORIDA • LAS OLAS BEACH CLUB, FORT LAUDERDALE, FLORIDA

• MARBELLA CLUB, MIAMI, FLORIDA • MARINA VILLAGE AT BOYNTON BEACH, BOYNTON BEACH, FLORIDA • MIAMI RIVER YACHT CLUB, MIAMI, FLORIDA • MURANO AT PORTOFINO, MIAMI BEACH, FLORIDA • **MURANO GRANDE, MIAMI BEACH, FLORIDA** • NEW HORIZONS, MIAMI, FLORIDA • OASIS ON THE BAY, MIAMI, FLORIDA • NEW PORT CONDOS, NEW PORT RICHEY, FLORIDA • OASIS, FORT MYERS, FLORIDA • OASIS ON THE BAY, MIAMI, FLORIDA • OCEAN ONE, SUNNY ISLES BEACH, FLORIDA • OCEAN TWO, SUNNY ISLES BEACH, FLORIDA • OCEAN THREE, SUNNY ISLES BEACH, FLORIDA • OCEAN FOUR, SUNNY ISLES BEACH, FLORIDA • **ONE CITYPLACE, ATLANTA, GEORGIA** • PALM LAKES APARTMENTS, MIAMI, FLORIDA • **ONE MIAMI, MIAMI, FLORIDA** • PORTO-FINO TOWER, MIAMI BEACH, FLORIDA • RIVERWALK 1, HOMESTEAD, FLORIDA

• SANTA CLARA, MIAMI, FLORIDA • SEAGRAPE VILLAGE, HOMESTEAD, FLORIDA • ST JAMES CLUB, BOCA RATON, FLORIDA • ST. ANDREWS AT BONAVENTURE, WESTON, FLORIDA • ST. ANDREWS AT BOYNTON BEACH, BOYNTON BEACH, FLORIDA •

ST. ANDREWS AT CAROLINA, MARGATE, FLORIDA • ST. ANDREWS AT JENSEN BEACH, JENSEN BEACH, FLORIDA • ST. ANDREWS AT KINGSPORT, TAMARAC, FLORIDA • ST. ANDREWS AT PALM AIRE, POMPANO BEACH, FLORIDA • ST. ANDREWS AT PALM BEACH LAKES, WEST PALM BEACH, FLORIDA • ST. ANDREWS AT QUIET WATERS, DEERFIELD BEACH, FLORIDA • ST. ANDREWS AT WINSTON PARK, COCONUT CREEK, FLORIDA • ST. ANDREWS PLACE, MIRAMAR, FLORIDA • **ST. REGIS RESORTS AND RESIDENCES, BAL HARBOUR, FLORIDA** • STRATFORD, MIAMI, FLORIDA • SUMMER CREEK, WEST PALM BEACH, FLORIDA • TAMPA SANCTUARY HOMES, TAMPA, FLORIDA • THE ENCLAVE AT MIRAMAR, MIRAMAR, FLORIDA • THE ENCLAVE AT NAPLES, NAPLES, FLORIDA • THE LOFTS DOWNTOWN, MIAMI, FLORIDA • THE LOFTS II, MIAMI, FLORIDA • THE LOFTS III, MIAMI, FLORIDA • THE MOORINGS AT LANTANA, LANTANA, FLORIDA • THE PLAZA ON BRICKELL, MIAMI, FLORIDA • THE MARK, MIAMI, FLORIDA • THE PRADO, WEST PALM BEACH, FLORIDA • THE PRESERVE AT COCONUT CREEK, COCONUT CREEK,

Bridget Conway

FLORIDA • THE PRESERVE AT MIRAMAR LAKES, MIRAMAR, FLORIDA • THE RESERVE AT NAPLES, NAPLES, FLORIDA • THE RESIDENCES AT CITYPLACE, WEST PALM BEACH, FLORIDA • THE RESIDENCES AT MIRAMAR, MIRAMAR, FLORIDA • THE TOWER CONDOMINIUM AT CITYPLACE, WEST PALM BEACH, FLORIDA • THE VENTURE, AVENTURA, FLORIDA • THE YACHT CLUB AT AVENTURA, AVENTURA, FLORIDA • THE YACHT CLUB AT BRICKELL, MIAMI, FLORIDA • THE YACHT CLUB AT HIGHLAND BEACH, HIGHLAND BEACH, FLORIDA • THE YACHT CLUB AT HYPOLUXO, HYPOLUXO, FLORIDA • THE YACHT CLUB AT PORTOFINO, MIAMI BEACH, FLORIDA • TRUMP HOLLYWOOD, HOLLYWOOD, FLORIDA • TRUMP TOWERS, SUNNY ISLES BEACH, FLORIDA • VICEROY SOUTH BEACH, MIAMI BEACH, FLORIDA • VILLA LOFTS, WEST PALM BEACH, FL • VILLAGE OF MERRICK PARK, CORAL GABLES, FLORIDA • VILLAS OF CAPRI, NAPLES, FLORIDA • WALDEN POND, MIAMI, FLORIDA • WEST BRICKELL APARTMENTS, MIAMI, FLORIDA •

"Jorge Pérez became one of the country's most successful developers through a strong combination of intelligence, drive, and enthusiasm for his business. Jorge knows how to read markets and make the most of his opportunities. Like the best businesspeople, he also knows that his success depends on the success of others—and he works hard to lift up the communities in which his company does business. It has been a privilege for Bank of America to serve Jorge's and his company's financial needs for so many years."
   —**Kenneth D. Lewis, Chairman and Chief Executive Officer, Bank of America**

"Everybody knows how energetic, flamboyant, and ambitious Jorge is. But what I most admire is his thoughtfulness, determination, financial might, and financial caution—in other words, his stability and dependability. Further, he has a devotion to the arts and architecture and design excellence—a passion really. He has shown an ability to see the future, in other words, a long-range planner and visionary. And man to man, he's awfully sexy."
   —**Steven Roth, Chairman and CEO, Vornado Realty Trust**